845
145

①

Return to
Judaism

The University of Chicago Press
Chicago and London

Return to
Judaism

Religious Renewal
in Israel

Janet Aviad

The University of Chicago Press, Chicago 60637
The University of Chicago Press, Ltd., London

©1983 by The University of Chicago
All rights reserved. Published 1983
Paperback edition 1985
Printed in the United States of America
94 93 92 91 90 89 88 87 86 85   6 5 4 3 2

Library of Congress Cataloging in Publication Data

Aviad, Janet O'Dea.
  Return to Judaism.

    Bibliography: p.
    Includes index.
    1. Orthodox Judaism–Israel.   2. Jewish religious
education of adults–Israel.   3. Jews–Return to Orthodox
Judaism.   4. Jews–Cultural assimilation.   I. Title.
BM390.A9   1983   296.7'1   82-17663
ISBN 0-226-03236-1 (cloth)   0-226-03235-3 (paper)

For Michael

Contents

Preface

This is a book about the conversion of secular Jews to Orthodox Judaism. It is an analysis of a phenomenon that has gripped observers of contemporary Jewry because of its size and visibility, and because of the extreme neotraditional direction it has taken. The current phenomenon is not the first or the only example of Jewish religious resistance to secularization and modernization.[1] It is, however, a steady, dramatic, and powerful example of such resistance, whose significance lies beyond the specific boundaries of Jewish cultural history and within the broader boundaries of the history of contemporary religious renewal.

Jews who have converted to Orthodox Judaism from a secular background are known as *baalei teshuvah* in Hebrew, "those who return." *Teshuvah,* the process of repentence for transgressions and return to the correct observance of Jewish ethical and ritual law, is a central category in Judaism. Any Jew who has veered from the law is commanded to return to it, so that teshuvah is built into the rhythm of the life of every religious Jew. The teshuvah of the contemporary baal teshuvah, however, is not return to a full and correct observance of the law after having veered from it. Contemporary baalei teshuvah have grown up or lived outside the framework of traditional Jewish belief and practice. They have lived outside a traditional Jewish community. Their "return" is thus to a Judaism with which they have had no acquaintance.

The present study focuses upon three groups of young Jews who have undertaken teshuvah: Americans, Israelis of European background, and Israelis of Asian or African background. I have attempted to identify common factors in the search and return of all three groups. At the same time, I have sought to characterize each in its distinctiveness. Following the paths of religious change, I have attempted to penetrate beneath the level of external behavior to the change of ideas and attitudes, which is the core of the process and that most difficult to observe.

The second focus of the study is the institutional framework that has emerged to nurture and frame the contemporary teshuvah phenomenon. This is the *yeshivah* for baalei teshuvah, modeled on the traditional Jewish academy of higher learning but reflecting the special needs of newcomers to Judaism. Without this institution the return of Jews to Judaism today would be sporadic, individualized, and sociologically far less significant than it is. The *yeshivot* have created those mechanisms of commitment through which youth, disenchanted with secular culture, have become enchanted with a highly traditional culture. And the yeshivot have created an objective fact—institutionalized return—and have made the teshuvah of large groups of secular Jews an experience and undertaking that is considered legitimate, plausible, and significant within contemporary Jewry.

Finally, the present study focuses upon the wider sociological and cultural processes within which the teshuvah phenomenon must be placed. Discontent with secular culture to the point of rejection and withdrawal is a phenomenon current in the East and West. And religious responses in a reactionary countermodern direction also are widespread today. Within this context, the teshuvah phenomenon must be analyzed as a reaction whose specific lineaments are set by the specific Jewish experience with modernity. The significance of the teshuvah phenomenon, however, lies both within the history of Jewish experience and beyond it in the realm of contemporary forms of religious conversion and reaction.

In embarking upon this study, it was decided to focus on baalei teshuvah and yeshivot located in Jerusalem. The decision was made in order to define a specific and ready-to-hand population. There is no doubt that large numbers of baalei teshuvah are not and have never been students in the yeshivot. The total number of such people is not available since records and statistics regarding teshuvah are not kept by any office. The population that is identifiable, however, is that presently studying in yeshivot for baalei teshuvah and those past students who can be traced today.

It was not simply accessibility that made the yeshivah population the likely and attractive one for the study. The yeshivot in Jerusalem are today the major force in shaping the teshuvah phenomenon. They are also its symbol. Baalei teshuvah of all types arrive at the yeshivah. In their background, motivation, and the mode of change they undergo they are representative of the total baal teshuvah population at present.

The estimated number of baalei teshuvah in the yeshivot at the time the fieldwork was conducted was twelve-hundred.[2] Three hundred and seventy-five questionnaires were completed. The sample consists of two-third Americans and one-third Israelis, which reflects the approximate proportions of these groups in the yeshivot. Fifty percent of the sample was American-born, 29 percent Israeli-born, 16 percent born in Europe or the British Commonwealth, and 5 percent born in Asia or Africa; 66 percent of the sample is male, 34 percent female. The proportion of women in baal teshuvah institutions is approximately 25 percent, so this sample is slightly overbalanced in favor of women. Fifteen percent of the sample was between the ages of eighteen and nineteen, 19 percent between the ages of twenty and twenty-one, 19 percent between twenty-two and twenty-three, and 18 percent between twenty-four and twenty-five.

Having determined to work in the yeshivot, the problem was to gain entré. Permission to interview students and staff, as well as to observe life in the yeshivot, had to be obtained from the director or directors of each institution. In almost every place great resistance was encountered. The actual degree of resistance and the variety of factors underlying it were not foreseen, perhaps fortunately, for the study might otherwise have been stopped before it was started.[3]

The rabbis in the yeshivot objected that researchers from the university world can only distort the subject because they cannot understand it in its own terms. In their view, university people are outsiders who study Judaism within a framework alien to it and therefore distorting of it. Further, the research demanded that the yeshivah expose itself to outside observers using what were considered to be foreign tools of analysis without offering anything valuable in return. There seemed to be no positive reason for cooperating.

Outsiders who had been permitted to observe the yeshivot and interview baalei teshuvah had misused their privilege in the eyes of the rabbis. They had written sensational and distorted descriptions, which had damaged the yeshivot. At least in the beginning there seemed to be no reason for trusting new outsiders to do a better or fairer job.

The main point of objection, however, was that teshuvah was not the sort of subject appropriate to the method being proposed. Questionnaires offended both rabbis and students in the yeshivot. Both claimed that teshuvah could not be reduced to a questionnaire and, more important, that a religious experience could not be grasped by those who had not themselves undergone it. It was only after long conversations about religious ideas and experiences that inroads were made and a minimal degree of trust established. When I hinted that I might myself be interested in teshuvah and that I had observed Jewish law somewhat at some times, these inroads were expanded.

Although it was never mentioned explicitly, no doubt the fact that

I was a woman did not help to advance my cause within the yeshivot, at least in the initial stages of contact. Again, after long conversations over a long period of time, the trust was established that overcame the liability of being a woman in a dominantly male world. Ironically, the fact of my being a woman may even have helped reduce resistance. Many times I sensed that I was permitted access because I was not taken seriously. As a woman I seemed to pose less of a threat than a man would have posed doing the same work.

Throughout the stage of contacting yeshivot and carrying out interviewing I was accompanied by several male yeshivah students. These were friends who had agreed to help me in establishing connections and in actually working in the yeshivot. They also vouched for my reliability and supported the value of the research project for the yeshivot. Without their help I am certain that I could not have broken into the yeshivah world.

The first year of the research was spent in negotiations for entry, observation of the yeshivot directly, formulating and reformulating the questionnaire. During the second year interviews were completed and analyzed. The third year was spent in reviewing material accumulated through written and oral interviews, participant observation, and discussions with others who had observed the teshuvah phenomenon. The result is this book.

I had been warned by friends and acquaintances that I would never be able to enter the yeshivot. And I had been warned by the same people that I was fundamentally an outsider to this world and could never *really* understand it. My academic friends echoed in their own language the objections to the study made by the yeshivah rabbis. I must confess that both groups were correct in estimating the difficulty of the task. I believe they were wrong in their suggestion that these difficulties could not be overcome.

The yeshivah world is complex and profound. Before it I often felt overawed, sometimes baffled, and always amazed. The same can be said of my feelings when confronting teshuvah itself, which like any conversion experience is in a sense private and unfathomable. In analyzing the expressions of the teshuvah experience, the process of change, and the yeshivot that have given it form, I have tried to be intellectually objective and humanly sympathetic. I have attempted to bring conceptual and analytic tools to the study, but have sought to preserve the sense of ultimate mystery that underlies religious engagement and relationship.

Other avenues of approach and other questions could have been asked of the subject. The problems I have chosen are those that seem most significant to me because of various gross and subtle coordinates of my own historical, social, and psychological position in the stream of life and fabric of culture of which I am a part. If the questions posed enable us to identify real problems and enlarge our view of them and the view of others who approach them from different perspectives, then they have such significance. I hope that this study has portrayed the process of change, which is teshuvah, faithfully and that it has analyzed one resolution of a community's struggle with modernity clearly.

I would like to express my deep gratitude to all those who helped me throughout the four years of research and writing. In the early stages of the project I worked closely with Ms. Elana Silber and Professor Arnold Eisen, to whom I owe thanks. Because the most tense and difficult stage of the project was penetrating the yeshivot and gaining access to staff and students, I am extremely grateful to the devoted work of two men, Mr. Shlomo Fisher and Rabbi Avi Weinstein. As an outsider and a woman, I was barred from easy entrance into the yeshivah altogether and from any entrance into its center, the study hall. I was dependent upon the fieldwork of Mr. Fisher and Rabbi Weinstein as well as upon their insights into the yeshiva world.

I would like to thank Dr. Shmuel Shye for his help in the statistical interpretation of the empirical data. I also want to thank Mr. Arnold Schwartz for his aid in reading and commenting upon the manuscript.

Finally, I wish to express my gratitude to The Van Leer Jerusalem Foundation and to its director, Professor Yehuda Elkana, without whose aid and encouragement I could neither have undertaken nor completed the project.

Janet Aviad

The Van Leer Jerusalem Foundation

1

Who Are the Baalei Teshuvah?

*Each torpid turn of the world has disinherited children, to whom
no longer what's been, and not yet, what's coming, belongs.*

Rilke, *Seventh Elegy*

Jerusalem is a modern city. Electricity and telephones, banking and
commerce, the printed word and the electronic impulse reach all corners. And yet, if one walks from the neighborhoods of Mattersdorf to
Ramot, or from Mea Shearim to Ramot Eshkol, one passes not only
through neighborhoods but through time. Although the residents of
these neighborhoods are linked by ethnic, historic, and civic bonds,
they live in significantly different worlds. Mea Shearim or Mattersdorf
are areas steeped in tradition, where opposition to modernity is evident
in dress, language, homes, school curriculum, bookshops, and even in
the absence of television antennae. Ramot and Ramot Eshkol resemble
a modern suburban apartment complex. The dress of the middle-class
inhabitants is modish; their language is spiced with modern Israeli slang;
the stores are big, bright, and modern; the atmosphere is open.

Sharp differences in values, ideas, and attitudes toward the world
divide populations in Israel. The Jew in Mattersdorf or Mea Shearim,
dressed in the black coat and hat that became fashionable in Poland
three centuries ago, lives his life according to the proscriptions and
prescriptions of Jewish law, the *halachah*. He seeks to ignore or reject
what he regards as intrusions of Western secular culture. He bemoans
the changes in thinking and behavior that, in his opinion, have brought
about the collapse of belief in the fundamental principles of Judaism
and the abrogation of Jewish law among his fellow Jews. He finds himself in basic opposition to the new and foreign culture within which his
fellows are immersed.

The Jew in Ramot—who dresses according to European or American
fashions, enjoys Western literature, TV, and movies, and longs for a
vacation in Europe—regards the Jew down the road in the black coat
as a relic. He may have some positive sentiment for that relic or, on the

1

other hand, may despise it. Either way, he sees no relationship between
the figure and neighborhood and modern Israeli life. Although he himself may pray occasionally, may observe rituals selectively, and may
consider himself related to the Jewish tradition in some positive way,
he does not feel the authority of the tradition as binding in his everyday life and refuses to accord the halachah absolute authority in a
modern pluralistic society.

The cultural and spiritual landscape of Jerusalem is rich in contrasts,
veined with divides. The modern and the traditional, the religious and
the secular mix, mingle, collide, repel, blend in endless variations. A
new element has entered this landscape in the past decade and a half,
one which has traversed the zones of the city, crossed its divides. These
are the *baalei teshuvah,* Jews from the Diaspora and Israel, who have
"returned" to Orthodox Judaism. Their presence is felt in the city.
As individuals, they may be noticed by the mixture of traditional and
modern they display in their dress, manners, style. As a group, they are
visible through the many new yeshivot established for them and planted
in orthodox neighborhoods.

The three major groups of baalei teshuvah found in Jerusalem today
may be distinguished, first, by the areas from which they came. One
group originates in American upper-class and middle-class suburban
neighborhoods, and must be considered as part of the American youth
culture of the late sixties and seventies. It was this group that was
addressed by the first rabbis to found institutions for baalei teshuvah.
The years were the mid-sixties when what has become known as the
counterculture emerged in full bloom. Youth—middle class, educated,
and liberal in orientation—protested in those years against what they
perceived as the failure of American society to solve its basic problems.
Protesting a war they regarded as immoral, a situation that permitted
terrible injustices to ethnic minorities, what appeared as a wasteful
and directionless use of technology—youth struck out in various directions.

One direction was toward new forms of religious life. Indeed, the
proliferation of cults and revivals was so great in the last two decades
that the period has been dubbed the "age of conversion." A sense of
the changes occurring during this period is conveyed by the comments
of one of its more astute observers: "At the level of our youth, we
begin to resemble nothing so much as the cultic hothouse of the Hellen-
istic period, where every manner of mystery and fakery, ritual and rite,
intermingled with marvelous indiscrimination.... What the counterculture offers us, then, is a remarkable defection from the long-standing

tradition of skeptical, secular intellectuality which has served as the prime vehicle for three hundred years of scientific and technical work in the West. Almost overnight a significant portion of the younger generation has opted out of that tradition."[1]

Out of this breeding ground emerged the baalei teshuvah who arrived in Israel in the sixties and seventies from the United States. A sense of who these American baalei teshuvah are and how they arrived at the yeshivot may be obtained from the self-description of a thirty-year-old man, who made his way to Jerusalem eight years ago.

After receiving a BA from the University I left the United States to travel. Half the time I spent reading. The first half year I was in Europe and the second in Greece. Traveling is the experience of moving through a tremendous number of different cultures. True, those that I saw were all Western cultures. But they were different spaces, meaning seeing different peoples living their lives in different conditions, rationalizing it, and seeing meaning in it. After this I realized that there might not be any one answer for all peoples. This was what the political solution was supposed to be.

There is a disorientation in travel and also a freedom of thought. I read a lot and entered the area of Eastern religion, Zen Buddhism, Mahayana Buddhism, and Southern Indian Buddhism. I started to read Gurdjieff—a Russian mystic close to the Sufi tradition. I was getting involved, practicing meditation and yoga on my own. I didn't seek out a master but rather, went slowly in a low key way, reading books and trying systems or ways. If I liked something I would do it and this continued for about a year. The culmination of the experience was six months in a small Greek island which was twenty miles around, and had about 2,000 people on it. In the summer there was a tremendous influx of tourists, but we were there in the winter. We ourselves were pretty similar. There were fun seekers and people who were just seekers. One poet drinking himself to death. As usual there were 50% Jews. One New York Jew who had been in Vietnam, others just getting out of the technocratic life. We founded a free university there, drank ouzo, went out to the hills and tried to figure things out. We wanted to do something serious with our lives. I was with a very good friend from the university. We would study at night—line by line with a candle in this idyllic setting—no electricity, draw our own water. Drugs weren't ample but were sufficient. LSD was a staple. It wasn't wild although there were a few outrageous moments. We were really trying to do something serious. Like—let's go to the hills, get drugged, and see what happens—not let's get drunk, go to town and break things.

Every book I read and system I studied stressed that for any serious progress, one needed a master and a school. Everyone agreed you couldn't do it on your own. You had to get a tradition and accept an authority. You had to get out of yourself long enough to accept authority. So at a certain point I knew I had to choose between staying on the island my whole life (and some did—I returned two and a half years later and met friends) or move on. I could have easily stayed. But it seemed that the logical place to go was to school, find a teacher, and give it a try. I was corresponding with an old college friend. We had gone through similar things: politics and spiritual activity. I had gotten a letter that he would come to Greece for a visit. Then I got a letter from Israel—he had decided to find a school.

All during my last three months in Greece I was getting letters about studying, praying, and celebrating the Sabbath. As my realization crystallized to go to school, it also came to me that I should do it in my own backyard. At that time I was reading nothing that had to do with Judaism, and I didn't know anything. I assumed that there must be an esoteric tradition in Judaism—what the truth is. So I decided I could look for it in a school.

I arrived in Tel Aviv in the evening and got to Jerusalem at two A.M. There was nowhere really to go, so I went to sleep near the yeshivah where my friend had gone. In the morning I tried to find him. A guy walked out with a *tallis** and *tefillin*[†] on. I had never seen anything like that before. You know, I had seen my grandfather put on tefillin, but I had never seen the whole get-up and of course, no one with a tallis over his head. My grandfather had worn a little American-type tallis and not a long wide one like this. Later, I found out this man was a rabbi, the head of the yeshivah. Now I would call this Providence, but then I called it karma.

Baalei teshuvah set out on a search. In the case of this young man, it took place over the course of several years and involved travel, experiments, and study of a wide range of religious traditions before it led, eventually, to his "own backyard." Both the search and the backyard are elements which recur in the descriptions of the baalei teshuvah. Not only do they seek a spiritual resolution for needs they feel, but they go looking, in the end at least, in their own backyard. They attempt to return home, even if it is to a home where they personally have never lived but which their fathers or grandfathers inhabited. Thus they experience genuine return to something they feel is theirs by birthright, although they have not really known it until adulthood.

In the search process, not all baalei teshuvah turned first to Judaism. On the contrary, Judaism was often only the end station of a long search that included stops and stations along the way. The youth culture in America has offered possibilities for those interested in experi-

---

*Fringed prayer shawl worn by males during services.
[†] Phylacteries worn by males during morning prayers.

menting, which are part of the passage of many who arrived at last at *teshuvah.*

> The choice seemed to be the drug scene in New York city or a mid-west commune. I had hung out with a leftist community while attending college. The spirituality which I had always seen as part of me needed to find a specific shape. Eastern religions seemed ridiculous. I couldn't really go for Christianity. All my friends were lapsed Catholics and I couldn't stand Protestant fundamentalists. I considered it somehow cosmically important to be Jewish. I had been part of a commune, but wasn't really into this organic culture stuff and the whole life-style to which I seemed to be heading. The normal hippie scene: rock, organic food and rejection of the values of the United States wasn't for me. So I decided to go to Israel and see what would happen.

Another student described his passage to Judaism with the same sense of choice and experiment:

> The change started six years ago with a spiritual awakening and into the spiritual counterculture on the West Coast. After four years of various paths, I came to Israel and lived in a yeshivah, where my brother had been studying. I began to go to the first year classes and that was it. But the main cause of the new relationship to Judaism occured earlier—an initial understanding of spiritual reality. Then I was open enough to spiritual ideas that I could accept and understand Judaism. I might as well mention that the spiritual experiences I had had to do with taking large amounts of LSD regularly for a year.

The milieu from which such baalei teshuvah emerge is one where choice between countercultural options is great and where a self-conscious pursuit of the spiritual is considered to be both worthwhile and legitimate. Drugs, Christian religious groups, and countercultural sects were available and were tried ways to achieve the sought-after "spiritual awakening" so as to arrive at the "spiritual reality." An openness to search in a religious direction and a readiness to change underlie the turning to Judaism.

The happenstance nature of the turning itself is an element that must be emphasized in introducing the baalei teshuvah. In statement after statement baalei teshuvah indicate that at a certain point it made sense to give Judaism a try because it was somehow a fact of their biographies. The precise cause of the turning was circumstantial: an unexpected event, a chance meeting, or an intellectual curiosity that seemed to lead to Jewish sources.

In the descriptions of what brought them to consider teshuvah, baalei teshuvah often speak of what brought them to a yeshivah. A majority report that an individual or a group was a decisive influence. Friends who were already studying invited others to come and see what happens in a yeshivah. Chance meetings with rabbis or religious Jews were often the factor that induced students to take a closer look at Judaism. For American baalei teshuvah the encounter with what they perceived as "real Judaism" or "real Jews" was most powerful.

The turning of hundreds of young Americans toward Judaism and teshuvah cannot be understood without taking into account the existence of the yeshivot as a social fact. They exist and are highly visible. Directors of the yeshivot have concerned themselves with public relations techniques in order to attain this visibility. Potential baalei teshuvah know about the existence of the yeshivot. They have become a subject of interest in the press in Israel, in the media, and are a recognized option for young people today, whether Israelis or Jews from the Diaspora.

Moreover, because baalei teshuvah are already a highly visible presence in Jerusalem, teshuvah itself appears to be a plausible option.[2] It is not a path an isolated individual has taken but one that attracts large numbers of young people from a variety of backgrounds. The objective presence of teshuvah in the persons of the baalei teshuvah and the presence of the yeshivot is of great significance in understanding the scope of the phenomenon.

It is not only the presence of the yeshivot, however, that is of critical importance in understanding the turning of seekers from the United States to Judaism. It is also the fact that the potential baal teshuvah has some consciousness of Judaism—memories, loyalties, knowledge— which leads him to Israel, to Jerusalem, or even directly to a yeshivah. Thus, American baalei teshuvah are not total strangers to Judaism and did not confront a totally new entity when they turned in the direction that led them to teshuvah. On the contrary, the resonance that the initial contact with Judaism had for them was based upon prior recognition. Most American baalei teshuvah in our sample had attended an afternoon school where some Jewish education was offered. Their parents were affiliated with Reform or Conservative synagogues and belonged to a Jewish organization (see Appendix). Certain Jewish holidays were observed or noted in some way at home. Nevertheless, none of these students claims to have grown up in a religious or traditional household where the authority of Jewish law was felt, and they considered themselves secular and far removed from Judaism and Jewish concerns prior to teshuvah.

In this brief introduction of American baalei teshuvah a second group ought to be mentioned. These are young Jews who come from homes that were orthodox or traditional. They are students who attended a Hebrew day school in the United States, who went to Jewish camps, and who felt at home among Jews and with Judaism before entering the yeshivah. They entered the baal teshuvah yeshivah in order to intensify their observance of Jewish law and to increase their knowledge of Jewish sources or, as they themselves say, to "strengthen" themselves.

Certain baal teshuvah yeshivot have sought out these students. Because of their background in Jewish studies, it is easier to teach them. Further, because they do not come as seekers and experimenters but as people committed to Orthodox Judaism who want to heighten their commitment, they add stability to the yeshivah. In their case, moreover, the yeshivah is relieved of the extremely difficult task of people-changing with which it is engaged when dealing with those who come as self-defined secular Jews.

Those who come seeking "strengthening" nevertheless define themselves as baalei teshuvah. The teshuvah to which they refer, however, is of a different order than that of one who comes from outside the structures of Judaism. In fact, the process involved with the "strengtheners" is closer to the traditional meaning of teshuvah—the return of those who knew and had observed the law but who had veered from it. In any event, these are not the people for whom the yeshivot for baalei teshivah were originally founded. The current teshuvah phenomenon grew in response to the needs of those who were raised outside the framework of traditional Judaism and outside the authority of Jewish law. Our analysis will focus upon these baalei teshuvah, those introduced as the first group of American baalei teshuvah, rather than upon those who have an orthodox background and come for "strengthening."

The second large group of baalei teshuvah in yeshivot today whom we shall analyze are Israelis of Western background. They have certain things in common with the American baalei teshuvah who define themselves as having been secular. The Israelis too are mainly from large cities, although some come from smaller settlements. They have completed high school, and some have attended a university for several years. Because they have been educated in Israel, they have studied the Bible and Jewish history in school, and are acquainted with the holidays, calendar, and symbols of Judaism. If the number of religious practices observed in their homes is a measure of the traditionality of their backgrounds, most of them would not be considered secular, certainly not wholly secular.

In only one-sixth of the homes, for instance, were no religious practices whatever observed, not even Yom Kippur, the most sacred day of the Jewish year. More important than this measure, however, for determining the religious-cultural state of the baal teshuvah prior to teshuvah is his own self-description. Israeli baalei teshuvah are quite clear and forceful in defining themselves as having been secular, meaning that their life was not determined by the commandments of Jewish law and that their actual behavior violated aspects of it. They state that their values and priorities were not what they considered to be those of a religious person. Finally, they state that they did not participate in religious communal life and probably had few, if any, religious friends.

Like the American baalei teshuvah, Israelis from this background embark upon a search, which leads them sooner or later to teshuvah. Israel does not have dozens of heterodox religious groups competing for the allegiance of the seekers. Options like the cults of America are not readily available, and Israelis do not live in a milieu in which shopping for spiritual alternatives is a common pursuit. A Judaism that appears vital and strong is available, however. And Israelis tend to turn to it directly, when the point of turning is reached. It should be noted, however, that some Israeli baalei teshuvah did seek out non-Jewish religious possibilities. In some accounts reading of Eastern religious traditions is mentioned. A few went to Zen sessions; some visited gurus when traveling abroad. If cults were more widespread in Israel, there is no reason to doubt that the passage to teshuvah would be marked by stopovers.

The Israelis add to the search theme a Jewish and especially Israeli articulation, sometimes associated with reformist intentions. They focus upon changes that must be made to alter Israeli society fundamentally. They link teshuvah to the realization that something more or beyond the reality around them, which they perceive as marred and disappointing, must be achieved if the Jewish state is to fulfill its destiny. Their descriptions abound in criticism of the State and in pining for something lost. The teshuvah of this group can only be understood in light of the climate in Israel after the Six Day War of 1967 and after the Yom Kippur War of 1973. Each of these wars was followed by a period of self-questioning within broad segments of the population,

albeit in a mood different in the latter years than in the years in between wars.

The record of an Israeli male, nineteen years old, offers a sense of
the experiences and problems which led members of this group to
teshuvah.

I came from a patriotic family. Both my parents had been raised
in religious homes, but our family was totally cut off from Jewish
tradition. I was not interested in Judaism at all until the Yom Kippur war. In the third day of the war I was sent into action. Eight
friends were killed and I was wounded seriously in the second hour
of fighting.

I was lying in the hospital. A friend came to visit and we started
talking about religious ideas. I decided that I wanted to study Maimonides' *Guide to the Perplexed,* but there was no one in the hospital with whom I could study. Instead I read Hesse's *Narcissus* and
found great spiritual wealth and direction there. While in the hospital
Lubavitcher *hasidim** came and urged me to pray. I decided that if
it didn't come from within me, from some inner motive, I would not
pray. I was burdened with lots of questions about the meaning of
life for which I had no answers. I thought that Judaism had the
weight which would enable me to wrestle with these questions,
but I had no one to help me. Yet I knew that something spiritual
was happening to me while I was lying there.

I went home to study for entrance exams at the university and
to do physiotherapy. I considered going to a kibbutz. But in the end
I decided to try the university, without much enthusiasm.

I became friendly with some religious students, and I began to
study Judaism myself. I can't tell you exactly what grabbed me.
I felt that there was a power there, a way of life, a force which could
guide men in life. What really attracted me was the power to shape
peoples' existence on a day-to-day basis.

I began to work alone on the fundamentals of the religion. It
was good that I began alone so that the change came from within me
and not from some outer force. At the same time, I became terribly
disgusted with what was going on in Israel. I love the land absolutely,
but I felt then very much opposed to the State as it was. I felt there
was no hope in trying to change things because whatever I might
attempt to do to change the country would weaken me. Now I
believe that only if the society returns to its source will the problems
be solved. I have no interest in politics. I used to be interested but it
decreased as I became more interested in religion. Politics seems to
me to be dirt and nonsense, and Zionism empty cliches. The Jewish
people was destined to be more than a state and an army. It was

*An enthusiastic religious group whose members engage in mission-
ary work among Jews, encouraging them to fulfill ritual commandments.

always a special people, morally and spiritually. It seems to me that
we have lost that.

The quotation must be seen against the post-Six Day War period,
in which several critical issues came to Israeli consciousness. One was
the State's deep isolation within the world of nations and its links and
dependence upon the Jewish people throughout the world. Another
was the persistence of the question of the legitimacy of the State of
Israel and its relationship to the Land of Israel. Israelis themselves and
outsiders sought to define these relationships in light of historical,
political, and religious considerations. Finally, the Six Day War, and
the Yom Kippur War after it destroyed the sense that the future of
Israel was guaranteed. Both demonstrated clearly that Israel's survival
is threatened and that the struggle for that survival will continue
to make great demands upon each individual and upon the collective.
The questions arose among many tired of that struggle: Why? What
for? Is it worthwhile? These are the questions which underlie the
teshuvah phenomenon among Israelis and to which teshuvah gives
a clear and radical answer.

We turn now to the third group of baalei teshuvah to be introduced
in this brief introduction, which is the second group of Israelis. These
are baalei teshuvah who originate in the disadvantaged neighborhoods
of large Israeli cities and in the development towns. Here are to be
found young people of Asian and African origin, children of traditional
families, of Moroccan, Persian, Iraqi, Yemenite, and Kurdistani immigrants. Their teshuvah is part of the reaction of the "second Israel"
to what is perceived by them as the "first Israel," namely, the European-
derived establishment of Israeli society.

For the individual coming from this background, teshuvah is a
religious change. It is a transformation that makes of a life experienced
as empty or meaningless one experienced as full, whole, and holy. As
a process undergone by a group coming from this ethnic background,
teshuvah is an assertion of traditional ways in the face of secular and
Western Israeli society.

An Israeli of Moroccan background described his own life and that
of his peers as "going down," until a sudden experience of purification
set him upon the path of renewal. Teshuvah became for him a way out
of personal confusion and degradation.

> I spent my free time reading love books which my brother
> brought home. The stories and the desires uprooted me from reality.
> Slowly I came to feel estranged from everything that used to be

precious and holy to me.... Soon I didn't recognize myself, and I asked myself repeatedly how I had lost my senses. I didn't know the reason for my own degeneration. I had become a person from whom one had to stay away. I hardly even went to school. I was confused, tired, and nervous.... No values, no respect and no work. Everything seemed the same to me.

The neighborhood where we lived was very loose. In the summer everyone was exposed. It unbalanced me. During this season I was most wild and often felt that I despised my own life, because it was without content. Then came drugs and I became even further removed from reality and wasted.

I thought the army would straighten me out and I would begin a new life. But after a few weeks they simply threw me out. I was totally broken.

Then I found myself on a ship for Europe. There I had ups and downs. Finally I landed in jail. I couldn't speak to the other prisoners because I didn't understand their language and I couldn't read. I was alone, and slowly found the way back to myself. It was as if I could see through an inner window into my interior.

Somehow I got back to my city and to my neighborhood. A friend told me about an "invasion" of a rabbi into the neighborhood. I really didn't know what the military term invasion meant here especially when, as my friend described it, it was accompanied by a band playing oriental music. But since I didn't have anything to do that night, and I still hadn't gotten into trouble, I went to listen. The rabbi spoke simply and quickly. He let the band play a lot....

The multitude of young people who had gathered together there, all looking like me with wild hair and clothes, found themselves singing the tune "Help me to life, to conquer the drive which tempts me toward wickedness." Then there was a break and the rabbi spoke. More correctly, he shouted in a decisive and convincing way. He compared the difference between the development of an animal and the development of man, showing how this reflects man's special destiny and mission.

The words were clear. It was as if they cried out—why didn't we pay attention to these words which were so correct and true? To be men and not animals. It seemed to me that he wasn't giving a speech but was rather hammering nails in the hearts of the listeners. All doubts left me. The music began again... I felt as if something was calling me. What were the tears flowing from my eyes—I the one who had been so blocked from emotions.

I went out purified and washed clean. That night I hardly slept. I cried a great deal. Toward morning I slept deeply and when I woke I felt as if I was beginning a new life. An inner force moved me, quietly...."

Three backgrounds and three paths leading to the same undertaking via the same institution. The search of young Jews for a new community and a new spiritual way is the story of protesting youth throughout the West. It is also the story of the protest and nostalgia of youth whose roots are in Islamic countries. The fascinating aspect of the story is not the protest itself, which is something familiar both in the East and the West in the past two decades. It is, rather, the radical direction in which the energy of protest has been channeled. This is in many respects the yeshivah's doing. In the next chapter we turn to a discussion of the teshuvah concept and the special tasks of the yeshivah for baalei teshuvah.

2
Yeshivot for Newcomers

Traditional and Contemporary Teshuvah

Teshuvah is that "turning" whereby the relationship of the individual Jew (as well as that of the group) with God is restored.[1] At the very core of Judaism, this notion rests upon the fundamental belief that faithfulness to God's law is essential for the Jew and for the Jewish people and that violations must be reversed through a full moral and ritual reformation—at one time by an expiatory blood sacrifice after the destruction of the Temple by teshuvah alone.[2] Neither the proper order of life in this world nor the longed-for redemption could be realized without teshuvah: "All the prophets commanded teshuvah, and Israel will not be delivered without teshuvah."[3]

Essentially, teshuvah is a decision to desist from acts that violate the law, the halachah, and a decision to return to observance of the halachah.[4] "Repentance is that the sinner forsakes his sin and puts it away out of his thoughts and fully resolves in his mind that he will not do it again; as it is written, "Let the wicked man forsake his way and the bad man his thoughts."[5] True "turning" and "return" assumes full repentance and determination not to stray from the path considered to be God's will for his people.

Teshuvah is a central moment in the religious life of every Jew because it is assumed that everyone sins and must, therefore, repent and return. Judaism has made provision for the act of teshuvah in the ritual framework within which the traditional Jew lives. A prayer for forgiveness of sins was introduced in the prayers recited daily. An entire ritual period of the year is dedicated to repentance, beginning on Rosh Hashanah, the first of the Ten Days of Repentance, and climaxing in Yom Kippur, when penitential prayers are recited all day.

Every Jew who repents and returns is considered a baal teshuvah. Jewish law does not distinguish between degrees or qualities of return—between one who returns from within the tradition and one who returns from without. The teshuvah of a Jew living in traditional Jewish society was almost always "teshuvah from within"—the repentance of one who recognized the authority of the halachah but who strayed from its precepts. A more drastic sort of teshuvah, "teshuvah from without," did occur, was noticed, and was encouraged even in traditional Jewish society. However, teshuvah of this sort was unusual, largely because so few Jews in traditional society lived outside the authority of the halachah. "Where a baal teshuvah stands not even a fully righteous man can stand."[6]

In the traditional situation individuals who departed from communal norms were obliged to repair their violation of accepted standards if they wished to "return to the fold." When the traditional Jewish community was intact, teshuvah was a turning to God, but also such a return to the fold, a returning to and affirmation of the social-cultural framework within which the Jews lived. However, the traditional Jewish community is not now intact, and as a result contemporary teshuvah is strikingly different from its traditional forerunner. The majority of the Jewish people is now "secular" and no longer accepts the basic principles of Judaism, nor does it follow the practices that are the translation of those principles into the language of daily life. The contemporary baal teshuvah, as contrasted to baalei teshuvah of earlier periods, does not return to the majority. Rather, by undertaking teshuvah, he in fact leaves the majority. He moves from that body that defines itself as orthodox and that sees itself in strong opposition to the majority. Within the current social context, the religious change he undertakes is, it might be said, a highly sectarian act.

Furthermore, the contemporary baal teshuvah did not grow up in a society where the world view and principles of Judaism were presupposed and where the authority of the halachah was accepted naturally. Judaism was neither an ethos nor a system lived and breathed from infancy and broken away from recently. Judaism had never been a reality that ordered his life. When he returns, therefore, he returns to a relatively new quantity. He may feel an affinity toward it, he may even recognize aspects of it, but he is fundamentally strange to it. His return must be a radical one covering a great distance. The change that occurs today, and to which one refers in speaking of contemporary teshuvah, is a radical break and a basic reordering of self around a new center. The contemporary baal teshuvah commits himself to a structure of ideas, interrelationships, and actions which were not his prior to teshuvah. In making this commitment he cuts himself off from the structure and framework within which he lived prior to the change.

These, however, are essentially sociological and sociologically induced psychological differences. Religiously, teshuvah today is still teshuvah. In his treatise on teshuvah, the great medieval sage Maimonides marked out the stages of the process.[7] The first is the act of recognition. Failures must be recognized, acknowledged, and then reversed through teshuvah. Regret follows recognition and implies that the individual has understood the gravity of his misdeed and can resolve not to repeat it. The third stage in the process is the determination not to transgress again and the attempt to extirpate the desire to transgress from the heart. Finally, a formal confession is required in order to externalize the inner determination to return and change. The confessional formula cited by Maimonides summarizes the essence of the entire process: "O God, I have sinned, I have done iniquity, I have transgressed before thee, and I have done thus and so. I am sorry and ashamed for my deed, and I will never do it again."[8]

The contemporary baal teshuvah resolves to cease living according to norms and structures which violate the halachah. He resolves to accept the framework of ideas and behaviors considered to be God's law, and to orient himself in the world by means of this framework. He comes to regard his past not as a period for which he is guilty but as a period of ignorance. Having reached a point of discontent with life as it was lived, the baal teshuvah turned in search of something more. And having determined to make a commitment, he resolved to forsake the past, put it behind him, and dedicate himself fully to a new present.

The elements structurally parallel to the elements of teshuvah in the tradition are obvious: recognition, regret, determination to change. Confession too is present in the contemporary process in discussions about the past, although not in the sense of a ritual formula reciting a litany of sins. The fit of traditional normative categories to the experience of contemporary baalei teshuvah was the real insight of those who believed that a movement of contemporary teshuvah could emerge if the proper institutional framework were established to nurture and guide it. It was clear that the category "baal teshuvah" meant something new in the current context. It was equally clear that the moment and movement of teshuvah could fit the contemporary situation and would have resonance for large numbers of Jews.

The primary task of the yeshivot established for baalei teshuvah was to channel the energy that brought young Jews from a nonreligious background to turn toward an orthodox establishment. In other words, the turning, whether in origin a protest against secular society or a vague spiritual quest, had to be transformed into teshuvah. The rabbis who founded the yeshivot believed that this task could be done, and they set about interpreting the traditional categories so as to make them meaningful to the experience of these newcomers.

Establishment of the Yeshivot for Baalei Teshuvah

The history of the yeshivot for baalei teshuvah begins in the middle 1960s. At that time two American rabbis, Noah Weinberg and Mordecai Goldstein, independently concluded that the time was ripe for a religious renewal within Judaism, that the movement of Jews away from Judaism could be reversed. They discerned a new openness to religion among middle- and upper-class young people in the United States generally, part of the generation's protest against the regnant materialistic and consumer-oriented culture. They felt strongly that Orthodox Judaism would appeal to the young Jews being drawn to non-Jewish religious groups, on the one hand, or registering for courses in Jewish studies on the other. To the two rabbis the problem seemed merely technical: how to make young people aware of orthodox values and beliefs as a way of life. No doubt existed in their minds that at this particular moment in history exposure to Orthodox Judaism would lead to a return to it. The question was whether the moment would be seized, whether other rabbis would respond to the challenge of reaching out to secular Jews and drawing them back to Judaism.

The story of the first baal teshuvah to approach these men reveals some of the problems they faced.[9] Rabbi Noah Weinberg of Baltimore, a student at Ner Yisrael yeshivah, had come to Jerusalem in the mid-sixties to investigate the possibilities of founding some kind of program for returning Jews. The idea of actually founding a separate baal teshuvah yeshivah was not yet certain in his mind. A young man who had heard of his talent as a teacher approached him and said that he wanted to study Judaism, that he had no previous acquaintance with orthodoxy and no knowledge of Jewish sources.

Rabbi Noah Weinberg advised the young man to speak with a neighbor, Rabbi Mordecai Goldstein, who might be willing to tutor him. Rabbi Goldstein was himself a student in the Hafetz Hayim yeshiva in Jerusalem, and was also very interested in the possibility of working with baalei teshuvah. He accepted this young man as his first student. Others soon gathered and a small class was organized. When Rabbi Goldstein felt that the first student, the man who had approached

Rabbi Weinberg originally, was ready to make his way in a standard yeshivah, he attempted to arrange for his acceptance. According to Rabbi Goldstein, several yeshivot refused to accept the baal teshuvah, reflecting their suspicion of his background more than of his ability to study. This refusal of the standard yeshivot to welcome baalei teshuvah convinced Rabbi Goldstein of the need to establish a separate institution for them. It was he, indeed, who founded the first baal teshuvah yeshivah on Mt. Zion in Jerusalem. This culminated several years of struggling and moving until a proper site had been located and funds secured for the new project. Rabbi Goldstein had sought out potential baalei teshuvah and had gathered enough to be given a room in the old Hebron yeshivah building, where he taught them. When that room became too small, he moved to a larger one in the Diskin Orphanage. After the Six Day War, the Ministry of Religion offered several abandoned buildings on Mt. Zion to Rabbi Goldstein as the site for a yeshivah. The ministry was anxious to have somebody take over these buildings and occupy them quickly. The offer was accepted, and funds were raised through the ministry and from tourists visiting the site to repair the war-damaged structures.[10]

The Diaspora Yeshivah was founded in 1967. In those years following the war, thousands of Jewish visitors roamed the Old City of Jerusalem. Among them were hundreds of long-haired young men, with guitars or packs on their backs, who were approached by Rabbi Goldstein to enter his yeshivah. The rabbi went out on the streets, spoke to young people, and convinced them to enter and try the yeshivah. Very few of those who arrived at the Diaspora yeshivah had any background in Jewish life or the study of Judaism. Many had been part of the counterculture in the United States and brought the accoutrements of the life-style associated with that culture to Mt. Zion.

Because of the background of the students, and the lack of any experience in organizing and ordering the new establishment, the first years on Mt. Zion were tumultuous. Establishing a study schedule, teaching Hebrew, enabling students to follow an argument in a talmudic text, eliminating drug use, maintaining a normal sleeping and waking schedule, educating these young people in the dietary laws of Judaism, the sabbath laws, dress customs, and so on—none of these was an easy task. Moreover, because the Diaspora Yeshivah was the first baal teshuvah establishment, and because its patterns were experimental and highly unusual in the religious world of Judaism, it captured much media interest. This created the image of the baal teshuvah yeshivah as a refuge for American "hippies" and created great suspicion among orthodox Jews as to the seriousness of the institution as a yeshivah.

Over the years a firm routine has been established in the Diaspora Yeshivah. As if to emphasize the order and conformity of the yeshivah to the standards of the ultraorthodox community, all students dress in dark suits and hats. They all follow a study schedule. Drugs have been eliminated. And yet, despite the order and organization which have been established and despite the routinization which has occurred over the years, the Diaspora Yeshivah remains distinctive among other baal teshuvah yeshivot. First, it still reaches out to everyone who passes by and is willing to take the risk of welcoming people whose behavior, at least initially, deviates greatly from that demanded by the yeshivah. While other yeshivot have become more careful and selective in their recruiting, Rabbi Goldstein retains the vision that was his when he founded the school in 1967. He believes that any Jew can become a baal teshuvah and is willing to take the risk of trying to convert him.

While Rabbi Goldstein was working on his project, Rabbi Noah Weinberg, with other rabbis from Ner Yisrael in Baltimore, attempted to found a new yeshivah in Jerusalem, which would have a baal teshuvah division. These rabbis were all interested in working with baalei teshuvah but were not certain that a separate and distinct institution would be the most effective way to do so. They conceived of a combination with a standard yeshivah, in order to give structure to the baal teshuvah branch and to legitimate it. In 1967, before the June war, they founded Mevasseret Yerushalayim. The effort failed, however, because of financial problems, and its founders, Rabbi Noah Weinberg, Rabbi Nota Shiller, and Rabbi Mendel Weinbach dispersed.

Reb Noah, as he is known in "teshuvah circles," remained in Israel, moved to Bnei Brak, and founded a small yeshivah for baalei teshuvah there, which is called Magen Avraham. This institution has remained small and for many years was the only baal teshuvah institution in the city of Bnei Brak, which is a center of standard yeshivot. Rabbi Noah left Magen Avraham after a year and returned to Jerusalem to work on the reestablishment of the baal teshuvah institution which had failed in 1967. In 1972, when Rabbi Shiller returned to Israel with the financial resources to guarantee the success of the new institution, the Shma Yisrael yeshivah was founded. Its name was changed to Ohr Sameah a year later, when Rabbi Noah left after an argument with his co-founders. He went on to found his fourth yeshivah, Aish Hatorah, where he has remained.

In the late sixties and early seventies, other rabbis conceived plans to establish educational programs and yeshivot for baalei teshuvah. It seemed to them that the ground was fertile and that whatever was planted flourished. Thus, in the summer of 1970, two English rabbis organized and taught a course for English university students in Jerusalem. The success of the program led to its development into a full-year institute. One of the founders, Rabbi Baruch Horowitz, became the head of Dvar Yerushalayim yeshivah for baalei teshuvah. This school has become a large institution, located in the midst of the orthodox neighborhood of Geulah, and containing programs in Hebrew, Russian, Spanish, and French as well as in English.

The other English rabbi involved in the summer program of 1970, Rabbi David Refson, was approached by several women who asked that he establish a program for them. The question of women within the baal teshuvah framework had to arise. Traditional Judaism places limitations on the nature of what women study and their obligation to study. Women traditionally do not study Talmud, certainly do not study with men, and are not obligated to study "day and night" as men are. Even an institution as innovative as the baal teshuvah yeshivah could not permit women to study alongside and equally with men. At the same time, the baal teshuvah yeshivah could not ignore the appeal and needs of women without eliminating a large population of potential baalei teshuvah.

The solution was to establish a separate school for women, whose program would be different than the program for men but which would be oriented toward accomplishing the same transformation, which is the essential task of the baal teshuvah yeshivah. The first and today the largest school for women, Nevei Yerushalayim, was established by Rabbi Refson. Today five such institutions exist, all attached organizationally and sharing staff with a male baal teshuvah yeshivah but run separately.

The task of the baal teshuvah institutions for women is to demonstrate the total reliability of the women who study and are trained within it to the orthodox community. This task is extremely important because of the critical role women play in the life of the family and in the education of children. Obviously the same task of demonstrating reliability holds for male baalei teshuvah but is of particular importance and is particularly sensitive regarding women. The orthodox community hesitates before accepting women, who have been part of another culture and society and who have not known the ways of Judaism since childhood, even more than it hesitates before accepting men.

Further, the task of the institutions for women is particularly difficult because of the nature of the change women need undergo in becoming baalei teshuvah. Women must learn to accept a system that has relegated them to a secondary role in ritual life and in the life of learning. Woman's function and the source of her status is homemaking and motherhood. The attitude toward women is grounded upon the assumption that biological differences between the sexes imply cultural and social differences and that this division is not only natural but also divinely ordained. Adopting this view and committing oneself to the way of life which goes with it demands great changes in the thinking and behavior of women, in many ways more difficult than the changes demanded of men.

In returning to the history of the development of the baal teshuvah yeshivah, we turn to the story of the Hartmann Institute because it conveys a sense of the spirit of the students and staffs in the early years of the yeshivah development as well as outlining how an institution actually emerged and grew. The Hartmann Institute was founded in Jerusalem as a program for American orthodox students studying at the Hebrew University, enabling them to study Talmud after university hours. A rabbi from New York's Yeshivah University, Rabbi Hayim Brovender, who was at the time a doctoral student at the Hebrew University, ran the Hartmann program. Very quickly, reflecting the spirit of the late sixties and early seventies, students with no religious background and education were drawn to the institute. These became baalei teshuvah, and their number soon exceeded the number of orthodox students for whom the program had been intended. The Hartmann Institute became a baal teshuvah institution in those years by force of student demand.

The personal relationships with the teachers in the Hartmann program and the esprit of study that was created were extremely important in helping students to overcome the initial difficulties and continuing demands of being a yeshivah student. When Rabbi Brovender decided to leave the institute, a core of loyal students insisted that he remain their teacher and that he establish another program in his spirit and according to his conception of education for baalei teshuvah. An apartment was rented in the Givat Hamivtar neighborhood of Jerusalem where eight students and Rabbi Brovender established a new yeshivah. The following year the core had expanded to thirty students and it was necessary to find larger quarters. The old building of the Navardock yeshivah, which had served several baal teshuvah institutions in their early stages of development, was rented.

Yeshivat Hamivtar, the name taken from the original location, developed over the next few years. It moved twice, trebled in size, and is now in the process of building its own quarters in an outlying neighborhood of Jerusalem. A women's branch, staffed by the same teachers who teach the men, was added in the second year of development. Having passed through several years when funds were scarce and physical conditions difficult, Yeshivat Hamivtar is now fully established. Most of its staff are young men who have been with Rabbi Brovender for many years. It attracts a very specific, highly intellectual population, and prides itself on its distinctive character.

The experiences of beginning as a small group around a rabbi, struggling for survival, passing from building to building, searching for funds, and defining a specific "way" for the yeshivah are shared by all baal teshuvah institutions. Nearly all have in the meantime established themselves, located stable sources of funds, draw a certain kind of student population, and have delineated a particular "way" as their own. While in the first decade of their development over fifteen baal teshuvah yeshivot were established, in the last year not a single major institution has come into being. Existing institutions are expanding in numbers rather than new ones being founded.

The earliest yeshivot for baalei teshuvah were founded for students from the Diaspora. By and large, they were populated nearly entirely by students from English-speaking countries, mainly from the United States. A very significant development in the history of these institutions was the emergence of yeshivot for Israeli baalei teshuvah. This development is linked to two major institutional frameworks: Ohr Sameah and Machon Meir, the baal teshuvah branch of Merkaz Harav yeshivah.[11] These were the pioneering institutions. Today one-third of the students in baal teshuvah institutions in Jerusalem are Israelis. Some of the Israeli schools are totally independent, others are linked to yeshivot for students from the Diaspora.

The origin of the first Israeli school was in the personal teshuvah of Ika Yisraeli, an Israeli painter associated with the political Left and a well-known figure in Tel Aviv's bohemia. Ika had become interested in what was going on in the Diaspora Yeshivah. He went to Mt. Zion and decided to study with Rabbi Goldstein. When several friends of his joined, Ika requested that a full program be set up for them in Hebrew. Rabbi Goldstein could not provide the resources. However, an Israeli rabbi, Avraham Ravitz, who had heard of the nascent group and who saw the potential for an Israeli movement parallel to the movement developing among American students, took the initiative and proposed an institutional arrangement with the American rabbis of Ohr Sameah.

Recognizing the significance of the Israeli development and the advantages of association to both sides, the American rabbis agreed to provide the initial funds and building for the fledgling Israeli institution.

The Israelis moved into the building the Americans vacated when they moved into the large complex across the street. Although Israelis and Americans study separately, the staffs meet together, and major policy decisions are taken together. The presence of the Israeli staff and students adds important dimensions to the institution. It has facilitated the integration of American students in the orthodox community by increasing the American institution's stature within the Jerusalem world. While rabbis from the United States are known and respected in the world of Jerusalem yeshivot, the association of Jerusalem rabbis with their institutions has definitely added to their status and guaranteed their legitimation. What is more, the Israelis have furthered programs which the American rabbis wished to carry out among the nonreligious Israeli public, establishing links with the army, *kibbutzim,* and outlying towns. Finally, the presence of Israeli baalei teshuvah and rabbis, working for the same aims and within the same framework, has created a sense of the pervasiveness of the teshuvah phenomenon. The individual undergoing a transformation as major as teshuvah requires a community to affirm his act, to make it appear sensible, reasonable, and real. A larger community does this more effectively than a smaller one.

Two major yeshivot for Israelis were founded in 1974, each with quite different and unique populations. The first was Machon Meir, founded by an Israeli baal teshuvah who had studied at the religious Zionist stronghold Merkaz Harav. Dov Bigon, inspired by a messianic view of the possibilities and significance of contemporary teshuvah and the importance of setting up special teshuvah institutions associated with the religious nationalist perspective, has been the force behind Machon Meir and its branches. The yeshivah has added a woman's institution and has organized evening classes in seven cities. The goal of those who have organized these classes is to interest as many Jews as possible in studying classical religious texts within a yeshivah setting, and to draw some toward teshuvah. Machon Meir is the most far-reaching teshuvah institution in Israel, having opened a branch in Eilat and a branch in Kiryat Shmonah. It has recently opened a program for English-speaking students, attempting to draw them not only to Judaism but to the specific religious-nationalist perspective.

Ohr Hahayim, the other major yeshivah for Israelis, differs from all large baal teshuvah yeshivot in its social composition, its specific goals, and its unusual spirit and atmosphere. This is a yeshivah founded exclusively for Oriental-Jewish youth and for youth on the fringes of society. The goal of its staff is to penetrate poor neighborhoods, areas of crime and drugs, and to speak to young people about a return to their roots, to the ways of their fathers. The yeshivah has grown to include over one hundred and fifty men and stretches over a solid block in Jerusalem's Bucharian quarter. It is the model for several smaller baal teshuvah institutions, which appeal to the same population for the same purpose.

The yeshivot, as physical representations of a spiritual and communal process, have given the teshuvah phenomenon both visibility and objectivity. One yeshivah in particular has become a codeword for contemporary teshuvah: Ohr Sameah. This institution was founded in 1972 as Shma Yisrael and changed its name to Ohr Sameah in 1974 after the reorganization of its directors. It stands in an old-new neighborhood of Jerusalem. The building, which serves as a dormitory and school for Israeli students, faces the older neighborhood and stands opposite the great old Navordeck yeshivah. The second and newer building, which serves as a dormitory and school for English-speaking students, stands almost as an extension of a modern housing project being constructed behind it. Close to four hundred students are to be found in these two buildings.

Some, about half, have arrived either on the suggestion of a friend or having read or otherwise heard about the institution. While in the early years of the yeshivah's existence all students were recruited from the streets of Jerusalem by a practiced and professional recruiter, today less than half arrive off the streets, reflecting the success of the public relations work of Ohr Sameah in the United States.

The Israeli building, rather cut off from the more modern, sprawling American complex, could be any dormitory school building in Israel; study halls and libraries on the bottom floors, classrooms, offices, and small apartments on the upper floors. The American branch could not be just any yeshivah or school. It is massive, well-kept, obviously well-supported, and seems clearly to be an import. And then there are those physical features that distinguish it from an ordinary yeshivah. A lot in the middle of the buildings is used as a baseball field; another empty lot is designated a wedding pavilion. In either place at certain moments one sees the odd collection of people: collegiate-looking young men, old traditional Jerusalem rabbis, modern orthodox rabbis dressed quite obviously as Americans, soldiers in uniform, and young men dressed in various degrees of traditional yeshivah garb.

The center of Ohr Sameah, as of every yeshivah, is the *beit midrash,* the study hall. Students spend most of the day and part of the night in the beit midrash. At any hour one may observe students and teachers bent over lecterns, sitting in small groups on benches, or huddled in a corner studying or arguing over the meaning of a passage. At almost any hour a low steady hum rises from the study hall as people work their way out loud through these passages.

And yet, if one looks carefully at the beit midrash in Ohr Sameah, certain highly distinctive features are evident that distinguish it from the beit midrash of a standard yeshivah. Again, one sees a rather strange mix of figures in a variety of fashions, unlike the uniform external appearance of men in a standard yeshivah. Some students wear corduroy pants or jeans and an open colored shirt. They look like students found on any college campus, except for the black *kippah* (skullcap) and the ritual fringes hanging out over their pants. Clean shaven or bearded, these students are clearly new to the beit midrash. Their gestures seem uncertain and even straining. Some, beginning to take on the appearance of their teachers, have exchanged the colored shirt for a white one and the corduroy pants for dark slacks. Yet, they still lack the confidence and naturalness of those who are truly at home in a study hall and truly comfortable in black suits and hats.

In the American beit midrash one also comes upon books rarely found in a standard yeshivah. Piled up on the benches and tables in Ohr Sameah are thick and expensive Hebrew-English dictionaries, interlinear translations, and cribs of various kinds. The books point to the struggle of the students with the very language of the texts and with the basic structure of argumentation they are attempting to understand. In the Israeli beit midrash the Hebrew-English dictionaries obviously are not necessary. There too, however, signs of the students' freshness and uncertainty are evident. One hears questions about matters known by children who have grown up in a "natural" orthodox environment. One hears interpretations of texts that reveal the novice at his craft. And in the Israeli beit midrash, too, the variety of dress and mannerism is that of an unusual population come together to study.

Ohr Sameah, like other baal teshuvah yeshivot, is located in the heart of an urban neighborhood. It is not isolated from city life or withdrawn from what goes on around it. Students walk in and out. Visitors walk in and out. As part of its education program, the Israeli army sends soldiers to hear lectures. People from the neighborhood use a path that cuts between the yeshivah's offices and study hall as a shortcut. The "secular world," as it were, is present by choice. The yeshivah could have been located elsewhere as a withdrawn retreat. The effect of its presence here is to reinforce the commitment of those who do not look and behave like the outsiders who walk in and around the buildings.

The presence of the secular world highlights the boundaries between worlds.

Exemplars of the choice of worlds baalei teshuvah are expected to make are highly visible in Ohr Sameah, and this is intentional. Prominent on the staff of the Israeli institution, for example, are two well-known baalei teshuvah who represent the radical change the yeshivah demands from the students. In an ordinary yeshivah, a baal teshuvah who is not, or is not yet, a recognized scholar would not gain such prominence. Here, however, these men are favorite figures and wield great influence over the students. One is Ika Yisraeli, who is today a respected member of the staff of Ohr Sameah. He has become a great advocate of ultra-orthodoxy, declaring that the only way to become a baal teshuvah is to change radically, to break all ties with the past, because such ties pull one back to a secular existence he believes must be renounced totally if a true religious change is to be made. Ika speaks of man as a weak creature who must be supported by a framework that will keep him from falling. Identification with this framework must be complete. Therefore, one must change one's dress, one's language and manner of speaking, one's associations, and one's interests to conform to the ways of the community. He himself stopped painting. When he does paint, he says, it is only as a concession to melancholy, hence an admission of weakness.

The other figure at Ohr Sameah who represents the radical one-hundred-and-eighty-degree change is Mordecai Arnon, known as "Pupick" from his days as a popular entertainer and film star. Reb Mordecai, as he is called in Ohr Sameah, denounces his past life. Further, he denounces the secular culture of Israel and the state that created and nurtures this culture. In absolute black and white terms he describes two worlds, two ways of living, one true and one false, and asks students to choose. He explains that no compromise with secular reality is possible, that moderation in one's demands upon oneself is weakness.

The message of Ika Yisraeli and Mordecai Arnon is not new. It is a radical version of the view of secular culture held by an entire community, a view which determines the nature of the relationships between this community and the non-ultraorthodox world outside it. The novelty is that Ika Yisraeli and Pupick Arnon enunciate the position and represent the stance. Baalei teshuvah know the pasts of these men, and they see where they are now. These are the heroes of Ohr Sameah. The change they symbolize is also represented by other figures in the yeshivah, whose "before" and "after" are part of the public lore of Ohr Sameah.

The success of Ohr Sameah and other baal teshuvah institutions cannot be understood without taking their geographical location into account. While a few teshuvah institutions exist outside Jerusalem, and while branches of Israeli yeshivot have been founded in New York, Los Angeles, and St. Louis, it is Jerusalem that is the center of the baal teshuvah phenomenon today. No major center or network of baal teshuvah yeshivot exists outside of Israel or outside Jerusalem.[12]

The sociological context Israel provides has been critical in nurturing and supporting the growth of the baal teshuvah yeshivot. First, there is the supportive effect of a Jewish environment and national culture for "returning" Jews who have grown up in a culture whose basic memories, symbols, and calendar are Christian. Israel's central symbols and fundamental identity references are clearly Jewish. Despite secularization, despite the transformation of meanings and values, the continuities with the manifold historical layers of Jewish religious-national culture are plainly evident and readily felt. This environment gives, as it were, objective support to the subjective processes of those discovering or returning to Judaism.

If this is the effect of Israel as a country, it is even more so of Jerusalem the city. Jerusalem is the *axis mundi* of the Jewish world.[13] Its historical, religious, and cultural "density," and the living presence in it of faces from the Jewish past and present heighten the experience of the physical and spiritual continuity—and renewal—of the Jewish people and of Judaism. To enter the world of Judaism at the center is no mean matter. Its impact often overpowers the past and helps the baal teshuvah overcome it. As an American baal teshuvah stated:

> There has to be environmental support for such a radical change.
> If one can't find reinforcement once he leaves the doors of the
> yeshivah, then he immediately identifies with who he was instead
> and who he is becoming. In Jerusalem the secular environment is also
> difficult for the baal teshuvah to relate to. So he feels more com-
> fortable in a religious neighborhood. If you are trying to change in
> America there is an immediate conflict when you see everyone else.
> It is very difficult when you feel more secure with what you were.
> In Israel, the Israeli secular culture is as foreign as the religious cul-
> tre. So there is no real problem of identifying with the culture here
> all the time. You aren't always pushing the river here, and that
> induces one to change more quickly and more securely.

Another most significant factor in assessing the importance of Israel for the teshuvah phenomenon, and the importance of Jerusalem particularly, is the presence of a vibrant populous and geographically extensive orthodox community. In Jerusalem there is a large concentration of orthodox Jews, and the religious presence is especially felt. There is no doubt that the very existence of masses of orthodox Jews, the objective reality of their presence, supports the subjective experience and choice of the newcomer. The orthodox world is discovered, as it were, by the baal tehuvah. Its very being and strength reinforces his own personal decision. By linking him as a subject to a strong objective reality, it heightens the plausibility of his choice. Moreover, for one who is in between worlds and world views, the presence of the orthodox community provides a real image of what he aspires to be. He is able to project himself into the new world, to see himself acting in that community which is new to him, according to norms which are strange to him. He is able to consider himself within new situations, to try them on, as it were, and to observe others for whom orthodoxy "works."

This process can be seen clearly in the relationship of baalei teshuvah who have come from the United States to the community of American immigrants in Jerusalem. The city contains a large concentration of immigrants from the United States who have come to Israel, and to Jerusalem in particular, because of their orthodox religious convictions and loyalties. Their presence is felt in certain heavily orthodox neighborhoods, such as Bayit Va-Gan and Mattersdorf, as well as in more nonsegregated neighborhoods, such as Talbieh and Ramot Eshkol. The American presence in Jerusalem is felt in the English language heard distinctly in the streets, in the synagogues, schools, and stores of Jerusalem. This same presence is felt in the number of English books to be found in all bookstores, but especially those that specialize in "Jewish" books. It is even felt in the growing number of health food stores that have opened in the city.

The American orthodox immigrants form a support system for baal teshuvah yeshivot whose clientele is English-speaking. Families invite baalei teshuvah for meals on the Sabbath and holidays. They provide a reservoir for social life and contacts in many spheres. Moreover, they form the objective reality of orthodoxy so important for baalei teshuvah. English-speaking baalei teshuvah can witness an orthodox life in their own language, can participate in it, and feel themselves at home among others who have "returned" to Jerusalem in order to live a full Jewish religious life. Thus, the American orthodox community facilitates the adjustment of baalei teshuvah both to orthodoxy and to society in Israel.

The same factor—the presence of a strong, vital, and visible orthodox community—enables the baal teshuvah yeshivah to present a future social world to the baal teshuvah. The yeshivah is not a self-sufficient world, nor is it intended to be a total and permanent community for the baal teshuvah. No yeshivah is a monastery or a retreat. Yeshivah students live with their families, participate in the life of the community, and most intend to work once they leave the yeshivah. Baalei teshuvah in particular are interested in becoming members of a community outside the yeshivah. The purpose of the yeshivah is to prepare them for such participation and to help them become integrated members of an orthodox community.

For all these reasons, the major baal teshuvah enterprises have been established in Israel and in Jerusalem, and all are located in neighborhoods where an orthodox population dominates.

A listing of yeshivot for baalei teshuvah with approximate student populations is given below. Because the yeshivot do not keep reliable records on enrollments and because the student population includes a transient group, exact figures are not available:[14]

1. Diaspora Yeshivah, Jerusalem; 60 men, 30 women (non-Israeli); founded 1968.

2. Tifferet Hateshuvah, Jerusalem; 35 men (Israeli); founded 1977.

3. Aish Hatorah, Jerusalem; 80 men (non-Israeli); founded 1974.

4. Dvar Yerushalayim, Jerusalem; 150 men, 30 women (Israeli and non-Israeli); founded 1971.

5. Nevei Yerushalayim, Jerusalem; 150 women (Israeli and non-Israeli); founded 1971.

6. Ohr Sameah, Jerusalem; 250 men (American), 80 men (Israelis); founded 1972.

7. Ohr Hahayim, Jerusalem; 80 men (Israeli); founded 1975.

8. Naase Venishma, Jerusalem; 25 men (Israeli); founded 1977.

9. Machon Meir, Jerusalem; 75 men, 30 women (Israeli); founded 1974.

10. Machon Bruria, Jerusalem; 50 women (American); founded 1975.

11. Yeshivat Hamivtar, Jerusalem; 100 men (American); founded 1975.

12. Darcei Noam, Jerusalem; 14 men (American); founded 1978.

13. Shapell, Jerusalem; 15 men (American); founded 1969.

Recruiting

There is no aspect of the work of the baal teshuvah yeshivot that distinguishes them more from the standard yeshivot than recruiting. From the start the baal teshuvah yeshivot had to make the very fact of their existence known.[15] They had to reach out in order to find young people who might be interested in trying their programs. Standard yeshivot are part of a network of institutions known within orthodox circles. They are institutions to which students apply and arrive.

The baal teshuvah yeshivot adopted a recruiting method not only because they had to secure students in order to establish a permanent body to guarantee the stability of the institution. They recruited openly because their self-defined mission demanded reaching out to areas where yeshivah students were not usually found and using methods foreign to the traditional yeshivah world. They entered a market situation feeling that discontent existed among young people and that some could be drawn toward Judaism. They defined their task as a war against assimilation, against secular culture, and went out fishing for souls who might indeed be lured away from that culture. If the yeshivot were to demonstrate that real interest existed, that it could be channeled into orthodox structures, and that the baal teshuvah yeshivah was indeed a necessary institution, recruiting had to be successful.

The recruiting method of those years was pioneered by Rabbi Noah Weinberg and Rabbi Meir Shuster, an American-born rabbi employed by yeshivot to recruit baalei teshuvah. The method was quite simple: a potential student was approached by a "rabbinic" looking figure, either Rabbi Shuster or Rabbi Weinberg, at one of several customary sites— the Western Wall, the central bus station, or the campus of the Hebrew University. The rabbi extended an invitation to visit a yeshivah, claiming that a Jew who visited Israel without being in a yeshivah had not seen the real Israel. Young people who responded to the proposal with interest were directed to one of a number of yeshivot, depending upon the judgment of the recruiter as to which would be most suitable for him.

Upon entering the yeshivah the student met the staff and the student body, and was invited to attend classes and study in the beit midrash. All aspects of the yeshivah and life in it were presented to the potential student openly and immediately. In contrast to recruiting methods practiced in certain new religious groups, no secretive entrance procedures exist in the baal teshuvah yeshivot, nor is any attempt made to entice students to stay by concealing the full and demanding nature of yeshivah life.

It was a familiar scene in those early days of the yeshivot when nearly all students were Americans: bearded, long-haired young men with guitars in hand and packs hanging from their backs entering a yeshivah accompanied by Rabbi Shuster. Some were genuinely interested and others were happy to have a free meal, enjoy an exotic experience, and leave. The recruiting rabbis accomplished the task of filling the yeshivot in the early years and helped them get established.

Israeli yeshivot have never relied on this recruiting method. Those Israeli institutions attached to Diaspora yeshivot have been able to rely upon the established name of the existing institutions. More important, the Israeli yeshivot for baalei teshuvah have developed their own techniques appropriate to Israeli taste and needs. Thus, army units are invited to yeshivot to be introduced to Orthodox Judaism and to the yeshivah. The army agrees to this program in order to enrich the knowledge of the soldiers. While the yeshivah endorses this goal, it also hopes to attract some soldiers to return to it later as baalei teshuvah. Another method developed by Israeli baal teshuvah yeshivot is to send rabbis to lecture throughout the country. Seminars have been offered by the yeshivah staff which lead some participants to eventually study within the yeshivah framework. Finally, the yeshivot have managed to reach the radio, press, and TV, promoting themselves in their work in returning Jews to Judaism.

One sign of the routinization of the teshuvah phenomenon, and of the establishment certainly of the major yeshivot, is the fact that the active recruitment policy has been partially abandoned. The yeshivot have increasingly come to expect that potential baalei teshuvah will turn to them on their own initiative. They have also come to rely upon another type of student, one who applies for admission. These are mainly American students who have at least a minimal education in Jewish studies, who have heard about the intense study program in the yeshivot, and who desire to come for a few years to "intensify" or "strengthen" the education they have. They chose a baal teshuvah institution intentionally, most often because their past education has not prepared them to fit into a standard Israeli yeshivah.

Israeli students reach the yeshivot in several ways, one of which is recruitment. Rabbi Elbaz is the only rabbi of a major institution who goes out on the street to "evangelize." Almost all of his students arrive after hearing his sermons on the streets of Jerusalem. However, most of the Israelis entering yeshivot come because they have heard of the institutions and are seeking a place to study. They do not apply formally, but make their way to the building, find a rabbi, and establish the connection. A few students come to the yeshivot as a result of a lecture they have heard by a yeshivah rabbi. Yeshivot send lecturers to kibbutzim, to settlements or cities, and invite groups of soldiers and students to the yeshivah, hoping to interest them in teshuvah.

Formation of Baalei Teshuvah

The task of the baal teshuvah yeshivah is to resocialize Jews who have not experienced Judaism as a religious system and who are ignorant of its ideas and worldview. The yeshivah is to transform the behavior, attitudes, and beliefs of such people, commit them to orthodoxy, and gain legitimation for them within the orthodox community. As an institution aspiring to change people totally, the baal teshuvah yeshivah shares certain general features with other institutions whose task is resocialization. Yet, because it is a yeshivah, change that takes place within it is subject to the constraints of Judaism and the norms of the wider orthodox community with which the yeshivah is linked. This insures that certain methods familiar from literature on thought reform and indoctrination will not be utilized by the yeshivah to break down an individual's self and substitute another.[16] The baal teshuvah yeshivah can manipulate change but cannot violate the methods and ideals of study normative in other yeshivot that are accepted within the orthodox world.

Structurally, the baal teshuvah yeshivah and the standard yeshivah are very close. First, the central activity of both is the study of sacred texts. Such study, *talmud torah,* is a commandment incumbent upon every Jew.[17] It became a commandment of the highest order in Judaism from the time that the written word, the canon of the Torah, became the center of religious culture and the bedrock of national existence. Religious knowledge for the Jew consists of the ability to understand and the ability to interpret the Torah and the sacred literature accumulated in the commentaries. Such knowledge is thought to provide an understanding of the "mighty acts of God" and their interpretation in later Jewish thought, and to enable one to know what is demanded by Jewish religious law. More than that, study is a ritual act in Judaism, an act of worship. It is devotion—a mode of piety that serves, as the tradition has it, to bring the student closer to God. Talmud torah is not only a religious act of the highest order in Judaism, it is a symbol embodying central experiences and behaviors of the entire religious system. As a form of worship it is pari passu the nexus for fundamental Jewish values, cognitive and axiological.

All Jews are commanded to study throughout their lives. Those who wish to fulfill the ideal of talmud torah as fully as possible enter a yeshivah for an unlimited period of time. They thereby participate in a sacred tradition in a charismatic setting. The yeshivah itself is linked to the sacred by virtue of the activity that takes place within it. More than that, the yeshivah is the ideal representation of that activity—the space wherein talmud torah occurs in a concentrated and intense form, unmodifed by secular or mundane elements.[18] Perhaps more than in any other period of Jewish history, the yeshivah today is recognized within orthodox and nonorthodox circles as the institution that both encompasses and embodies the symbols at the heart of Judaism and is most successful in preserving them.

Those who established yeshivot as the institutional context of the contemporary teshuvah process chose an institution wherein the baal teshuvah immediately encounters the sacred sources of the tradition and its ideal representatives. Baalei teshuvah are introduced to Judaism at its very center. They cross from the secular world into a reality that is experienced not only as extraordinary and fascinating but as authentically Jewish. The inhabitants seem to be "real Jews," occupied with something "really Jewish." When the newcomer opens a book in the beit midrash, no matter how elementary, he participates in the ritual of study. At that moment he becomes part of the sacred community, in actual touch with the charismatic tradition. He is a *bahur yeshivah,* a yeshivah student, in an institution where he perceives true ideas and values as being present.

While the beit midrash into which the baal teshuvah enters appears similar to the beit midrash of any standard yeshivah, it is different in certain significant aspects. And the baal teshuvah as a bahur yeshivah differs in certain significant aspects from the veteran student of orthodox background. The baal teshuvah lacks the fundamental knowledge which Jews born into the traditional framework imbibe from infanthood and which they have learned from an early age in formal and informal situations. He enters a yeshivah in order to survive within a religious culture in which knowledge is demanded and valued. He seeks to gain basic information, such as the literal meaning of the biblical narrative, and to acquire basic skills, such as when and how to pray. None of this would be a subject of formal study for an orthodox child beyond elementary school. Thus, for the traditional Jew, talmud torah is an ongoing process, and one who enters a yeshivah as a young man builds upon the foundations established in earlier years. For the baal teshuvah, study in the yeshivah establishes the foundations, and then only in adulthood. The student in a standard yeshivah aspires to become a *talmid hacham,* a learned scholar. The baal teshuvah knows that this ideal is far, far from his grasp. He starts from the beginning and hopes to gain a *basic* knowledge of Judaism and to acquire the tools with which he can continue learning after he leaves the yeshivah.

This means that the program of study in a baal teshuvah yeshivah must necessarily be different from that of a standard yeshivah. Baalei teshuvah must learn the elementary texts upon which the entire structure of Judaism rests. The yeshivah may have to teach them the Pentateuch—books all orthodox Jews learn even before they enter school, and certainly study during the earliest years of elementary school. Baalei teshuvah must begin to study the *Mishnah*, also learned at an early age by orthodox Jews. Finally, baalei teshuvah must learn the special language and methods of *Talmud* study, in order to be able to follow the complicated arguments within that text and the later commentaries upon it. For students from the United States, all of these tasks are doubly difficult because they do not know Hebrew well and therefore have to struggle not only with the text but with the language in which it was written.

The difficulties in the study process are not hidden from a novice entering the yeshivah.[19] On the contrary, the gap between him and those studying in the beit midrash is evident immediately. If he remains, it is despite the intellectual difficulties he faces. Moreover, he does so despite the difficulties encountered in entering a new cultural and social reality where he is a stranger to the most elementary patterns of behavior, accepted norms, accepted styles, and basic climate.

In seeking to understand why baalei teshuvah are willing to overcome the difficulties, one must point to the enormous power the yeshivah and the beit midrash exercise over the newcomer, even at first meeting. Impressions recorded by baalei teshuvah give some insight into the force of the traditional institution upon the entering student.

> I was amazed at the fact of all this noise and at the same time everyone is concentrating and studying. I looked deeper—and saw real passion in learning which is something you never experienced before in your life. You may have seen an impassioned lecturer but you've never seen an impassioned student. It is the manner of study and that it is done all day. And it is a social exercise and not just solitary. It is the first time that you see people actively enjoying study. It is not passive. There is a vitality in an arena where you've never seen it before. And then you have to assume that that energy comes from a sacred source.

This quotation indicates one of the strongest points of attraction pulling the stranger into the yeshivah. The place appears to be a con-

text where truth is pursued intensely and passionately. Further, it
appears to be a community where such pursuit matters. It is precisely
this framework and form of study baalei teshuvah seek. They have
turned to a religious institution because they believe that therein questions affecting their everyday existence and questions explaining their
relationship to their world will be both discussed and resolved.

Many baalei teshuvah are people who have left the university dis-
appointed because study there was detached from what they considered
real existence. The yeshivah appears as a total contrast to the university
world because it is linked directly to values, moral behavior, and the
search for meaning. The attraction of the yeshivah for refugees from
the university is expressed most lucidly in the following statement:
"Much of education is a matter of words—the better the words are
shaped, the better the result. In our time, words with educational
import or claims have swollen beyond measure. One can produce and
consume them, utter and evaluate them, select and ignore them with an
ease and an uncertainty which, I suspect is historically unprecedented.
But in the yeshivah, words are urgent acts. The restoration of words
is more than refreshment for the word-swamped person—it is part of
the reconstruction of existence."[20]

One who experiences study in the beit midrash in this way and
determines to stay there accepts the regimen of the yeshivah framework. The schedule of the baal teshuvah yeshivah is parallel to that of a
standard yeshivah. The day is divided into three blocks of study time,
broken for prayers, meals, and rest. The day begins at six with prayers.
Following breakfast advanced students go to the beit midrash to study
alone or in small groups, while beginning students attend classes designed to introduce them to the study of the Pentateuch, the meaning
of prayers, or certain themes in Jewish thought. None of these subjects
would be taught in a classroom situation in a standard yeshivah. Although in a standard yeshivah lectures are given by the head of the
yeshivah, these do not take place in the morning and usually not in
a classroom but in the beit midrash for all students to hear. For the
baal teshuvah, however, these classroom lectures are essential. They
offer an opportunity to get a grip on the elementary ideas and skills
necessary for the newcomer to have in order to live in the orthodox
world.

The morning session is followed by lunch and afternoon prayers.
After a brief rest period, around three o'clock, the afternoon study
session begins. In most baal teshuvah yeshivot the afternoon session is
devoted to individual study in the beit midrash. Tutors are available to

help students work their way through difficult texts. In several yeshivot Hebrew language classes are offered late in the afternoon, and in some places lectures on the Pentateuch, Jewish ethics, or Jewish thought are offered. At seven, evening prayers are recited and dinner served. After another short break, the third and concluding study session in held, it too devoted to individual study.

The critical figure in the educational process within the baal teshuvah yeshivah is the rabbi. Here a comparison with the role of the rabbi in a standard yeshivah is most important. The rabbi who attaches himself to a standard yeshivah is primarily a scholar, a talmid hacham, dedicated to study as a full and permanent life's occupation.[21] In a yeshivah he finds a place to study. He is asked to lecture occasionally, although his main function is to study, not to teach. The talmid hacham is expected to be a model of piety, the assumption being that a master of words is a master of living. He is to represent the chief values of the religious system—his piety to be imitated, his learning to be an inspiration as well as a source of wisdom.

The rabbi active in the baal teshuvah framework cannot dedicate himself to study fully and cannot fulfill his educational role indirectly as a model to be emulated. He is asked to teach daily, to be a counselor and a curer of souls. He is "on call," as it were, twenty-four hours a day. Rabbis are expected to teach formal classes and to guide students attempting to study independently in the beit midrash. They are also expected to guide students when they are relaxing outside the classroom, talking in the hall, eating in the communal dining room, on the Sabbath and holidays. They must be concerned with the student's relationship to studies, to old and new friends, and to family. They must tend to the physical welfare of the students as well as to their religious progress.

Rabbis who choose to work within a baal teshuvah institution are people driven by a calling and interested in education per se. The calling is no more or no less than the saving of a generation from assimilation for Judaism. They are people determined to save souls, believing that in the baal teshuvah institution they have developed the techniques that can return a generation to Judaism.

The founders of the baal teshuvah yeshivot are without exception highly charismatic men. They are enthusiastic, open, and warm, gifted with the power to persuade through words and example. Some are spontaneous and passionate, some scholarly and reserved. All possess characteristics that link them with two worlds and account for their ability to tap young people from modern secular backgrounds and draw them toward a traditional orthodox reality. They use expressions and examples that reveal an acquaintance with the language and situation of the modern secular young person. They poke fun at or criticize aspects of modern life that demonstrate this basic familiarity with it as well as contempt for it. They point to stereotypic weaknesses in current secular society and contrast these with the strengths of the orthodox world, which they make available to the potential baal teshuvah.

The power of the staff in a baal teshuvah yeshivah to influence is enormous. The rabbi is the channel through which Judaism is presented to the baal teshuvah. That body of laws and principles the baal teshuvah thinks he wants to appropriate as his own is handed to him literally by his teacher, according to the latter's discretion. Judaism is not one meaning and not one way. Each yeshivah embodies a particular perspective and attitude that reflects the religious orientation and style of its founders and staff. This orientation, in turn, determines what is stressed and what is deemphasized in the yeshivah as well as the style of teaching and the general climate within the institution. Since the Judaism the baal teshuvah encounters in the yeshivah is likely to be his first steady taste of it, particular interpretations, attitudes, and stresses are crucial in shaping his relationship to Judaism as a whole.

Moreover, the rabbis quite consciously assume responsibility for the entire process of transformation they hope baalei teshuvah will undertake. They become the spiritual authority for the student, meaning, in fact, the authority in every area of the student's life. The rabbi in this situation becomes a father, replacing the natural father from whom the student has broken in some sense. The student-teacher relationship in the baal teshuvah yeshivah most closely fits the paradigm suggested in the Mishna: "[He who seeks] his father's lost property and that of his teacher, his teacher's has first place, for his father did but bring him into this world, but his teacher taught him wisdom that brings him into the world to come."[22]

The staffs of the yeshivot are large enough to provide individual counseling for every student. It is the students, however, who initiate relationships, approaching teachers with whom they feel free to converse and advise. The intensity and directiveness of the relationship depend upon each partner's needs and desires. Certainly in the beginning stages of the students' stay in the yeshivah little pressure is exercised. Every student is expected to observe certain "house rules," which include public observance of the Sabbath, dietary laws, and modesty rules. As time passes, changes in attitude, values, and perspective are expected to occur. Teachers gradually broach subjects that penetrate

to deeper levels of the person's self and attempt to direct transformations in the social, cultural, and political life of the student, seeking to
bring all areas into conformity with the expectations of the orthodox
community.

Intervention in these areas is understood to be the heart of the work
of the baal teshuvah rabbi and is accepted as appropriate by those who
remain in the yeshivah. People who find this involvement overbearing
or offensive can disengage and leave freely. Those who stay submit
to the ongoing pressures for change, which is the explicit goal of the
baal teshuvah institution. Certain limitations, however, are built into
the situation of the rabbi who works in a baal teshuvah yeshivah. None
work in a vacuum. All live in a community upon which they depend
and with which they are interrelated in numerous ways. If any rabbi
violated the prescriptions of the law, or somehow violated the rights of
the individual granted by Jewish law, he could be censured and isolated.
No rabbi in a baal teshuvah yeshivah, therefore, can create a law in his
own name. The free-wheeling whim and will of the cult leader, or the
personalized subjectivized spirituality of the guru, is illegitimate in the
framework of Judaism and is not found in any baal teshuvah institution.[23]

Limitations upon the power of the baal teshuvah rabbi derive from
the traditional authority of the halachah, Jewish law. This law is
beyond the manipulation of any single individual. Interpretations of it
must be recognized and legitimated by other halachic authorities. Thus,
the power of the baal teshuvah rabbi to create new forms or twist
existing forms is limited by the halachah and its recognized inter-
pretors. The baal teshuvah rabbi does not speak in his own name and
does not innovate. He is not the way himself (nor is he the pathmaker,
initiating or opening new ways in his own name). Rather, he points to
the way by force of his moral and spiritual being, his learning, and his
powers of persuasion. He is an exemplary figure whose extraordinary
personal qualities press the baal teshuvah to follow him.[24]

All baal teshuvah yeshivot must attempt to accomplish three central
tasks. They must provide the framework and conditions for teaching.
They must provide a community for students during a time of transition, which might also be a time of turmoil. And they must provide
entrée for the baal teshuvah into the orthodox community. All the
yeshivot for baalei teshuvah create a total environment where learning,
formal and informal, is ongoing, direct, and nonfragmented. All assume
that students enter because they are interested in changing their lives in
a fundamental way. They also assume that students are willing to aban-

don activities with which they have become discontent and which conflict with the framework they are in the course of considering or
adopting.[25]

Underlying all yeshivot for baalei teshuvah is the assumption that
the students require therapy, healing from the ills of secular society,
and that the remedy is full participation in the life of the orthodox
Jewish community. The disorder of the generation is clear to those who
work in the yeshivot—rejection of the Torah and imitation of Western
culture. The individual Jew, born outside the structures of orthodoxy
and sick with the sicknesses of secularity, must be returned to the
community and framework of Judaism.

The task of the yeshivot is to cure the student by committing him
to the behavior, beliefs, values, and attitudes of Judaism as embodied in
the orthodox Jewish community.[26] The curriculum of the yeshivah,
the degree of intervention in the life of the student, even the recruitment policy of the yeshivah, are all shaped by this therapeutic understanding. Differences between yeshivot are not in the diagnosis of the
sickness but in the evaluation of how a cure is worked. Curriculum,
intervention, and recruitment reflect differences between yeshivot in
this evaluation. The goal, however, is common to all. In the language
of the baal teshuvah world, the task is to make the student *frum*. Being
frum means being pious. It implies fulfillment of the ritual and ethical
law, an inner state of belief, and a complete acceptance of the authority of traditional structures. It also implies an at-homeness within the
traditions and structures of orthodoxy. All of these the yeshivah aims
to convey to the student.

Cure of Souls: Three Approaches

That yeshivah where the analysis of the illness and the therapy proposed are most explicit, full, and clear is Aish Hatorah. The yeshivah
is shaped almost exclusively by Rabbi Noah Weinberg, the pioneer of
yeshivot for baalei teshuvah. Reb Noah marches to his own drum, to
the degree possible within the framework of the halachah. He is distinctive among rabbis who work with baalei teshuvah in his approach to
study, to talmud torah, in his style, and in the force of his person.
Reb Noah is recognized as a titan in the development of baal teshuvah
institutions by those involved in the contemporary teshuvah enterprise.
His work has drawn the attention of the media in Israel, and his approach and character have stamped the public image of the teshuvah
institutions.

Aish Hatorah is located in the rebuilt Jewish quarter of the Old City of Jerusalem. About one hundred and fifty young men study in the rather cramped quarters of the yeshivah, and the door remains open to newcomers. Recruits, in fact, are actively sought among tourists and students. Reb Noah totally dominates Aish Hatorah. The cornerstone of his approach is the assumption that the Western world is fundamentally ill. All who actively participate in its life are said to share the sickness. This is especially true, in Noah's view, of Jews who have abandoned Jewish culture and society in order to assimilate into the West. Noah describes the basic illness of modern Western man as confusion, loss of purpose, and loss of ethical standards. He stresses that the loss of clarity and understanding has left modern man bereft of the fundamental knowledge of how to live and what to value. As a result, modern man has become insane. According to Reb Noah, the sad fact is that, by its own doing, by appropriating the values and ideas of the West and abandoning Jewish tradition, modern Jewry voluntarily shares in this insanity.

For Reb Noah, the baal teshuvah yeshivah is where refugees from the folly, evil, and insanity of the Western world can be taught to transform themselves, to return to truth, and thereby be restored to sanity. The task of the baal teshuvah yeshivah, and of the baalei teshuvah themselves, is to reach all Jews. Reb Noah encourages his students to leave the yeshivah after a relatively short period of study, urging them to work at the primary task: bringining others to the recognition that Western culture is fundamentally sick. He believes this recognition may lead them to save themselves from the spiritual death Western culture imposes. The task Reb Noah has taken upon himself, and which he transmits to his students, is to bring about a confrontation between two diametrically opposed ways of life.

Reb Noah very explicitly focuses on the question of meaning and promises to reveal true and certain ideas to those who will hear him. He constantly stresses the need for clarity, which brings in its wake satisfaction and power. To enjoy the world God gave man to enjoy, according to Reb Noah, one must have proper knowledge of oneself and of one's world. The path to clarity, order, and control is set out by Reb Noah in his course, the Forty-Eight Ways.[27] The title of the course is drawn from the *Ethics of the Fathers*, where, in chapter 6, forty-eight ways to the Torah are elaborated. Reb Noah takes subjects from this list of forty-eight ways and interprets them in his own very distinctive way. Reb Noah believes that his formulations and interpretations of the

Forty-Eight Ways are a vehicle for accomplishing the transformation of the baal teshuvah from nonreligious to religious, from ailing to healthy, from insane to sane. Whether or not that is so, his lectures do form a handbook of elementary concepts of Judaism and a manual for those entering its world.

Reb Noah introduces the student not directly to the Torah itself but to its interpretations via the Forty-Eight Ways. Self-transformation is to take place through understanding the words of Reb Noah and by absorbing the ideas he presents in the Forty-Eight Ways and in his lectures on the proofs of God's existence. It is this approach that makes Reb Noah a charismatic figure. Not only is he effective through his persuasive powers of influencing baalei teshuvah. No other rabbi has composed a course comprised primarily of his own interpretations, at a remove from the sources, and has presented that as a systematic introduction to Judaism.

More than anyone else working with baalei teshuvah, Reb Noah has mastered the techniques of salesmanship. His sales catalogue is the Forty-Eight Ways and the proofs of God's existence. Noah states that these ways will provide what the Jew needs: sanity and happiness through clear ideas. This instrumental appeal, reminding one of the popular approach to Christianity of Norman Vincent Peale, is most effective and powerful.[28] There is no room for ambiguity and confusion in Noah's presentation. Life is black and white, darkness and light, and the student is told to choose. For Noah there seems to be no dark night of the soul, no wrestling with the angels, and he seeks to convey this same clarity and certainty to his students. Once one is cured of the ills of Western civilization, one is completely cured. The therapy is total.

Reb Noah's approach is based upon utter faith in the power of rationalistic arguments to convince and thereby to bring to teshuvah. This rationalistic approach is adopted only in Aish Hatorah, but there it apparently is effective. As one of the students of the yeshivah wrote to his parents: "I've been staying at, of all things, an Orthodox Jewish yeshivah—when I got to Jerusalem I went to visit the Wailing Wall and got invited—they hang around there looking for unsuspecting tourists to proselytize. It's sort of a Jewish Jesus-freak type outfit—dedicated to bringing real Judaism to backsliding Jews. I haven't been especially impressed by the message, but it's been an interesting week." A few weeks later the same student wrote home: "I've read and talked about it enough to realize that the arguments for the existence of G-d (a spelling which shows how superstitious I'm becoming—and the Jewish version of it at that—are very plausible and intellectually if not emotionally convincing. . . . It's frightening, because while I can convince myself of the possibility and even probability of the religion, I don't like it—its 613 commandments, its puritanism, its political conservatism, its Jews-first philosophy. On the other hand, if it is the truth, not to follow it means turning your back on the truth."[29]

The rationalistic approach that convinced Mike Willis and led him toward a way of life he claimed he did not like is therapeutic. It is a cure for those who have lived in error. And it is a fairly safe and quick cure. Mike Willis and other followers of Reb Noah are certain that they have gained absolute and entirely defensible knowledge of the truth. Their compact and simplified formulas are a protective shield against doubt and the lance with which they go out to convince others.

Other baal teshuvah institutions which function upon the therapeutic principle do not try to administer a cure by means of a simplified, albeit systematic, rational theology. In Dvar Yerushalayim, Ohr Sameah, or Nevei Yerushalayim for instance, the student is directed to study basic texts. No manual has been prepared to ease students toward Judaism. Sheets with instructions on how to observe particular rituals are prepared, and xeroxed outlines that help explain a particular passage might be prepared for a particular course. These, however, hardly comprise a simplified guide to Judaism whose purpose is to clarify and guarantee faith.

The program of study in these therapeutic yeshivot is tailored to the students' abilities and knowledge. Adjustments in curriculum, tutoring, and counseloring, are services offered to each individual according to his needs. The effort is upon affecting behavior and making frum. While acknowledging that baalei teshuvah can become talmidei hachamim, the approach to them assumes that they are forever locked out of the depth and scope of knowledge of someone who has grown up in the tradition. They can learn certain amounts but, even if they spend years at it, can never really "catch up." From the beginning, therefore, the effort is to offer and insist upon enough to cure the sickness and make frum. Programs of study are directed toward achieving this goal. Intervention in the lives of the students is directed toward the same goal. Directly or indirectly, rabbis guide the student toward enacting the changes that will transform his behavior to frum. And by force of peer pressure the students themselves enact the same changes without direct intervention. It is clear to all that the goal is to be initiated into the life of frum Jews. To become wise Jews is a luxury usually not to be afforded, given the starting point of the baal teshuvah.

The baal teshuvah yeshivah for Israelis that comes closest to the
therapeutic pose is Ohr Hahayim, founded by Rabbi Reuven Elbaz.
When considering this institution, one enters a world unlike that of
any baal teshuvah institution for Jews from Diaspora countries and
unique within the world of yeshivot generally. Rabbi Elbaz went beyond all existing frameworks, even existing baal teshuvah frameworks,
when he set out to establish an institution for Oriental Jews from
lower-class background, usually uneducated, and often well-known to
the police. The faces at Ohr Hahayim are not the faces in any kind of a
standard yeshivah. Here one finds rough, street-wise youth; their speech
in the dialect of Jerusalem's oriental neighborhoods; their manners,
mannerisms, and dress those of the *shuk,* the open-air market. The
faces and people are described in sociological literature as the "second
Israel," youth from the "disadvantaged neighborhoods." These Rabbi
Elbaz has attracted to his yeshivah.

Elbaz immigrated from Morocco to Israel and was a young neighborhood rabbi in Jerusalem. He managed to interest several young men,
semidelinquents who hang around the market area in Jerusalem, to study
and eventually to become baalei teshuvah. His success in this marked
the beginning of his attempt to "return" young men from these areas
to Judaism. Rabbi Elbaz developed a unique recruiting method, taking
to the streets with a band and bandstand, and using oriental music to
draw large crowds. Having selected a certain neighborhood, Elbaz and
his students arrive, set up their platform, begin the music, and, when
the crowd has gathered, he launches into a hell-and-brimstone address,
calling for teshuvah. By means of these "commando raids," as he calls
them, Elbaz has attracted hundreds of youth to hear him and tens to
study in his yeshivah.

The rabbi's address is a mixture of warnings and harangues, hope and
love. He describes the "animal," "materialistic," "dark," miserable
existence of drug addicts, dropouts, criminals, and others familiar to
his audience. He attacks their goals—the Western standards of success,
such as money, cars, a big apartment, which he states are false standards. He then urges his listeners to extricate themselves from the hell
of such an existence through teshuvah. In very graphic and hard-hitting
images, he depicts the life awaiting those who do not turn while there is
still time. Like many preachers before him, Elbaz browbeats his audience
and then offers them love but demands that they shed their old ways.

"You were animals and you want to be like the animals of Rehavia."
According to Elbaz, everyone immersed in the material world is sub-

human, whether he be a poor young man in Katamon or a well-to-do fellow in Rehavia. The animal-like, materialistic, empty, and dark existence of the secular world is contrasted in absolute and simplified terms with the spiritual world of truth and light of Judaism. Elbaz offers pure truth and an absolute standard of excellence to young people who have had no idea of what to do or of how to achieve excellence.

The identification of materialism with Rehavia is extremely important in the approach of the "missionizing" and "magical" rabbi to his students. He gives direction and articulation to their existing anger at Rehavia, which symbolizes prosperous and Western Israel. Rehavia is not to be condemned simply because it represents the haves versus the have-nots, but because it represents erring and corrupt secular and materialistic Israeli society.

Elbaz appeals to the pride and self-consciousness of the Oriental Jew in Israel. He presents oriental culture not only as honorable but as identified with Judaism, and therefore as true and superior to Western culture. The values and ideas that were their grandfathers' in Morocco, and that their fathers forgot in Israel, are presented as truth. That which was thrust upon them by Western and Westernizing Israelis, and which they could never assimilate, is actually inferior to their own roots. Ohr Hahayim is a refuge for those who feel themselves outsiders in Israel. It offers them a way to be "insiders" in the deepest sense.

Ohr Hahayim is a rehabilitation center in which the rehabilitation is constant but indirect. As in any yeshivah, the essential activity here is study. When a student enters Ohr Hahayim he is given a place to live as well as food and spending money. He is set to work over books in the study hall of the yeshivah, given a tutor if he cannot read well. His time is filled from early in the morning to late at night. Every activity is sanctified, every act measured by an absolute code. For some students, this may be the first time they have wanted to read or had the experience of reading something that was significant to them. For others, it is the first time they have submitted willingly to the demands and limits the discipline of study in the yeshivah requires. Study, talmud torah, is a challenge that grips these young men, a routine they are willing to embrace, because it is a means whereby they can rebuild themselves.

In Ohr Hahayim explicit emphasis is placed upon teshuvah in its most fundamental meaning. This is a yeshivah where a student confesses sins, repents, and atones vividly and repeatedly. The sin is easily identifiable. Even the source of the ill is recognizable. Rabbi Elbaz depicts students as those who walked in darkness, who erred out of ignorance, and who were helped neither by the government, social workers, nor the prison rehabilitation system. Society, secular Western "Ashkenazi" society, failed them.

For the students at Ohr Hahayim, teshuvah is a genuine change of self in which the past is repudiated and a new life begun. Rehabilitation in the most basic sense is the professed aim of the yeshivah and the conscious goal of the students. Rabbi Elbaz presents a formula, a traditional way, and urges his students to adopt it. They, feeling themselves oppressed and depressed, identify with the rabbi who "understands" them. They accept the rabbi's definition of values and ideas, familiar to some from their own not too distant past. They are determined to "make it" within this framework, the assumption being that it is possible to start again.

Judaism functions for the students at Ohr Hahayim as a way leading from various forms of misery to a life of dignity and self-respect. Baalei teshuvah find themselves honored in their neighborhoods and among their friends. Rabbi Elbaz actually presents the success stories to the neighborhood in the most uncomplicated way: pictures of baalei teshuvah before the turnabout and pictures after. The portraits are supposed to convey the message to others who recognize the faces of well-known neighborhood drug addicts, criminals, or heroes who now appear, in their postteshuvah picture as respectable, stable, and satisfied men. The rabbi touts the pictures around the neighborhood, tells the stories of the people, and is respected for his work.

Students too take pride in the before and after portraits. They are happy to recite a confession of their past sins and point to their present redeemed state. They assert their new identity over and over again, as if attempting to prove to themselves and to their listener that the transformation undergone is real and complete.[30] The assertion is not only a personal one but has a collective reference. The students of Ohr Hahayim affirm an ethnic identification and the traditional ways, which were those of an ethnic-religious community in Morocco, Persia, Iraq, Yemen, and so on. The specific differences between various oriental countries are swallowed up in the overall identification of Eastern versus Western or of Oriental versus Ashkenazi. Ohr Hahayim is a proud ethnic establishment, which in its denial of Western culture for traditional Jewish culture tacitly asserts the superiority of the old, ethnic ways.[31]

Like in other baal teshuvah yeshivot where the people-changing aspect is salient, in Ohr Hahayim, too, where the educational level is generally low, the curriculum is tailored to the students' needs. The subjects studied focus on ethical and theological matters significant and relevant to the lives of the students. Beginners study Torah as a spring-board for the discussion of religious and ethical issues. They study *Ethics of the Fathers* in order to raise ethical issues immediately. They study *Proverbs* for the same reason. The *Shulhan Aruch* is taught as a direct guide to life. The law is taught as an absolute norm which orders life in as nearly perfect a way as possible in this world.

The students in Ohr Hahayim have not been educated in Western universities. Neither have their teachers. They are not possessed of the need for proofs of God's existence or for complicated theoretical arguments on any theological issue. Most have always believed in God, have always known that Israel is a chosen people and that the Messiah will come. Rabbi Elbaz taps what is known viscerally. He activates beliefs and explains them simply to those ready to accept the "truth."

Ohr Hahayim has grown rapidly, responding to a need in the oriental community of Jerusalem and its environs. It provides the learning and training necessary to produce observant Jews. It provides the total environment necessary to provide a home for those who wish to change places in order to change themselves. It also provides vocational train-ing. Elbaz is concerned with the financial well-being, the occupation, the marriage, and the children of his students. His concern is to rehabili-tate them—not, however, so that they will be good citizens but that they will be traditional Jews. The effect of his approach has impressed the Israeli police to the extent that they entrust him with prisoners, who are paroled to the yeshivah. While all baal teshuvah institutions are in the business of people-changing, not all view the student as requiring therapy. Some minimize explicit people-changing and minimize actual intervention in the lives of students. Some have a "supermarket ap-proach," offering rabbis and programs which are more directive and others which are less. The student chooses according to his own pref-erence.

That yeshivah which least stresses explicit people-changing and which is, at the same time, the most intellectual of the yeshivot for baalei teshuva is Yeshivat Hamivtar and its women's branch, Machon Bruria. Here it is assumed that changes in the lives of the students are the outcome of learning and will be initiated by the students them-selves. The atmosphere of the institution and the behavior of those frum people in it set patterns that will be imitated. There is no need for explicit directing. These institutions pride themselves on being un-abashedly intellectual, meaning that their goals and methods are the same as those of any yeshivah. They strive to attract students with

high intellectual standards and motivation who seek learning of a sort
not found in a university.

The nature of both Machon Bruria and Yeshivat Hamivtar have been
shaped by the peculiar view of the teshuvah pehnomenon held by their
founder, Rabbi Hayim Brovender, who claims that the teshuvah phenomenon has changed a great deal over the past decade. It is in light of
this change that he has molded the yeshivah which can create talmidei
hachamim out of those who define themselves as baalei teshuvah. Rabbi
Brovender characterized the growth of the teshuvah phenomenon in the
following way:

> In the sixties there was a movement, whereas now there is not. There
> is a promotion campaign which says that the world is changing be-
> cause of the teshuvah movement. I don't believe it. I don't say that
> there shouldn't be such a movement, but that in reality there is none.
> The kids whom I see coming are graduates of Orthodox day schools
> in the United States, who don't know anything, and who are not
> frum from any point of view. There are a much smaller number of
> kids from a Conservative background who are becoming orthodox.
> I started the first baal teshuvah yeshivah eight years ago, where they
> were seven guys all who had no background. I always thought my
> task was to teach people how to learn. I never thought that I was to
> help build a teshuvah movement which would be international. In
> my school there are a few requisites which are assumed: halachah is
> clearly part of the deal; learning; *davening* (praying) and shabbos are
> part of the learning process. The students don't have to believe any-
> thing.
>   In the sixties 90 percent of the guys knew nothing, and weren't
> frum. In those days, guys were willing to try anything—*ashram* or
> *tzitzit**—it didn't make much difference. Now it is different. Now
> most of the people are religious but don't want to be *amei ha-aretz.*†
> Only Reb Noah has a genuine baal teshuvah yeshivah where guys
> make the full turn. Like Uri Zohar. What do I do? I don't see myself
> as a guide to tell someone what to do with his life. He should solve
> these problems himself. I don't see why people who came to yeshivot
> have to end up *soferim*‡ and not musicians, artists, or writers. It is very
> strange and oppressive—those who want to manipulate others. I urge
> people not to erase their past, not to dull their sensibilities. The job
> of the yeshivah is only to give them opportunities in Jewish learning.

This statement reflects the hesitation of one rabbi about "people-
changing," which he calls "manipulation." He objects to the training
that encourages students to truncate themselves and which he assumes

*A ritual fringe on ceremonial garments worn by Jewish males according to
the commandment in Num. 15:37–41.
†Uneducated Jews.
‡A scribe who writes sacred books.

is given in other yeshivot for baalei teshuvah. Rabbi Brovender is a scathing critic. He has pointed to a possibility in yeshivah education which he is determined to avoid. His statement also reflects his judgment about the change in the type of students who arrive at yeshivot for baalei teshuvah. In the view of Rabbi Brovender, the student who knows nothing and makes a total change is no longer the dominant type, and in his place has come the student who received a little Jewish education, wants more, and wants to become frum.

Given these perceptions, it is not surprising that Rabbi Brovender has attempted to create a yeshivah where the intellectual task is paramount and explicit people-changing is minimal. Nor is it surprising that Rabbi Brovender is interested not in drawing "people off the street with starry eyes" but in people who have studied previously. In fact, however, and contrary to Rabbi Brovender's own evaluation of the situation, more than half the students in Yeshivat Hamivtar and Machon Bruria come from nontraditional backgrounds and have had very little Jewish education, certainly not day school education. Yeshivat Hamivtar and Machon Bruria are baal teshuvah institutions.

The goal of the staff in Yeshivat Hamivtar is the creation of talmidei hachamim, with the recognition that the process may take more years than it takes in standard yeshivot, given the late start of the students. It is assumed that the only problems baalei teshuvah face are those of the initial stages of learning when they must acquire the basic skills an orthodox person gets naturally in the normal course of his growing up. Hebrew, methods of reading, and interpretation must be taught to beginning students, who are forewarned that the first six months may be tedious and difficult. They are also told that with perseverance they can become talmidei hachamim. That several former beginners have been certified as rabbis is the most effective demonstration of that possibility.

Because the task of the staff is defined as guiding intellectual progress, there is little intervention in the life of the students outside the study hall. This is not to say that links are not cultivated between students and teachers. On the contrary, as in any baal teshuvah yeshivah students are invited to the homes of staff members and camaraderie is established. These links, however, do not mean that students feel the pressure of the staff in their leisure time activities, their social life, or their future plans. The most clear sign of the nonintervention policy is the refraining in Yeshivat Hamivtar from active matchmaking. The success of the yeshivah is not measured by the number of couples produced and integrated into the orthodox community of Jerusalem.

Gentle Persuasion

Yeshivot intervene more or less and apply pressures to change more or less depending upon the educational ideology which guides the staff. There is little pressure and intervention in Yeshivat Hamivtar, whereas in Ohr Sameah, Mt. Zion, and Ohr Hahayim there is a great deal. One might well ask whether in the course of the process of resocialization violations of the individual's freedom occur and whether brainwashing or indoctrination techniques are used. Thought reform, or brainwashing, is an organized effort to change people from one set of beliefs to another through intellectual, emotional, and psychological manipulation, often with recourse to physical force and coercion.

As described by Lifton, the individual is stripped of his identity until he reaches a breaking point. Then "he is totally cut off from the essential succor of affectionate communication and relatedness, without which he cannot survive. And at the same time, his increasing self-betrayal, sense of guilt, and his loss of identity all join to estrange him from himself—or at least from the self which he has known. He can contemplate the future with only hopelessness and dread."[32] At this point, according to Lifton, when the individual feels powerless and alone a new identity is pressed upon him, which he comes to assume either easily and with a sense of relief or with difficulty.

No physical coercion is used in any yeshivah. The yeshivah itself is open—nothing hidden and no one isolated. Moreover, yeshivot are found in the midst of a city, and students are exposed daily to nonreligious Jews and to activities not sanctioned by the halachah. No efforts have been made to locate yeshivot away from the "temptations" of the nonreligious world in order to gain tight control over students. Further, the baal teshuvah enters the yeshivah voluntarily and leaves whenever he wishes. Traffic flows constantly. Large numbers of people are invited to see the establishment, including potential students, reporters, and patrons. Students go in and out for visits and vacations. Family and friends are invited to the yeshivah, permitting contact with nonorthodox people and those who might desire to draw the student away.

Given the voluntary nature of contemporary teshuvah, emphasized by the physical openness of the yeshivah, the method of effecting total change must be reconsidered in light of the method used in thought reform. First, in contrast to thought reform, baalei teshuvah are not subjected to a frontal attack upon their personal biographies in order to weaken the self through guilt. Students are not asked to identify and confess sins publicly. Nor are they encouraged to focus upon them privately. Baalei teshuvah confess sins regularly but in no way more than any Jew who recites a standard prayer found in the daily service. This is particularly important because teshuvah as a religious paradigm, built upon the notion of sin and repentence, could easily be used as the foundation of a "cult of confession"[33] and other sin-related rituals in the yeshivot for baalei teshuvah.

Sin and guilt are the subject of intense discussions, harangues, and account-taking in the yeshivot. The focus, however, is not the individual and his sinful past but the generation, the community, and its acts. Jews have sinned, the generation is confused, the Jewish people has betrayed itself and is lost. One who recognizes this situation is urged to take the step of cutting himself off from the collective that has submerged itself in secular culture. This is the message to baalei teshuvah. The implication that the individual is guilty and must repent over having been born within the secular culture and society is not drawn out. Time in the yeshivah is spent, therefore, in berating the collective "out there," and in urging the individual to withdraw from it and join the minority which has remained true to Torah culture and to the true calling of the Jewish people.

Bringing the baal teshuvah to reject his past is a process worked at in the yeshivah indirectly more than directly. The constant denial of the value of Western culture and the constant debunking of secular or assimilated Jews is a denial and debunking of the background of the baal teshuvah. The constant attack upon modern patterns of socializing, leisure activities, cultural choices, and sexual mores is an attack upon the way the baal teshuvah spent time. Further, the presentation of a total black/white contrast between past and present, secular and religious, righteous and sinful, valuable and valueless is a way of denying legitimacy and worth to the baal teshuvah's past as well as denying the possibility of maintaining it in the present. The baal teshuvah is placed in a position of having to choose, when the choice is either/or.

At the same time as the negation process continues, a positive building up of the baal teshuvah takes place. First, through study the student is filled with information about Judaism and preached to regarding its ultimate truth and absolute value as a way of life. Yeshivot for baalei teshuvah are doctrinaire and indoctrinating. Their explicit and self-conscious task is the selling of Judaism. Their staffs are composed of people whose talents and interests lie in persuading a generation of young people to return to orthodoxy. People-changing is the raison d'être of the baal teshuvah institution. Their aim is to create a "true believer," not a liberal, open-minded, and self-questioning individual. Within the yeshivot, the contrast is often made between the yeshivah and the university, the former teaching truth and the latter doubt.

The purpose of the education of the baal teshuvah is to build into the individual an acceptance of tradition, which is as automatic and absolute as possible, given the background of the baal teshuvah. Mustering whatever powers of persuasion are available, rabbis and teachers attempt to create a commitment which is total and closed. They attempt to create dependencies upon themselves as authority figures. They attempt to involve themselves intimately with the students and guide them through complicated personal decisions and changes. They attempt to become models of an uncompromising, militant, and radical Judaism.

Baalei teshuvah are easily impressed, even awed by what they perceive as the great wisdom of their teachers and by the sanctity of the life style they represent. They are drawn to and enrapped in the warmth and concern the rabbis extend to them. They tend to be submissive students, reserving questions, suspicions, and hesitations until they "know more." They are taught that this is the proper approach to Judaism. That is, they are told that the practice of a Jewish way of life is more significant initially than certainty about specific principles of faith. And they are told that as they study texts and accumulate knowledge, answers to theological problems will come. Belief can be suspended, temporarily, since it is assured to come as one lives and learns. And rabbis tend to provide simplified resolutions to theological problems, which satisfy those who are drawn to an environment that bespeaks its own plausibility.

The yeshivot often take advantage of the students' ignorance and malleability to spoonfeed Judaism and to truncate its deepest and profound insights. They define themselves as being in the business of selling a product and not in the business of teaching a course on Judaism. An example in which a student resisted simplification illustrates both the dangers and the possibilities of the baal teshuvah yeshivah situation. As told by the student, a certain rabbi had explained to the class that the prize of the covenant with God had been given to Jacob and not to Esau. "We have it and they don't," he said. "Eventually they will realize the truth and wisdom of the Torah." The student, at this point, "decided to challenge him and I asked about the Christian saints—how do you explain this great spirituality?" The rabbi replied that "they would have been greater if they weren't Christians. If it weren't for Christianity, the pagans could have evolved the worship of *Hashem*,* which wouldn't have been Judaism but which would have recognized the Jewish God. Christianity is false religion."

The student went on to say:

> I decided to pursue the conversation, and after class asked him questions. He never ducks questions, but his true flavor only comes through when he talks in private. Then he told me that Jesus was a genius and had great spiritual gifts. He could call upon the name of God. But, his powers were invested in him by the devil. The proof is that Christianity is what Christians do. The rabbi made an emotional case of it, and this is dangerous because most kids in the yeshivah do not have enough spiritual powers to challenge him. On the gut level, it is a simple rejection of everything else going on in the world. Everything is seen as fighting against us, and we have to maintain our integrity. Once the rabbi presented the following argument: "there was a great orthodox rabbi in the nineteenth century named Hirsch† who led the effort to accommodate to the West, to internalize Western culture, and somehow marry both. In Eastern Europe too there was an initial openness. Rabbi Yisrael Salanter‡ sent his greatest student to study medicine. But he was broken and became a Christian. Salanter then closed the blinds and became only inward. The nazis are the judgment upon our efforts to make a synthesis. Hirsch's dream failed.

The student continued to describe the classroom and the reaction to the rabbi's posing the world against the Jews. "The kids in the yeshivah have lost faith in the Western dream, but they haven't thought it out well. The rabbis have lots of weight. The kids are bright but not educated. For them teshuvah makes sense of everything."

This student remained in the yeshivah for several months, objecting to its superficiality but finding that what he learned made remaining worthwhile. Finally, he left for another yeshivah where he felt the approach was more sophisticated. Students know of the existence of other yeshivot for baalei teshuvah, and distinguish between them in terms of style, approach, and student bodies. Moreover, students know of the existence of the nonyeshivah framework for the study of Judaism. The university is one. Special institutes and schools, which encourage some form of commitment to Judaism and which are not self-defined people-changing institutions, exist in Jerusalem and are well-known in the student milieu.

*Literally, "the Name," used by orthodox Jews as pious designation of God.
†Leading thinker and organizer of neoorthodoxy in Germany (1808–88).
‡Founder of Musar movement (1810–83).

How many students leave the yeshivah framework cannot be known precisely. No yeshivah keeps records on in-out traffic. Those that recruit heavily admit that many more leave than remain. The entire approach of the baal teshuvah institution is that of a revolving door, the assumption being that everyone gains something by stepping in.

Ideological education is one avenue of building commitment in the yeshivot. Engaging the student in study is another. As important is the process of actually changing behavior, dropping activities and substituting others for them. From the moment he enters, the newcomer is instructed in Jewish law. He is asked to observe what are considered to be minimals: *Shabbat* regulations, dietary laws, personal modesty laws. Gradually the student is drawn into a full and demanding routine. With no special test to pass or initiation to undergo, the baal teshuvah becomes an "insider," behaving as a member of the community even before he makes a final commitment to it.

Great care is taken by the staffs of the yeshivot not to force an immediate or sudden amputation of the past, and not to force an immediate or sudden appropriation of an entire new way of life. Demands are added gradually. Thus, it is seldom that baalei teshuvah reach a breaking point due to tensions brought on by the transformation process. Rabbis attempt to avoid open confrontations and disciplinary actions. Quiet consultations, glances of approval and disapproval, and peer pressure are used to advance religious "progress."

The premise of the process, however, is that progress must be made and that the transformation must be complete and thorough. As gentle as the rabbis may be, as understanding, and as open, their goal is total change according to the fixed lines of behavior of orthodoxy, and in the image of accepted attitudes, values, and ideas of orthodoxy. The baal teshuvah is directed to identify with the orthodox world's definition of itself as represented by the yeshivah. He is not directed to freely or selectively accommodate himself but rather to accept fixed formulas and fixed patterns.

The complete integration within the orthodox community, which is intended to be achieved by every baal teshuvah yeshivah, is integration with a specific subgroup within orthodoxy. As a channel of passage from the nonreligious to the orthodox world, the yeshivah monitors that passage from its own ideological and religious perspective. Its links are with an orthodox community of the same orientation, attitude, and style. Because of the wide differences within the orthodox world regarding social, cultural, and political issues, the channel to a specific community is of the greatest significance to the future of the baal teshuvah. The choice of a yeshivah a baal teshuvah makes will determine not only the way and what he will learn, but also the stance he will adopt toward the non-Jewish world and toward those who define themselves as religious.

It is this ideological thrust of the baal teshuvah yeshivot that we shall examine in the next chapter.

3
Battling Assimilation

Baal teshuvah institutions mirror major ideological conflicts within orthodoxy regarding secular culture, modern society, and Zionism. The orthodox world is divided on these issues, and when choosing a yeshivah the baal teshuvah wittingly or not opts for a particular ideological and sociological stance. This he cannot avoid, whether he chooses an institution identified with "ultraorthodoxy" or one that assigns religious value to Zionism and some positive value to secular culture. In either case he takes a stand with regard to historic controversies. Moreover, the teshuvah phenomenon itself has become part of these controversies. Orthodox Jews treat the baal teshuvah as a symbolic figure and relate to him within their own historical perspective. In both Zionist and non-Zionist orthodox communities the teshuvah phenomenon is viewed as a sign of the impending and inevitable triumph over secular culture. Further, the baal teshuvah is viewed as one who has discovered the path of truth and who has rejected false paths, secular or religious. The ideological education provided by the communities and their yeshivot is shaped by their views on the issue of secular culture and of the role of the baal teshuvah in the historic fight with secularization for the Jewish soul.

Jewish Responses to Secularization

Secularization is a process in which religious authorities gradually lose control over more and more societal domains. The concomitant development on the individual level is diminution of religious belief and practice.[1] Secularization is precisely what was happening in the eighteenth and nineteenth centuries in Jewish and non-Jewish society alike.[2] Changes in economic life, transportation, communication, and learning—to name only some of the major spheres—freed vital areas of social, political, economic, and cultural life from the control of religious institutions and the domination of religious ideas.

Traditional forms were threatened by these developments. Skeptical about religious beliefs, or simply no longer interested in them, sections of the Jewish population in Europe began to share the aspirations and interests of non-Jewish Europeans. Wanting to be free of the limitations of a separate Jewish existence, these Jews, moreover, sought entry into European culture and society. To start with, they changed their dress and language and adapted their patterns of education and entertainment to those of the Europeans. These signs of acculturation, seemingly external, signaled changes of much deeper significance. First, there was the change in the authority legitimating and controlling norms and expectations. For secular Jews a transcendent authority, or the representatives of a tradition purported to be grounded in a transcendent source—in other words, God and the rabbis—made way for secular sources of authority: the law of the state, or ethical codes believed to be the product of human reason. The second deep change was in patterns of interaction. Jews sought recognition, acceptance, and friendship among non-Jews, and referred to non-Jewish standards, manners, and customs when determining their own behavior. In sociological jargon it might be said that the reference group newly salient for them bore little likeness to that of the traditional Jew. The result of these two major changes was that the fundamental identity of the Torah, culture, and society, which had provided the structures of Jewish existence and the raison d'être of that existence, was shattered. Orthodox Judaism emerged in this context as the reaction of those bent on defending traditional Jewish institutions, structures, and values against the corrosive influence of secularization in the general culture and of liberalizing tendencies within Judaism itself.

All Jews, not only the orthodox, had to respond to these influences. Their responses covered a wide range of options. For those for whom in the new situation Jewish identity was burdensome, inconvenient, insignificant, the baptismal font seemed a way to remove the obstacles to full participation in European society. This path of acculturation, assimilation, and conversion was adopted by Jews in Germany, France, and England, in particular. A less radical response was acculturation and assimilation, but without conversion. Jews who in effect abandoned Judaism as a framework of belief and a way of living, refused to take the final step that would negate their Jewish identity.[3]

Another approach to the same problems was the affirmation of a religious self-definition as a Jew, coupled with denial of Jewish ethnicity. Rethinking of religious principles, reforming religious law, and negating the ethnic foundation of Judaism were aspects of the changes introduced by liberal Jewish thinkers in the nineteenth century in Germany.[4] The explicit justification for such changes was the desire to liberate Judaism from what was regarded as narrow ethnic provincialism in order to enable it to realize its universal potential. But there was another motive as well: the desire of people who no longer lived within a traditional religious universe to be freed of ties of a total community that religious tradition had created.

A largely Eastern European version of the assimilation mode combined acculturation and revolution. Rather than accepting existing patterns and frameworks, Jews joined radical movements seeking to create a universal just society. Jewish radicalism did not necessarily imply a total break from either Judaism or the Jewish people, but did imply that a surrogate ideology fulfilled many of the functions fulfilled in the past by Judaism itself.[5]

Modern Jewish nationalism was also in part a response to the currents of change which secularization and modernization introduced into European and European Jewish life. The desire to create a Jewish homeland where new forms of Jewish existence could develop, in contact with and drawing upon European cultural developments, was the product of a desire to maintain Jewish cultural integrity within the modern situation. Zionism was a movement both of secularization and of resistance to assimilation.[6]

Another possible response to secularization was resistance in the name of Judaism and the tradition. The powerful forces of traditional Judaism in Europe attempted to stave off large-scale abandonment of the tradition on the part of assimilating and secularizing Jews. The forces of resistance, however, were themselves divided in their approach to and evaluation of secular culture and in their relationship to secular society. Two fundamental positions on these issues may be delineated, with, of course, all the usual caveats about the dangers of oversimplification.

By *neoorthodoxy* is meant a variety of attempts to maintain side by side both a positive relationship to secular culture and the structures and authority of Jewish law and traditional Jewish life.[7] The starting point of neoorthodoxy is appreciation of the possible merits of secular culture and consequent desire to appropriate aspects of it. It is a response characteristic of Jews open—even if only to some extent—to new cultural influences, experiences, and sensibilities. It is characteristic of those whose trust and confidence in their own tradition permits them to encounter new cultural trends without fear, with the option even of accepting and integrating elements or aspects of them. It entails an implicit admission that in the modern situation changes within Jewish society—within limits set by the halachah—are necessary and unavoidable.

Here the term "neoorthodox" is being used to cover several historical groups of Jews. One is the neoorthodox movement which developed in Germany and Hungary.[8] In those countries Jews came into contact with an attractive majority culture whose language and ways they had to appropriate as a condition for being granted political emancipation. Those Jews who wished to remain orthodox assumed that knowledge of aspects of Western culture and some changes in external behavior would not impinge upon the inner fabric of Judaism and the order of Jewish life.

In Eastern Europe a neoorthodox ideology did not develop. Certain attitudes and a perspective that may be described as neoorthodox emerged, however: an awareness of the challenge new intellectual and cultural currents presented to traditional Jewish life and an attempt to respond to them. Rabbi Avraham Yitzhak Kook (1865-1935), for instance, displayed an appreciation of secular culture and knowledge of selected aspects of it, on the one hand, and a total dedication to Torah culture, on the other hand.[9] His theology is based upon the assumption that the Torah is total and eternal truth, which includes all partial truths within itself so that no necessary contradiction between secular culture and Judaism exists. Other rabbis in Eastern Europe, also aware of the positive values of secular culture and of its attraction to young Jews, attempted to respond by renewing halachic learning, demonstrating its fullness and superiority over secular learning. The very necessity to respond not through negation but through inner renewal is a manifestation of a neoorthodox approach.[10]

The second basic position orthodox Jews assumed via-à-vis Western culture and modernity was total opposition, an unequivocal "no" to the new ideas and social-cultural values that emanated from "foreign" cultures. In this view, the Jewish Enlightenment, the *Haskalah*, was neither enlightening nor enhancing but rather destructive both of Jewish tradition and of the unity of the Jewish people. The only appropriate response to the insidious forces which had drawn multitudes away from the fold was staunch opposition. They must be kept at bay.

This position, which rejected secular culture and tried to shut it out, intellectually and sociologically, may be called *ultraorthodoxy*. The basic goal of ultraorthodoxy was to maintain the certain and known patterns and truths of Judaism, despite changes in the surrounding world. Perhaps the clearest statement of the principled position was made by an early representative of these rejectionists, the Hatam Sofer (1762-1839): "May your mind not turn to evil and never engage in corruptible partnership with those fond of innovations, who, as penalty for our many sins, have strayed from the almighty and His law.... Never

say 'times have changed.' We have an old Father—praised be his name—
who has never changed and never will change."[11]

This form of orthodoxy may be described as restorative. Its goal is
to restore and recreate an older traditional context that no longer exists
in a "natural" way, a total civilizational context wherein Judaism and
Jewish culture are identical and the contents of belief are self-evident
from experience. Restorative orthodoxy is fundamentalistic. One
motive underlying the effort to resist and the determination to reject
so prominent in its basic stance is the motive underlying fundamentalistic efforts generally: the strong desire to fix boundaries, to establish
limits, to protect known truths.[12]

Both the neoorthodox and the ultraorthodox positions were confronted with the issue of modern Jewish nationalism. As indicated, the
modern Jewish nationalist movement arose to preserve the cultural and
physical integrity of the Jewish people against the threat of disintegration posed by assimilation and anti-Semitism.[13] Zionism emerged as a
force of resistance against trends that seemed to be dissolving particular
Jewish meaning, vocation, and community. Orthodoxy was a force of
resistance against the same trends of dissolution. However, relations between the two, between Zionism and orthodoxy, were highly problematic because of their clashing visions of Judaism and of the Jewish
people.

The Zionist movement presented itself as a secular movement, and
so it was perceived by orthodox Jews. It appeared to them to be one
more manifestation of the penetration of modern ideas and values,
another secular cause, another form of assimilation. Jews whose
response to modern secular culture was militant negation opposed Zionism with the same militancy. While the central target for these Jews was
Westernization and assimilation, Zionism was the concrete embodiment
of both.

Moreover, Zionism, in seeking to end the state of exile, was clearly
involving itself in a redemptive process. That process, according to this
orthodox view, was to be initiated and carried out by God or the messiah, his agent, and not by a secular movement led by secular men. It
seemed obvious that ultraorthodox forces would have to oppose the
Zionist movement. This they did actively on two fronts: in Europe,
within the Jewish communities when the movement was gathering
strength, and in Palestine, where the ultraorthodox "faithful" felt particularly threatened by the influx of new Zionist settlers.

In order to oppose Zionist activity effectively, orthodox anti-Zionists in Europe organized an umbrella organization in 1912 called

Agudat Yisrael.[14] The rationale for the anti-Zionist position was enunciated most clearly in the manifesto of the organization: "The Jewish people stands outside the framework of the political peoples of the world and differs essentially from them. The Sovereign of the Jewish people is the Almighty, the Torah the law that governs them, and the Holy Land has been at all times destined for the Jewish people. It is the Torah which determines all actions for Agudat Yisrael."[15]

A different position toward Zionism developed among Eastern European Jews who here have been called neoorthodox.[16] Driven by a deep desire to return to a full national existence, these Jews viewed the Zionist movement as a legitimate organized attempt to break out of the basically negative condition of exilic existence in order to restore a desired wholeness and fullness to Jewish life.[17] These Jews also were driven by a sense of alarm at the destruction of Jewish life being wrought by anti-Semitism and assimilation. Their understanding of contemporary secularism allowed them to come to a modus vivendi with secular Jews in order to work together for a common goal, the return of the Jewish people to its homeland.

The most well-known and significant theological interpretation of modern Zionism is that of Rabbi A.Y. Kook. Kook viewed modern Zionism as part of the messianic process and saw the period of Zionism as the beginning of the messianic redemption. In his view, all Jews who participate in redeeming the Land of Israel and in the ingathering of the exiles of the Jewish people, whether they are religious or not, are agents in God's scheme of redemption. Fulfillment of the commandments of settling the Land of Israel and making it fruitful overrode hesitations regarding cooperation with secular Jews.[18]

Neoorthodox Jews who desired to return to a full national existence, and who wished to cooperate with the Zionist movement, formed the Mizrahi party in 1902, under the leadership of Rabbi Yitzhak Yosef Reines.[19] The Mizrahi cooperated in the political and economic efforts of the Zionists but opposed their nonreligious cultural program. The ideal of the religious Zionists was always the eventual transformation of the Zionist movement (and later the State) from a secular to a sacred entity. "The land of Israel for the people of Israel according to the Torah of Israel."[20] Recognizing that reality was far from these aspirations, religious Zionists resolved not to separate themselves from the task and from the commandment of resettling the land and redeeming the Jewish people. As stated by Rabbi Reines, "There is no greater sacrilege than to allege that Zionism is part and parcel of secularism for the truth is that it is precisely the holiness of the land that induces the

secularists to participate in the movement. .... It is in this that we may
see the greatness of Zionism, for it succeeded in uniting people of
diverse views, directing them towards a noble aim—the saving of the
people—and this is its glory.[21]

In summarizing these positions, it must be emphasized that orthodoxy as a whole can be viewed as forming a defensive line against secular ideas, attitudes, and life-style which were perceived as threatening
the very foundations of Jewish life and Judaism. However, if one is to
understand Jewish resistance to secularism, a variety of ways and of
camps must be distinguished within orthodoxy. The extreme response,
as indicated, is that of ultraorthodoxy. Utterly fearful of change, and
hence utterly defensive, ultraorthodox Jews negate the value of Western
learning for Jews, limit contact between Jews and non-Jews to
secondary relationships, close themselves off in exclusivist neighborhoods, dress in a manner that exemplifies peculiarity, exclusiveness, and
faithfulness to old forms, and vigorously oppose Zionism.[22]

Since ultraorthodoxy considers compromise on cultural issues illegitimate, it opposes all pluralism within Judaism. Hence, ultraorthodox
Jews do not cooperate with orthodox groups outside their camp. They
do not participate in the state religious school system, and refuse to recognize the authority of the chief rabbinate in Israel, an office considered
to be a symbol of compromise with Zionism. The ultraorthodox have
in effect cut themselves off, as a group, from the cultural and social
developments occurring within the Jewish people, which they hold to
be valueless.

Neoorthodox Jews begin at a different point. They tend to affirm
the legitimacy of Western learning. They also affirm limited participation in Western cultural forms and the accommodation of traditional
structures to such forms when possible without violating the halachah.
The religious kibbutz, the religious youth movements, and the curriculum of the state religious school in Israel are examples of attempts to
incorporate secular cultural values into the religious tradition and to
adapt religious forms to a new historical situation. Such attempts have
been made on the twin assumption that adjustments and innovations
may be valuable for the religious tradition itself, and that by working
within the secular context in Israel, by interacting within this context, a
transformation of the secular may eventually be accomplished.

Counteroffensive against Secularism

It is of great significance that the world out of which most rabbis who
work with baalei teshuvah come, and the world to which they remain
loyal, is that of ultraorthodoxy. Despite the fundamental inward-turn-

ing of the ultraorthodox posture, it was the rabbis from ultraorthodox yeshivot in the United States, and later in Israel, who turned outward toward the potential "returnees." It was these men who noticed a change in the spiritual climate, first in the United States and then in Israel, and who were prepared to consider new ways to act in order to channel the new interest in religion toward Orthodox Judaism.[23]

The ideological position of the yeshivot for baalei teshuvah is consistent with that of the community with which they are linked. Thus, in those yeshivot dominated by rabbis whose fundamental orientation is ultraorthodox, a basic negation of the value of Western culture is not only tacitly expressed, it is also enunciated outright. The message, conveyed in many ways and from the first day that the student is in the yeshivah, is that Western culture is alien to Jews and that assimilation to Western culture is a betrayal of Judaism. The traditional world of Judaism contains all truth, so the message continues, and traditional Jews are the saving remnant of the Jewish people. It is precisely this message, both parts, that resonates loudly and positively for the majority of baalei teshuvah who are protesting the cultural values of the societies from which they have emerged. The idiom used to express the protest may be new to the baalei teshuvah, but the content of the message is apparently welcome to them. The West is portrayed as the source of confusion and false ideologies. Absolutely no value is accorded secular values or achievements. In the literature of the yeshivot, and in classrooms and private discussions, the West is depicted as overrun by drugs, crime, degenerate sexual mores, spiritual ignorance. In this view, assimilation to the West is personal suicide, a condemning of oneself to a valueless and meaningless existence.

Classrooms often become arenas for a purge of the West. The indictment is simple and simplified. It begins with the evident collapse of Western values, which baalei teshuvah are supposed to recognize firsthand. It proceeds to condemn the West for what it has done to the Jewish people. Western secular learning has in recent years led the Jews to the gas chambers. In premodern times Christianity led to pogroms. The only possible conclusion is that the West is totally hostile to the Jewish people and that Western values are fundamentally corrupt.

The yeshivot present themselves as fortresses against the West. Assimilation, coterminus in their rhetoric with Westernization, is equated with a list of modern "evils," reminding one of the Syllabus of Errors of Pope Pius IX. In a leaflet describing a major women's school in Jerusalem to a prospective student or contributor, the following questions are posed: "Assimilation? Intermarriage? What shall become of our Jewish daughters?" The pamphlet continues with a list of possibilities for the future, those which go with Judaism and those which accompany assimilation. "Judaism? Marriage? Family Life? Tradition? Israel? Atheism? Permissiveness? Kibbutz? Moonism? Jesus Freaks? Drugs? Trial Marriages?"[24]

The rhetoric of the yeshivot in describing their own position vis-à-vis assimilation is one of battle. "Defend your heritage, join the corps leading the battle for Jewish survival"; "Equipped with the most powerful armament in the annals of mankind, Jewish knowledge, graduates deploy to the four corners of the globe in a concerted effort to immunize youth against the plague of assimilation and intermarriage by sharing with them the joy of discovery of authentic Jewish values and guidelines"; "Previously condemned to assimilation by adult apathy and ultimately disillusioned in their encounters with alien philosophies..."[25]

The damage done to Jewish youth is a central focus in diatribes against assimilation. "Young Jews in particular, living in a secular and permissive atmosphere of youth revolt and student unrest, in an insecure and confused world, without clear values or cultural roots, feel more isolated and vulnerable than others. Some succumb to the movements of secular humanism, the New Left, hippiedom and drug addiction. Many feel that they live in a spiritual vacuum. Most grope for a firm anchorage, for a clear pattern of ethical, spiritual, and religious life through which their existence may gain meaning, and seek fulfillment in the Land of Israel."[26]

Opposition to assimilation is the flag, as it were, of the yeshivot for baalei teshuvah. Public relations items depict the yeshivot as the major force in the battle for the survival of the Jewish people against a long list of cultural evils which threaten that survival. The public relations material is simple, direct, and absolutely clear. It is a war of the children of light against the children of darkness.

Baalei teshuvah are projected as those who have awakened to the truth about the West. They are those who have turned away from the culture and society within which they were born, more's the misfortune, to return to the culture that is really theirs, more's the fortune. The significance of the teshuvah phenomenon and of the return of the individual within the context of the modern period for the Jews is presented in a book written expressly for baalei teshuvah.[27] In the introduction Yoel Schwartz reviews the modern situation, presenting the historiographical perspective prevalent in the yeshivot for baalei teshuvah.

> A very difficult period has passed over our people. First, the spiritual holocaust beginning with the Enlightenment and Reform movement and continuing with secular nationalism destroyed great parts of our

people, cutting them off from faith and Torah. The physical problems stuck—World War I and afterwards, the terrible Holocaust committed by the beast-man, Edom-Germany.... these troubles all but destroyed the centers of Torah of the Jewish people. Now it appears that a revival has begun. Thank God, the yeshivot are flowering. Throughout the world the voice of the Torah breaks from the mouths of thousands of Jewish youth. But, most important, the flight from Judaism has ceased. The opposite is occurring—a process of return to faith in God and the fulfillment of the Torah.[28]

As the linkage between physical and spiritual holocaust clearly suggests, in the eyes of the author the gravity of the spiritual loss can be compared to the gravity of the loss of lives. There is a difference, however, in the modes of response available. The Jewish people can respond to the spiritual loss by returning, rebuilding, and overcoming the waves of assimilation which have destroyed so much in the past and which continue to wreak havoc at present. The intention of those who use the image of the Holocaust in connection with assimilation, and it is used repeatedly, is to channel the negative feelings evoked by Holocaust memories onto assimilation. Assimilation is derided in yeshivot for baalei teshuvah. It is viewed as a process leading to betrayal of one's people and falsification of one's self. For the rabbis, assimilation is an evil force threatening the Jewish people and Judaism and must be fought through active combat. In their eyes, it is not enough to sit back and fortify oneself and one's own, as the orthodox have been doing since the threat actualized itself. Nor is it enough to build more moats around the fortress. Rather, the battle must be taken outward, a counteroffensive must be launched.

The yeshivot, in the view of those who work in them, are the new and major weapon in the counteroffensive. The imagery of combat is used constantly when describing the role of the baal teshuvah institution and the situation of contemporary Jewry. The sides are clearly divided and the choice, as depicted, does not involve subtle distinctions or complex deliberations. The historical record has been read and the verdict is obvious. Baalei teshuvah are asked to choose between truth and falsehood, between spiritual life and death. Nothing less. Furthermore, it is made quite clear that the choice carries with it responsibility for the life of an entire people.

Counteroffensive against Zionism

There is no doubt in the baal teshuvah yeshivot about the lessons to be learned from modern history, as there is no doubt about the lessons to be learned from Revelation. Since the Jewish Enlightenment, the Haskalah, the majority of the Jews have been on a downward path as a result of having sold out their birthright. Only a remnant has remained faithful. Hope lies in reversing the direction, in bringing back the masses, even if that requires working one by one. The historical perspective and vision involved in the contemporary teshuvah movement is revealed quite clearly by the revival of interest in teshuvah circles in the biography and writings of Natan Birenbaum. The surfacing of Birenbaum in this context—he is presented as the prototypical baal teshuvah—is one of the most fascinating elements in the current teshuvah phenomenon. It also highlights the anti-Zionist motif, which is so strong a current within it.

Natan Birenbaum (1864–1937) was born in Vienna and passed his youth among Jews who aspired to assimilate into the general culture and society of Vienna. Birenbaum himself received a European education, became a lawyer, but quite self-consciously rejected the path of assimilation. Birenbaum had developed a theory of ethnic unity and felt himself closely bound up with the Jewish people. He founded Kadimah, a Jewish student organization at the University of Vienna, which promoted a Jewish nationalist doctrine. Birenbaum wrote and published a short-lived periodical called *Self-Emancipation* in which, in 1885, he coined the word "Zionism" for the nationalist program he espoused. In that same year he joined Herzl and until 1898 functioned as a leading intellectual in activist Zionist circles.

During the last years of his political activity, Birenbaum moved from political Zionism toward a cultural nationalist position that led him to an affirmation of diaspora Jewish centers. The solution for the Jewish problem seemed to him to lie in the creation of strong and semiautonomous centers of Jewish population in Europe rather than in a mass exodus of all Jews to a Jewish homeland. An aspect of this basic change of position was Birenbaum's newfound dedication to Yiddish as the national tongue of the Jewish people and his opposition to its replacement by Hebrew.

Birenbaum toured Europe lecturing about cultural nationalism. Having developed a closeness to Eastern European Jews, he moved to Czernowitz in 1908, where he came to know intimately the inner life of the Eastern European Jew. He reports that for many years he had doubts about his own atheistic and materialistic philosophies of life but had not been convinced of a true religious faith. In 1908, however, he underwent a genuine religious experience. Birenbaum soon became an orthodox Jew, joined Agudat Yisrael, and began to speak out against political Zionism. He thus reversed his previous life's work. In 1919, the man who had been secretary of the Zionist movement in its earliest years became first secretary of Agudat Yisrael.

The stages in Birenbaum's biography serve many contemporary baalei teshuvah as a model for their own spiritual odyssey and self-conception. Birenbaum abandoned "atheism," in his terms, for Orthodox Judaism. He abandoned political Zionism for anti-Zionism. He equated Zionists with assimilationists and both with idolators. Thus, he states that "I do not include in the category of 'Jews who worship idols' only those who are called assimilationists. I do not doubt that those who intended to make the Jews the same as the nations of the world ...are idolators. I do not deny their good will nor their power and facility, which is a direct result of their will. But I see that regarding the question of questions, the matter of God and the world, they are not different than the assimilators, whom they curse. I sense in all their words and movements a rebellion. I sense in all their words, in their ethical conceptions, and in their spirituality, that they follow the ways of the idolators."[29] It is this renunciation of political Zionism as a form of secularization and, hence, as a form of the collective assimilation of the Jewish people, which is the heart of the matter for the yeshivot. This is the view conveyed to baalei teshuvah. Birenbaum, former secretary of the Zionist movement who became secretary of the anti-Zionist Agudat Yisrael, is a symbol for the rabbis of the baal teshuvah yeshivot of the awakening of modern Jews to the folly of secular culture and to the truth of traditional Judaism. Similarly, he is a symbol of the awakening of modern Jews to the false foundation and inherent error of modern Zionism.

A lecture presented to Israelis on Israeli Independence Day in one baal teshuvah yeshivah can serve to underscore the strength and significance of the anti-Zionist motif being pressed upon some (not all!) baalei teshuvah. Not all students in the yeshivah were invited to the lecture, which was entitled "Why We Should Mourn on Independence Day." Only those judged capable of understanding, those who had been in the yeshivah long enough to have already absorbed the main thrust of the message, were invited to attend. The lecture, in fact, was offered as a kind of "gnosis" for those who had demonstrated their interest and capacity to understand and absorb its message:

> Let it be understood that I do not negate the achievement or character or path of Zionism, I come to negate its very essence. As a faithful religious Jew, I am more anti-Zionist than I am anti-Christian. I know this is a very sharp statement. The distinction is in types of destruction. Christians and Muslims have attempted to destroy Jews

physically. But they have never been able to destroy the soul of the Jew simply because they cannot reach it. Goyim cannot hurt us in terms of values, because their level is the physical, and they cannot reach the level of the Jews. Therefore they cannot touch us.... Furthermore, when Christians attempt to convert Jews they attempt to negate the Jew but not Judaism. They could not destroy Judaism as an idea, so suggested replacing it with another idea.

Zionism, on the other hand, made history by separating Judaism from the Jew and sought to kill the first while saving the second. This is indeed its historical accomplishment. The goy never meant to hurt Judaism but just Jews. Zionism didn't intend to hurt Jews but to hurt Judaism.... In the Holocaust six million Jews were destroyed. Zionism has destroyed tens of thousands by making them goyim. They do this without harming physically, so that Jews do not notice that they are being hurt. Christians didn't try to destroy Judaism but to say it was wrong. Zionists tried to destroy the idea of Judaism by saying it is something else. The Zionists say that I don't want Judaism but want to remain a Jew—this is its innovation.

In the view of the rabbi giving this lecture, the essence of Judaism is the Torah:

As Rabbi Saadia Gaon stated, a Jew is a Jew because of his Torah. The reason the Jews are a nation is because one will created a unity, the divine will. This will doesn't effect the goy.... And without the religious idea, there is no significance to the Jewish people. This is Judaism. One must accept it or not, but this is it. Every goy knows this. Zionism has reversed the whole thing, making the people the essence, Torah and culture secondary. Yitzhak Breuer said, "Zionism has created collective assimilation." It is impossible to compare the Jewish people with other nations of the world, and this is just what Zionism has done. In seeking to be like unto all the nations one ceases to be a Jew because you have lost the idea and the value.

Little elaboration on the basic content is needed. Zionism is charged with having severed the essential unity of the Jewish people and its religious idea. Because it carried and forwarded secularization, Zionism is fundamentally fouled. According to this view, there is only one order for Israel—God's law as interpreted by the recognized communal authorities; any other order established by Jews for Jews must at least be decried, if no other means to act against it are available. The opposition to Zionism enunciated here is not new. The innovation is not the content but the context—a baal teshuvah audience, people raised in an environment where anti-Zionism was not a plausible option but, rather, where such statements would have been considered a betrayal.

To appreciate the force of the rabbi's address to baalei teshuvah, attention must be paid to the way it interweaves meaning, vocation, and the identity of the Jewish people. Vocation and community are the real starting and focal points of the rabbi's remarks. "But without the idea there is no significance for the Jewish people." Baalei teshuvah seek a new solidarity, one which provides meaning and a meaningful task. They respond positively to the presentation of Judaism as an idea and the Jewish people as a unique people who in its communal life embodies and is the bearer of important values.

The force of the rabbi's words lies also in their clarity, firmness, even their extremeness. "This is Judaism. One must accept it or not, but this is it. Every goy knows this." Total, final, and absolute—the definition of Judaism is so obvious that even the goy recognizes it. The negation too is powerful. The faithful remnant negates the ideology and life-style of the majority of the Jewish people in the name of an ancient ideal and calling. The punch of the address lies in the fact that it presents a militant negation of Zionism and Western culture to those who formerly lived and knew only this. Judaism gains in attractiveness when it is a counter to another world view and way of life.

The anti-Zionist motif is not often presented in this radical form in the yeshivot for baalei teshuvah. However, even when it is not stated as strongly or directly, it is constantly being signaled. The negative response when the subject of political events is raised, the disdain evidenced toward those who dedicate themselves to matters of the state, the silence that breaks out when the subject of army service is mentioned are all signs of a basic stance. Still, one of the distinguishing marks of a baal teshuvah yeshivah is the conscious effort to transmit a message about the stance that should be taken toward a secular Jewish state. In an institution where a major effort must be made to transmit a particular ideological message, an address on Zionism, such as the one cited above, would be delivered. In a standard yeshivah that shares the same intellectual orientation, students study as usual on Independence Day, ignoring the holiday; they are offered no special lecture. The concern of the baal teshuvah institution is not only to teach a young Jew to observe the commandments of the halachah but also to ascribe certain values to activities, ideas, and groups in the world. The concern is to convey to the student a world view and social posture of a community so that its perspective and position will become his. In the case of that community that strongly opposes secularization and Zionism, these issues must become salient in the hidden and open curriculum of the yeshivah linked to that community.

The anti- or non-Zionist perspective is certainly not the only ideology available to baalei teshuvah. Ultraorthodox Jews were not the only ones to recognize the potential for contemporary teshuvah nor the only ones to establish institutions to nurture it. One major yeshivah for Israelis and several smaller yeshivot for students from the Diaspora have been founded which do not preach sectarian denial and withdrawal. They represent a religious Zionist ideology.

Machon Meir was established in 1974 by a baal teshuvah who felt that an active program ought to be launched by a Zionist institution to compete with the non-Zionist yeshivot already established. Dov Bigon's idea was to set up an independent institute whose concern would be exclusively with baalei teshuvah. The attitude of the rabbis in Merkaz Harav toward the teshuvah possibility was positive both on practical and theoretical grounds. The theology of Rabbi Avraham Yitzhak Kook centered around the concept of teshuvah. Certain that man could not fulfill himself apart from God, Rabbi Kook taught that secularism among Jews was a passing phenomenon. He viewed Zionism as an inherently religious movement. Return to the land and to the language were first steps which would eventually end in full return to the Torah.[30]

Moreover, the gains of the ultraorthodox, and the direction of non-Zionism or anti-Zionism which the ultraorthodox yeshivot encouraged made it clear that a counter to this trend was necessary.

The critical difference between Machon Meir and non-Zionist baal teshuvah institutions is the conception held in the former of the return of the Jewish people to Israel and of the establishment of the State of Israel, a conception linking both, and the teshuvah phenomenon itself, to the theology of redemption of Rabbi Kook. The interrelatedness of teshuvah, redemption, and return is stressed in all published material of Machon Meir. Sources in Jewish thought are selected that focus on the notions of the chosenness and uniqueness of Israel, on the uniqueness of the promised land, and on the renewal of the Jewish people that occurred with the settlement of the land of Israel as a step toward redemption.

In no other yeshivah is Jewish theological thought so central to the curriculum as in Machon Meir. In no other is the ideological focus so explicit and intense. Machon Meir has launched a campaign to attract baalei teshuvah to a religious Zionist position in an attempt to combat the influence of those baal teshuvah yeshivot whose orientation is non- or anti-Zionist. It is attempting to demonstrate that a return to Judaism is indeed a choice between worlds and world views but not necessarily according to the terms set out by the ultraorthodox. The return to Judaism need not involve a complete about-face, a total denial of one's past or a rejection of secular culture in its totality. The return to Judaism need not entail a denial of the value of a Jewish state created by a secular national movement; on the contrary, the value of that state can be affirmed from a religious point of view.

For the baal teshuvah the positive value attributed to Zionism has direct sociological and psychological implications. Since neither total withdrawal from secular society or total rejection of the cultural patterns which have evolved in the state is an explicit ideal, the baal teshuvah need not see teshuvah as leading sooner or later to an abandonment of his past. He need not buy a black suit as a sign of such an abandonment. The opposite—the ideal is some degree of participation in the state without, of course, compromising religious values. And the ideal is to innovate in religious customs and practices in order to meet new conditions, whenever this is possible.

Despite the positive value accorded to participation in the life of the general society, the antisecular thrust of Machon Meir is strong, and the rejection of Western culture is similar to that found in yeshivot associated with the ultraorthodox community. "Our parents left the values upon which they were reared for a new ideal—socialism. We have left socialism, and remain with a void; we are left barren, and without any belief." These are the opening lines of a Machon Meir public relations brochure which set the stage for a description of the institution. Secularism, and socialism, are viewed as totally bankrupt and their children disinherited. The brochure continues,

> The lack of spiritual meaning in the daily life of much of the nation is seen and felt, and the problem has been ignored far too long. The time calls for renewal and rejuvenation. There is a danger which calls for our most urgent attention. For almost two thousand years we were a committed people without a land. Now we face the possibility of becoming a land without a committed people. *The Solution*— a new institution, dedicated to the spiritual needs of the people of Israel, influenced by the ideals of the late Chief Rabbi Avraham Yitzhak Kook—the love of Torah, the love of the people, and the love of homeland—has been established to meet this great need.[31]

The central theme of the rejection of secular Israeli culture and of secular culture generally clearly emerges from these statements. The theme is repeated in lectures and informal discussions, and is reflected in negative attitudes displayed toward secular values and activities. In Machon Meir, as in ultraorthodox baal teshuvah yeshivot, secular culture and society are portrayed as fundamentally askew and consequently degenerate. Even within a framework where a greater openness to secular culture and an appreciation of its merits might be expected, such openness and appreciation are actually lacking in almost all areas.

But because Machon Meir is a religious Zionist yeshivah, certain secular enterprises are indeed valued. The state, as such, represents the return of the Jewish people to a full and sovereign existence, and is valued. The Israeli Defense Force, as the defender of the state, is also valued. While negating the value system and world view of secular Israel, religious Zionists participate to some degree in the activities and society of secular Israel. They certainly do not assume a sectarian stance toward the nonreligious world. Students in Machon Meir, therefore, are directed to serve in the Israel Defense Force. They are encouraged to participate in settlement activity on the West Bank. They are not directed or encouraged to live in exclusive religious neighborhoods. While being taught that secular values are fundamentally mistaken and that a secular way of life, in whatever version, is fundamentally bankrupt, baalei teshuvah in Machon Meir are not taught to withdraw from Israeli society completely. The intellectual and sociological closure is partial, creating a major difference in attitude and behavior between baalei teshuvah educated within this religious Zionist framework and those educated in the ultraorthodox framework.

Now the question that arises is why the majority of baalei teshuvah are drawn to yeshivot oriented to the ultraorthodox community and why they are ready to undergo the radical changes expected by that community. In seeking answers to these questions we must return to the question, Who are the baalei teshuvah? In the next chapter we will analyze questionnaire data obtained through a survey conducted in the yeshivot and oral interview material in order to understand the motivations of baalei teshuvah and their paths toward teshuvah.

4
The Passage

Discontents

In describing the motives underlying teshuvah and in turning to the yeshivot, we return to the three groups delineated in Chapter 1. This includes baalei teshuvah from the United States, Israelis of Western origin, and Israelis of Asian-African origin.[1] Running through the discussions of baalei teshuvah from all three groups is a sense of social malaise and protest related to specific issues, such as the sickness of a society that overvalues consumption, or the evils of a society that fails to resolve civil rights issues, and carries on an unjust war in Vietnam. Even more pervasive, however, is a shrill but general criticism of "degenerate" or "empty" society.

Several statements by American baalei teshuvah will convey the tone and the content of the social criticism emmanating from this group.

> When you watch TV in the States you are being subtly manipulated, being presented with a whole set of values. They are emptying garbage into your living room. Like I watched *The Graduate* four times and really liked it. Then I was trying to explain it and I realized how sick it was. ... I have stopped TV, movies, and theater. ... I was searching for a way of life in which man did not lower himself to the level of an animal and in which existence had a purpose other than acquiring wealth. When I came to Israel to a kibbutz *ulpan**
> I found that we were running all the time from something and hoping to find something in Israel we could not define quite, but which would endow our lives with a sense of purpose and meaning, which we were unable to find in our home countries.

A sense of life wasted in amusements and activities which do not ennoble but rather lean to the moral degeneration of the individual is a steady theme in the descriptions of their own middle-class background. For this baal teshuvah the movie *The Graduate* represented sexual looseness, moral confusion, and a total lack of direction. He sought to

*Hebrew language course given to newcomers to Israel.

escape all three—first in a kibbutz and later in a yeshivah. The same themes are repeated in the following two quotations from students of the same background.

> Frustration with undefined middle-class American philosophies of life as opposed to a developed and useful one that I increasingly saw as revealed by God in Judaism. Besides, it was my birthright. Why not use what made me special? What was given to me? America is decadent—it has raped the rest of the world for its riches. The country has no moral direction and lives in a basically nonspiritual way.

> Why do kids come to the yeshivah? Because of the community and life and sense of direction we have here. Boys come from completely atomized families, where they give you money and TV and where the parents vanish. Here are your things—and go. The kids get burned out. Most of the boys here are middle- and upper-middle-class backgrounds. Some are the protest type kids, and some are hooligans. There is a heavy rejection of American values. They used to teach us to be good, clean our nails, work hard, and make money. Then we grow up and see cheating and lies. Do whatever you want as long as you don't get caught. This is the Western ethic—in America everything is relative. A judge tells you it is wrong to steal—but if I am on a higher level than the judge, I can steal. Good is not relative—it is absolute.

The repeated references are to the "emptiness of life," "lack of values," "illusions," "waste of time and energy," "looseness of society," and "decadence." Baalei teshuvah express real hostility to the bourgeois life-style they experienced in Jewish and general American society. They feel angry at what they perceive to be the fundamentally askew goals of American society, and indicate the evils technology and affluence have produced. The society seems wasteful, directionless, or going in the wrong direction, and morally corrupt. The themes occurring over and over again among American baalei teshuvah, and later among Israelis in a different form, reveal people whose sense of emptiness seems to mean aimlessness. They are people who came to feel that whatever they were doing had no purpose at all or none that was meaningful to them.

In reviewing the self-descriptions of baalei teshuvah, discussing their own perception of why they turned toward teshuvah, one finds a litany of plaints far from original. Its notes were sounded by large numbers of protesting youth in the sixties and seventies who sought alternatives, often in a radical direction. Thus, in describing the motivation, the explicit complaints and charges of baalei teshuvah, one struggles hard to find something that distinguishes them from thousands of other young people who have expressed their anger with and alienation from American society. Volumes have been written describing radical youth, alienated youth, countercultural youth, postmodern youth in the last two decades when the disaffection of these groups became socially troublesome.[2]

Equivalent studies of Israeli youth are not yet available. Israeli baalei teshuvah, however, express many of the themes prominant in the self-descriptions of the Americans mentioned above. Israelis issue the same plaints against secular middle-class Israeli society, while adding to them a specific local idiom. The cries of materialism, emptiness, dishonesty, and hypocrisy are heard with little variation or innovation. Recurring in the Israeli descriptions, however, is the specific charge that Israeli society has become "like unto the nations." The claim is that Israel is sick, weak, or corrupt because it has abandoned special ideals assigned to the Jewish people in exchange for the values of the non-Jews.

"The generation declines and is less," said one student, quoting a poem by the Hebrew poet Shaul Tchernichovsky. The student continued, "Anyone who observes what is going on today in society and family, and the general degenerate condition of this generation from a spiritual point of view...and the persistant effort to be like the nations." The motif touches on a perennial tension in Jewish history and one the Zionist undertaking in particular raised to the surface in modern times. The tension between a transcendent ideal and an earthly reality surfaces in the words of baalei teshuvah. They locate the source of their disappointment in the assimilation of Israel to the ways of the nations of the world, its desertion of its peculiar vocation. Over and over one hears that Israel must be better, that Israeli society must strive to reach some special standards, and that the disparity between the ideal and the real is too great.

"I remember what is written in the *Kuzari**—that the purpose of Israel is to fulfill the commandment of the Torah. I asked my friends what we were really doing. .... Our education is corrupted and mistaken because it has gone the way of the goyim. Assimilation is the path of the goyim."

The secular Israeli, conscious of the meaning of chosenness for the Jews, uses the language to articulate the traditional opposition between the ways of the nations and the vocation and destiny of Israel. He uses that language to express disappointment with the present Israeli reality and to pose the basic and specific question of why he should remain in Israel at all.

---

*A major philosophical work by Rabbi Yehuda Halevi (1075–1141).

Thus, another Israeli young man writes, "When I was in the army I started to seek a deeper reason why I am here. A more rooted reason. This thinking brought me to my being Jewish—and then I decided to learn about Judaism. The most important factor was the lack of purpose and fulfillment from a spiritual point of view in my life and in the life of the society. This is what led me to the search. The declining and disintegrating society in which I found myself—it made me look elsewhere to seek and understand."

Among Israeli baalei teshuvah, both those of middle- and those of lower-class backgrounds, there was a tendency to identify Zionism and the Zionist movement with the reality of life in Israel. Condemning what they felt were the evil or disappointing aspects of life in Israel, they also condemned the root from which in their view those problems had sprung—Zionist ideology. Zionism had produced a secular state which failed to fulfill the ideals of the Jewish people. Therefore, Zionism as a secular movement was to be condemned and resolutions of personal, social, and cultural ills to be sought beyond it.

Israelis of Eastern background restate many of the plaints against Israel and the condemnation of Zionism issued by Israelis of Western background. The former, however, tend to see reality in black and white terms and to view Israel as totally rotten. Among no other group of baalei teshuvah is classical religious terminology invoked more often to describe experiences prior to and after teshuvah. Those who feel themselves actually oppressed by society also view themselves as personally sinful. They feel they had no chance in Israel; therefore, they sunk into a life of degradation. Code words are used, like "discotheques" and "soccer games," to stand for that which is materialistic and degenerate in their past. It is as if these activities symbolize an entire existence. Baalei teshuvah depict life prior to teshuvah as sinful and life after as true, secure, and good. And in the course of describing the former existence they treat Israeli society, which they believe has mistreated them, to a sound lashing.

> Only God can determine if I will really be able to overcome my past and change myself. The hardest thing to overcome is the evil inclination. But once I have accomplished this, I want to work to return others to Judaism.... Who are the Zionists? Where are all the Zionists? They are all liars. How many have left Israel? How many murders are there here? What about crime? What about the drugs—how many guys are stuck on them? Why didn't they teach us this in school—about the real Zionists? How many of their children are no longer Jewish because they are either Christian or living with Christians? The only true Zionism is Torah. There is nothing else. Politics,

government, means filth and lies. In God's Torah there are no
political parties. All Israel is one. Actually, when I think about it,
the only good thing in Israel are the yeshivot. The bad things are obvious: robbery, murder, adultery, prostitution, abominable films,
poor relations between parents and children, wasting time in schools
with lies.

Again, Zionism is held responsible for all social evils: drugs, crime,
emigration from the country, prostitution, and so on. No area of life
is spared. Again, Zionism is said to have produced Jews who are no
longer Jews, literally or metaphorically. It is not only that the Zionist
state is rotten but that it has ceased to be a Jewish state. The force with
which the attack is made here is intense. Other baalei teshuvah repeat
the content with less intensity but with the same meaning. Behind it
lies the anger and desperation of those who feel personally degraded
and lost and who blame society for leading them astray, for ignoring
them, for corrupting them.

Thus, a student states that "Sabbath eves were marked by wild
parties and by the loss of all self-control. There were no boundaries, no
limits, no authority." And then proceeds to berate Israeli society for
providing no limits, no authority, and no boundaries. Or another
begins, "The soccer games and players became the most important
thing in my life. Every detail of the lives of the players in the national
and international leagues interested me. It was idolatry, with the spirit
of crazy ecstasy. It is enough to think of what goes on in the chaos of
the soccer stadium in order to grasp the chaos and emptiness of the
souls of those involved." He continues with a grand condemnation
of the society that nurtures such games, such ecstasy, and such evil.
The personal disorder and crisis are identified with social and cultural
illness and crisis. The resolution of both seems to these baalei teshuvah
to be total change and total reform.

In concluding this section, it must be emphasized that the motivation of baalei teshuvah to seek an alternative to their given reality is
not very far from the motivation of thousands of young people, a high
proportion of Jews among them, who have undergone some form of
religious conversion in the past two decades. The dissatisfaction is
shared among religious seekers and converts. It is also shared with those
who do not turn to religion but who adopt another framework within
which they find the direction, meaning, and values they seek, in opposition to those they have received. All of these people react to secular
society by seeking a new center outside that society, which contains
ultimate moral and spiritual meaning for them.[3]

Baalei teshuvah find their center in a highly traditional form of Judaism, which represents both a counter to the counterculture and a counter to liberal secularized Western culture and society. As to the latter, Orthodox Judaism is a reenchantment of the world. It is also a system in which revealed knowledge, authority, structure, and control are givens, accepted not only as necessary but as right, good, and true. As to the former, Orthodox Judaism is a highly rationalized and traditionalistic order, which does not elevate subjectivity and self-realization to supreme values. Thus, much more than the motivation, it is the direction baalei teshuvah chose to resolve their discontent, which distinguishes them from other alienated youth today.

Search for Meaning

The same differentiation between baalei teshuvah, those who did return, and others who took other paths to resolve their discontent, must be made when considering the second major factor mentioned over and over when baalei teshuvah described the motivations which led them to teshuvah. Both baalei teshuvah and nonbaalei teshuvah seekers are driven by a desire to find meaning which could give order and direction to their lives. This is the quest described by many sociologists who analyzed the youth culture of the past twenty years. Its character emerges in the following description of the counterculture:

> The counterculture was clear and united in its stand that the old myths and social arrangements and ways of life they had fostered were no longer viable and acceptable. It was unable to come up with an agreed on substitute to fill the void it created, although it insisted in a kind of desperation that the void be filled. In the absence of a vision to be derived from a scientific understanding of the world, nearly everything that afforded even a slight promise of answers to questions of meaning were subject to being tried and experimented with.[4]

Baalei teshuvah are differentiated from other disenchanted and discontent youth not in their quest for meaning but in the direction eventually taken in the pursuit of saving knowledge.

The need to know "the truth," to find certainty and full understanding, is emphasized in the self-descriptions of baalei teshuvah: "I was looking for what I could call truthful and absolute. This coincided with my realizing that all my previous knowledge of Judaism was total ignorance and misconception." "I realized that I wanted a consistent way of approaching all questions." Or, as another baal teshuvah expressed it:

I was approached at the Wall and asked to attend a class at the yeshivah. After listening to the rabbi I began to consider some of the
questions that were asked: "What was I living for; what is the
purpose of life; what is reality; why do I feel Jews are different than
others?" These questions forced me to introspect my present beliefs,
goals, and ideas. I found a great attraction to answer these questions
and the yeshivah provided the stimulus, atmosphere, and environment to do so. The rabbis dealt with questions of reality, truth, and
meaning, something usually not encountered elsewhere.

Across ethnic and sexual lines, baalei teshuvah attested to the desire
to know and understand "the truth," which would give them a handle
on the world. The knowledge sought was to enable them to distinguish
between good and evil and between the worthwhile and worthless. The
search is for a truth that will release them from ignorance regarding the
fundamental questions of existence: Who am I? Where do I belong?
How shall I act? In this sense what is sought is saving knowledge. It is
knowledge that will deliver from an existence experienced as problematic in very modern terms. Thus, baalei teshuvah seek religious wisdom—sacred knowledge which will release them from aimlessness and
alienation.

Some baalei teshuvah seek a more specific form of knowledge. They
want to understand the meaning of being Jewish and the individual's
relationship to Judaism, Jewish history, and Jewish identity.

An Israeli male phrased it clearly:

It is very difficult for me to separate my life into periods. As I progress in the way of Torah, I see more and more things that occurred
to me in the past, which influenced me toward the present. These
were things which when they occurred meant nothing to me. I was
especially bothered by social questions and the situation of society,
which gave me no rest. I also wanted to know why I am a Jew?
Does this obligate me to something? I wondered about the difference between Israel and Japan, between Tel Aviv and Kiryat Arba,
and why fast on Yom Kippur? Why not eat pig? What is the connection between me and the socialism which I have been taught all my
life? Is the village where I grew up faithful to its ideals? Israeli
society has no answers to these questions.

The questions put so forthrightly here are questions for which Israeli
society provides many answers. Essayists, journalists, philosophers,
theologians, and even politicians have filled volumes seeking to define
the meaning of chosenness and Jewish particularity today, the Jewishness of the Jewish state, the meaning of socialism today, and so on.[5]
And yet the questions remain questions, and society periodically ago-

nizes over them. Some baalei teshuvah agonize over them individually and make their way to Jewish sources for answers or to Judaism as an authoritative answer.

Another Israeli baal teshuvah posed the question of the meaning of Jewish survival in the context of anti-Semitism and explained how it brought him toward teshuvah.

> I was thinking increasingly about Jews. The probabilities were one in a million that the Jews should have survived. The most powerful civilizations had hated us. This is a constant in history. I began to conclude that there must be a God who wanted us to survive, but then I didn't know how Judaism related to God. Once I had reached the conclusion that we are a metaphysical people, because of our survival despite anti-Semitism, I also realized we are a religion-people. Then I knew that assimilation was a failure and must be a failure.
>
> But I didn't know why orthodoxy then. I started to ask myself questions about assimilation and about Zionism. Zionism, it is true, was successful in the operative sense of bringing Jews together and making the land fertile. But Zionism is collective assimilation. It is the assimilation of the Jews to the ways of the nations. It seemed to me then, before I came to the yeshivah, that this was wrong and that we had to return to our genius, our treasure.

Several elements emerge from this statement which must be noted. First, the saliency of Jewish history for the student and the need to explain it. He stated several times earlier that anti-Semitism and especially the Holocaust had to be explained. The only explanation he could come up with was the religious one—that God exists and that he guides the Jewish people. The Jews must be a "religion-people." He believes that this is a rational conclusion and not a leap of faith. Second, the implication from the conclusion that the Jews must be religious is that assimilation is a self-betrayal. Therefore, he personally must give up his own assimilated ways and enter an orthodox framework.

Beneath the argument is a strong desire to make sense of history and to find one's place within it. Beneath it also is a strong rejection of Western ways and a desire to return to the authentic Jewish genius. These motives characterize other baalei teshuvah who describe their need to understand themselves and their relationship to Judaism and the Jewish people.

> My change began when I felt a need to understand myself, my history, and the way it affected my life. As a nonreligious person everything seemed meaningless to me. It is not that everything is clear now, but that studying Judaism has given me the tools whereby I may approach the same questions in a different manner.

Again, this time through American baalei teshuvah, the cognitive need to account for history and one's place in it. American students reported a specific occasion for the surfacing of these questions and issues, related to their living in a Christian culture.

"I was confronted with questions which I couldn't answer and realized that there was a great lack in my education and in my relationship to God. There were no good schools and religious education where I lived. In college I came into contact with Christians and Jews who asked questions for which I had little knowledge and understanding to respond." Naturally, only students from the United States described the meeting with Christian culture as the catalyst for an intellectual search which ended in a religious leap. Israelis described a different curiosity and search for what they called "meaning." Thus, one typical statement begins: "I didn't like the way of life and the emptiness of secular society. It seemed to me that the religious life was whole, and that Judaism filled life with meaning."

Among both the Americans and the Israelis the drive to diminish ignorance is related to the positive pull of what we may term "roots." Somehow the sense of belonging to a people about which one knew little, or to whom one had felt little common binding previously, propelled students toward Judaism. Thus, "It seemed to be a constant awareness and feeling of my Jewishness. The knowledge of a different realm of Jewishness was desired, and a knowledge of the vastness of the literature." Another American student described the sense of belonging that preceded teshuvah as "two personal realizations.... One was that I was a Jew when I didn't know what the word meant. The second, when I began to see that the only reason the Jewish people had survived was because it had clung to the Torah—that from the Torah came all that Jews had to offer the world. I had the empty feeling that Western life had left with me." Another student put it as follows: "I experienced a kind of psychic distress—that whatever I had done, in the end, I remained in the midst of a void. Then, suddenly, it seemed that beside me and all around me, there was a world which might be absolute truth. What is more, that was the place from where I had come—without it I would not be. There was only one conclusion—to study."

Another variation of this theme by American students is associated with a visit to Israel and followed by a decision to study Judaism: "When I came to Israel for the first time in my life I came in contact with Jews and I wanted to understand what a Jew is or was. I was on a kibbutz. After getting no satisfactory answers I left and came to Jerusalem." Those baalei teshuvah who felt drawn to study or to become involved in religious life in Israel often did so after living on a kibbutz, participating in a youth program, or attending university for a certain time. "Confronting the reality of Israel–it necessitated a decision on the religious question. That decision required knowledge and a place to learn."

As is evident from all these statements, the quest for meaning is a powerful force in moving people toward teshuvah. The knowledge sought is not oriented toward a career or profession. Nor is it general intellectual or cultural information that is sought. Baalei teshuvah seek compelling knowledge that makes sense of the world and their place in it, and they turn for knowledge to the religious sphere. Sacred absolute truths attract and hold them because they order their world and define ways of behaving in it. Baalei teshuvah are willing to break into the universe of Judaism, despite all the difficulties involved in entering a religious system, because they perceive that universe to be ultimately meaningful and to be their own.

Religious Experience

The importance of the cognitive quest cannot be overestimated in understanding baalei teshuvah. The current teshuvah phenomenon, especially that aspect of it which encompasses young people, is oriented toward those Jews interested in learning and who are prepared to invest time in studying. The quest and the structures within which it takes place are religious. The baal teshuvah enters a symbolic universe, which is religious. He takes part in a learning activity defined as sacred, which is itself the gateway to piety. While the cognitive is a major focus in understanding the present teshuvah phenomenon, the attunement to the religious dimension and its experiential aspect must also be emphasized.

Baalei teshuvah are people who are interested in religion and who respond to a religious calling. As indicated previously, many other paths could have appealed to the young people who, sooner or later, turned to Judaism.

Political revolutionary movements have been available throughout the past two decades for those whose goal it is to change society. If the goal is to change oneself, a variety of psychologically oriented groups and treatments have emerged in the past two decades that can be tried.[6] And if the goal is to secede from society to a community of like-minded and like-hearted people, the communes that have mushroomed in the past years offer a variety of forms of communal living.[7] Revolution, reform, and other avenues for delivering the self or changing the world have been available in abundance in this period of competing ideologies and life-styles during which thousands of young people set out in search of such deliverance.[8]

Baalei teshuvah opt for a traditional religious culture. One factor underlying their choice is attunement to spiritual concerns. Judaism provides ideas and rituals through which a relationship to transcendence and to a community that understands itself as oriented toward transcendence is established. It is not surprising, therefore, that baalei teshuvah interviewed described some sort of religious experience as accompanying the teshuvah process. Religious experiences occur in a peculiar mode, which is felt to be radically different from the modes of ordinary everyday experience. In describing these experiences, baalei teshuvah have used the words "sacred" or "totally other" in referring to something that pulled them, lured them, and demanded something of them. The imperative to act in certain ways is always a part of the experience.[9]

Sixty-three percent of those interviewed in our survey reported having had religious experiences. Forty-six percent interpreted them as revelations of God, some in the form of specific visions and some as more generalized and abstract communications. The revelations were described as having given direction or push to an ongoing process rather than as immediate causes of the teshuvah process. In some cases the experience assumed very specific Jewish articulation, and in others it was quite specific but did not take a Jewish form. The experiences reported by baalei teshuvah who have not been raised within the framework of Jewish symbols and paradigms are outside the traditional idiom. None of these baalei teshuvah reported a reexperience or reenactment of the most cherished religious experiences of Jewish collective memory. They did not encounter God's "presence" or the Lord seated upon a throne, or a chariot ascending to the heavens. While some used Jewish symbols and images, the experiences they reported were personal and individual.

Among the experiences that did not assume a particular Jewish cast were illumination experiences. Baalei teshuvah come to sense the impingement of external forces of great power, which conveyed to them special knowledge of things they did not know previously, or which they knew "through a glass darkly": "My eyes were simply opened." "An inner light—that there is God." More dramatic and detailed descriptions focused on the clarity achieved with the revelation: "I experienced the reality of a spiritual experience. I am not a superstitious type but I reached the finer celestial levels where there was a clarity of perception which was both dramatic and overwhelming." Or,

I can't describe it, but it was approximately emotional, a feeling of bright clarity, almost psychedelic in nature, sustaining and nourishing. During my early davening I almost cried for long periods. Is seeing God constantly in the world a revelation? If you see something that was always there, but you see it now—how did you see it?

In a moment of despair, when I seemed to be in great controversy with God, I felt as if some sort of light had entered my body. The beginning of the change was influenced in part by an event. It was during the High Holidays—during intensive teshuvah and feeling the results as well as sensing within myself a growing intuitive awareness and certainty that God exists. During the ten days between Rosh Hashanah and Yom Kippur a few prayers were answered... which at the time was a welcome surprise to my skepticism. I felt growth as I learned more about Judaism—knowing that an observant Jewish life is an ideal if one is up to the responsibility—sensing Judaism had much to offer me in preparation for manhood, married life, and family life. I felt a tremendous blossoming of creative potential and inner strength and inner determination as a result of the High Holidays. My prayers were answered and a feeling of actually making emotional contact with my transgressions (sins of the past and feeling cleansed as a result—a sense of purging I guess, with subsequent emotional high and social openness). It would be a little strong to call what I experienced a revelation of God. Better said that I had a growing awareness of the possibility that God exists and does aid those who believe in him and follow his commandments.

In the third year of the university, I suddenly felt again the need to study Judaism and to get to know it from within. It was something like an illumination—that there is a God and that one must explain things to the end. That was when I made the decision that no matter what would be, I must turn to Judaism.

Some students described a very real but vague feeling of closeness to God, of being engulfed by a divine presence, which had no specific form. They depicted an overwhelming sense of the sacred that seemed to press in upon them, a sort of oceanic consciousness they linked with God. Very few students described an experience of vision. Most depicted a fragile or vague intuition, which had been forceful in confirming their previous religious sense or insight. While some refused to describe the religious experiences they had undergone, most were not reticent and reported the experiences they remembered clearly. The openness in this reporting, the clarity of the experiences, and the perception of the connection between the experiences and changes in their life indicate that these are people for whom religious experience is not only legitimate but is also felt to be a vital form of human experience.

Among baalei teshuvah reporting religious experiences, some described highly specific revelations having a Jewish articulation, which they perceived as messages and imperatives from God. The religious imagination revealed in these visions is very particularized, colorful, and Jewishly informed. "I dreamt that there were many idols, Greek statues, arranged in a room, which suddenly moved around, striking out, combating. Suddenly they fell down, defeated by a force which I understood to be God." This variation of the legend of Abraham in which the Chaldean idols fought among themselves was reported by an American youth who claimed to have had no acquaintance with the Jewish legend. He also claimed not that this dream convinced him of God's existence but that it impelled him to study.

Three reports of dreams of Israeli students contain powerful religious experiences in a clear Jewish articulation. "A year ago I had a dream in which the letters of several names of God combined to form one letter. To me this affirmed God's unity and his strength. This happened before I entered the yeshivah." "It was one day when I felt God was present and helping me every minute. And this feeling did not stop until I fell asleep and then *pesukim* [Bible verses] were going out of me, when I had no intellectual control over them for ten minutes and then my soul rested."

"When I returned from Sebastia,* my eyes darkened, I felt I was in the desert, tired, and without water. I fought against habits. I knew I was in darkness. In spare time I tried to recall the incident and the same picture of the beit midrash called to me from the depths. Like a man who walked in a forest lost in darkness and winter. Suddenly lightning appeared which enlightened far away places and afterwards total darkness, but at least I knew the direction. At the same time, I got to know a young man from Merkaz who invited me to come for Shabbat to the yeshivah. Throughout this period the picture of the beit midrash stayed with me."

American baalei teshuvah recalled experiences that occurred in relationship to Israel, to Jerusalem, and to the Western Wall. It was not only the sense of being with Jews, where one belonged, but being with them in holy places where one's "soul returned": "My experience took place at the *Kotel*.† I was overcome with a certain strange feeling of confirmation of my feeling to become frum."

Study itself, the act of learning within the yeshivah, constitutes an extraordinary, fascinating, and sometimes elating experience for many

*A new Jewish settlement on the West Bank.
†Western Wall.

baalei teshuvah. It must be recalled that the yeshivah is charismatic space and that all yeshivah students participate in it. While studying they act out a ritual of Jewish piety. Baalei teshuvah share in the experience of the charismatic and in the piety of study. For many baalei teshuvah, however, *talmud torah* is also an illuminatory experience which actually moves them toward teshuvah or which reinforces the decision already reached to undertake teshuvah. Some described a sense of being enwrapped by God while studying; others described a sense of elevation and extraordinary happiness subsequent to learning. "It was a good feeling of getting close to truth, close to God, which brought me great happiness. I had no direct religious experience, but my coming to God and elevations of my soul came through studying." "It is a sense of elevation difficult to describe. The happiness which comes with the removal of all doubts." "I have had different types of experiences, from the realization of God's presence in this well-ordained earth, to remorse over past actions, to having my mind blasted by understanding a piece of *gemarrah** or a nuance of *Humash*."†

For many students that experience is the intellectual clarity that comes through learning or through some kind of cognitive breakthrough. "No visions and no voices, but meanings speak and in one second you grasp complicated essences in a very clear form." "Yes, I had a religious experience, but not a spiritual awakening or revelation but rather an intellectual religious experience through study and the observance of mitzvot." "The description of inner feelings is done by an artist and it is difficult for me to suddenly be a writer. But so that there won't be any misunderstanding, the movement of my life from eighteen until today has been full of religious experiences, despite the fact that I didn't belong to a specific religion. The definition of a religious experience about which I speak is the full clear understanding of a total life according to what I know is true. This is a sudden situation of ending all doubts, a small fullness on the way to fullness."

This selection of statements demonstrates clearly that religious experience plays a role in the contemporary teshuvah process, among students both of Eastern and Western backgrounds. The character of these experiences differs widely. Their effect, and that of the entire process of rejection, protest, and turning toward Judaism, has been eloquently described by William James. "Let us hereafter, in speaking of the hot place in a man's consciousness, the group of ideas to which he devotes

---

*Talmudic commentary on the *Mishnah*.
†Pentateuch.

himself, and from which he works, call it the *habitual centre of his personal energy.* It makes a great deal of difference to a man whether one set of ideas, or another, be the centre of his energy; and it makes a great difference, as regards any set of ideas which he may possess, whether they become central or remain peripheral to him. To say that a man is "converted" means, in these terms, that religious ideas, previously peripheral in his consciousness, now take a central place, and that religious aims form the habitual centre of his energy."[10]

Modes of Teshuvah

The motifs mentioned above as preceding or accompanying teshuvah may be organized into a set of concepts in terms of which one may analyze the process of teshuvah. Each concept concerns a distinct aspect of teshuvah, while together the set encompasses the entire notion of teshuvah. The method utilized in arriving at this set of concepts was the SSA (Smallest Space Analysis). The SSA permits an empirically testable structuring of observed items and the concepts they represent. The ordering of the derived concepts is in a manner that can be represented geometrically.

Forty-four variables concerning behavior that could ensue from or accompany teshuvah were selected for the multivariate analysis. All of these variables were actually observed through direct questionning of the subjects who participated in the study. All contained ordered response categories which could be interpreted unambiguously as ranging from "high" to "low," in respect to the manifestation of teshuvah-associated behavior.[11]

The results of the exploratory SSA are shown on figure 1. Here each of the initial set of forty-four variables is represented by a point on the plane in such a way that the larger the observed coefficient between two variables, the closer the points representing them on the plane. Once such a picture was obtained we attempted to partition the space into regions, each containing variables with a common specific meaning. In other words, interpretable correspondences were sought between the geometric contiguity patterns of the variables and the content of the variables. Because it was assumed that much "noise" would be present, effort was directed at establishing broad generalities concerning sought correspondences rather than a perfect fit. We arrived at certain general conclusions, which were then retested on a subset of selected variables.

Surveying the distribution of the variables over the two-dimensional space (fig. 1), it became apparent that a simple partitioning of that space into four sections would produce a classification of the variables

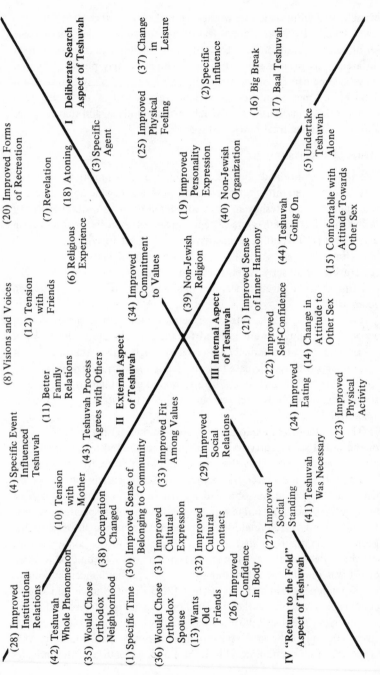

Figure 1. Smallest Space Analysis of forty-four variables.

by an overall content criterion. At this stage of the exploration there was no insistence upon a 100 percent fit between regions and content, since not all original variables could be expected to be "pure types," with respect to the conceptual constructs to be derived.

On the basis of observing the SSA of figure 1, the following conclusions emerged in this stage:

1. Those variables located in Region I associate teshuvah with a deliberate and conscious search for a religious or value system, seemingly unlinked to prior preferences (var. 39 and 40). In such a search the influence exercised by specific people (var. 2 and 3) plays a particularly important role. Teshuvah is perceived as having improved the subject's self-expression (var. 19), and the whole process is perceived as a visible and concrete break from former patterns of life (var. 17 and 37).

2. The variables in Region II associate teshuvah with phenomena external to the individual. Although teshuvah is a personal and internal process, it may be influenced or accompanied by what are perceived by the baal teshuvah as external factors. Some phenomena are interpreted as conducive to teshuvah (var. 4, 6, and 7), others as accompanying teshuvah (var. 18), and still others as resulting from teshuvah (var. 11 and 20). All of these variables point to roles played by factors external to the individual during the course of teshuvah.

3. Variables in Region III associate teshuvah with the individual's personal identity (var. 14, 15, and 22) and integration (var. 21). The focus in this region is upon the internal processes including the individual's inner world. Further, these variables indicate points in the development within the individual of teshuvah (5 and 41 refer to the beginning; 44 to the development; 21 and 22 to the product of the process).

4. Variables in Region IV associate teshuvah with social structure, in this case a religious community. They include variables concerning the outcome of the teshuvah process, mainly in the social and cultural areas (30, 31, 32, and 35) as well as variables that deal with projected behavior (35 and 36).

These variables reflect a reaffirmation on the part of the baal teshuvah of structures once known or to which he feels an affinity (13).

Below is a schematic diagram of the interpretation of figure 1.

	external interaction	
return to the fold (community)		search for value system
	internal interaction	

The selection of the original forty-four variables was not guided explicitly by the conceptual categories that emerged from the SSA. Therefore, it was necessary to reverse the procedure described in the last section and reexamine the categories. First, a selection was made of "pure" variables, that is, those that conformed best to the content of the four components of teshuvah outlined above (I: search; II: external interactions; III: internal world; IV: community). Second, a reanalysis with respect to these variables was conducted.

The goal of this reanalysis was to discern a clear partitioning of the selected variables in accordance with the conjectured components of teshuvah. Such a partition would support the formulation of these components. However, only further replications, with different sets of both variables and populations, could confirm the emerging hypothesis concerning the internal structure of teshuvah. In the following paragraphs twelve variables selected as having a relatively high definitional reliability will be indicated and described.

Region I: The Search Mode of Teshuvah

Variable 2

Was the change in your relationship to Judaism influenced by a specific person or group? [definitely yes... definitely no]

The existence and awareness of specific influences are typical indicators of an "autonomous" individual, who consciously explores and seeks out value systems before choosing his own. Having made the choice consciously, he is likely to be able to account for its origin.

Variable 14

The second variable selected was a computed measure of the improvement in the course of teshuvah in the individual's functioning in the personal-expressive mode. This mode concerns, by definition, the exercise of power within the system that constitutes the individual's distinctive personal characteristics. The act of reaching out for religious values on the part of the individual, when guided mainly by distinct personal considerations, constitutes an instance of functioning in the autonomous mode. Improvement in the self-expressive behavior of the baal teshuvah, which concurs with teshuvah, is interpretable as an instance of the search mode that is teshuvah.

Variable 16

To what extent is your life today [after teshuvah] a break from your life in the past? [to a great extent... not at all]

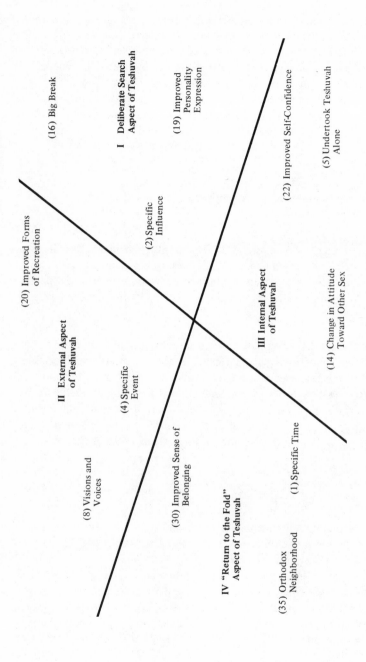

Figure 2. Smallest Space Analysis of twelve variables selected by structural hypothesis and reanalyzed.

The more deliberate and conscious the search, the greater the sense of break. The notion of the big break was chosen as an indicator of the search mode because it assumed that those who deliberately adopted a new ideology or value system after having embarked upon a quest for it are more aware of having found what they sought. They are, in fact, more likely to experience a big break from their past experience than those who "slid" into an ideology or value system unaware.

Region II: The External Mode of Teshuvah

Variable 4

> Was the change influenced by a specific event? [definitely yes...
> definitely no]

The event was understood by all participants in the study to refer to an external factor. Some associated the "event" with an empirical happening, such as the Yom Kippur War. But many who said that their change in relationship to Judaism was influenced by an event referred specifically to something that was not only external but also transcendent.

Variable 20

This variable is a computed measure of the improvement in the baal teshuvah's functioning in the personality adaptive mode, which occurred during the teshuvah process. This mode concerns the interaction between the personality system and external factors, such as the utilization by the individual of forms of recreation or renewal. Improvement in this area, because it involves relationship to outside resources and constraints, lies within the range of the external mode of teshuvah.

Variable 8

> Did you ever experience visions of voices in the course of the
> change? [definitely yes... definitely no]

In questioning respondents about the influence of an event upon teshuvah, several probe questions were posed. One was whether the respondent had undergone religious experiences during the process, another was whether that experience was interpreted as a revelation of God. Despite the hesitancy to claim a revelation and to describe it, 63 percent of the respondents answered positively. As a more specific probe, the above question on visions or voices was asked. This variable belongs within the domain of the external forces, because visions and voices were subjectively perceived as originating outside or beyond the individual.

Region III: The Internal Mode of Teshuvah

Variable 5

Did you go through the process of teshuvah alone or with some or one of your friends? [alone, with one friend, several friends]

This question was included in the region covering "internal mode" because it was assumed that when a person undergoes teshuvah alone the process is more unified, compact, and less likely to break up as a result of social complexity. He who undergoes teshuvah alone is more likely to be motivated by factors stemming from his personal internal self, in contrast to one who might be conforming to peer pressure, or receiving encouragement from friends.

Variable 21

This variable represents a computed measure of the improvement in the individual's functioning in the integrative personality mode. This mode concerns interactions between various personality components *within* the individual. A sense of inner harmony, relative freedom from excessive anxiety, and general psychic well-being are indications of satisfactory functioning in this mode. Improvement in this internally oriented mode of human functioning, which accompanies teshuvah, is interpretable as pertaining to the internal dimension of teshuvah.

Variable 14

Since the change in your attitude toward Judaism, have you changed your relationship to men/women? [very much . . . not at all]

We have interpreted a change in one's attitude toward the other sex as an indication of a change in an aspect of one's own identity. Hence, this variable too provides (at least indirectly) an indication of change in the inner self.

Variable 35

Do you want to live in an orthodox Jewish neighborhood in the future? [definitely yes . . . definitely no]

The desire to live in an orthodox Jewish neighborhood is a firm indicator of commitment to the total way of life embodied and acted out in such a neighborhood. Therefore, this factor is included in the "community-belongingness" mode of teshuvah.

Region IV: Community Structure Mode

Variable 1

Did the change in your relationship to Judaism occur over a short or extended period of time? [in one day . . . more than 2 years]

Inherent in the process of teshuvah is the notion that somewhere or some time there exists a "holy community" to which one returns. This region refers to teshuvah as a "return" to the fold," assuming that "the fold" exists in their consciousness to one degree or another. To the extent that this traditional component in teshuvah is really experienced as homecoming (return), it will be experienced as occurring in a shorter time frame. This is inferred from the fact that a clearer recognition of formal ties with Judaism and a Jewish way of life, even if they have been abandoned for sometime, facilitates a quicker adoption of both. Moreover, a prior understanding of Judaism and the Jewish community enables a quicker and surer integration into the religious community.

Variable 30

This is a computed measure of the improvement, which accompanies teshuvah, in the societal-conservative mode of functioning of the individual. This mode concerns the confidence of the baal teshuvah in his community and the strength of his sense of belonging to it. Improvement in this mode of human functioning is interpreted as pertaining to the "community-belongingness" mode of teshuvah.

Each region within the SSA represents constellations of responses suggestive of certain emphases in contemporary teshuvah. It should be pointed out, however, that the teshuvah of any particular individual may partake of one or any number of these emphases or modes, which have been labeled as the search mode, the external-world mode, the internal-world mode, and the community mode.

The search mode denotes a deliberate and conscious search undertaken by an individual, which ends in teshuvah. As indicated, the search is a process in which a person may pursue various options until arriving at teshuvah. The decision to undertake teshuvah is viewed as a visible and concrete break from former patterns of life. Often the decision for teshuvah is related to the influence of a specific individual or group, of which the seeking individual is well aware.

In the external mode, teshuvah is associated with phenomena seemingly external to the individual. In some cases the altered relationship to Judaism is seen to be influenced by an external event. Often it is related to the felt intrusion upon the individual's life of an extraordinary external force. This intrusion is taken to be a religious experience. By providing a relationship to the transcendent, Judaism, like any religion, can contribute to a sense of selfhood, one attuned with being and open to growth and expansion. Moreover, teshuvah brings one into a framework in which sex roles are clearly delineated and firm differentiations are made between men and women. This, too, can lead to a sharpened sense of self or identity. That component of teshuvah involving personal consolidation and integration will be referred to as the *inner-world* mode.

Inherent in the process of teshuvah is the notion that there exists a "holy community" to which one returns. This sense of "returning to the fold" may well be the most distinctively Jewish component of the teshuvah process, setting it off from other "conversion" phenomena. Judaism entails commitment to a community. When such commitment is salient in the teshuvah process, we speak of the *community* mode.

Each of the baal teshuvah respondents was given a score "high" or "low"—for each of these modes on the basis of his responses to select items in the questionnaire (see Appendix for the items). The distribution of scores for each mode is presented in table 1.

Table 1
Distribution of Scores in the Four Modes of Teshuvah (%)

	Search	External	Inner World	Community
High	51	40	40	64
Low	49	60	60	36

Earlier we noted that the community mode was the most distinctively Jewish component of the teshuvah process. Here it may be noted that it was salient for almost two-thirds of the baalei teshuvah. Examination of the relationship between the modes and various background variables (table 2) suggests that the community mode—the most salient for all groups of respondents—was more salient for women than for men, more for those with lesser education, more for those of Eastern than of Western origin, and more for those whose fathers were traditional. The reason for this differentiation may lie in the higher degree

Table 2
Percentages of Baalei Teshuvah "High" on Teshuvah modes, by background variables

Background Variables and Mode	Search	External	Inner World	Community
Sex:				
Male	50	42	38	59
Female	51	36	44	74
Education:				
High (more than high school)	49	37	36	58
Low (less than high school)	53	43	42	70
Origin:				
Western	53	43	41	60
Eastern	39	30	34	75
Father:				
Traditional	45	34	42	71
Nontraditional	54	40	37	56
Self prior to teshuvah				
Traditional	44	39	40	61
Nontraditional	58	40	41	67

of individuation associated with greater education and diminishing traditionality. Individuation is certainly more characteristic of Western societies than of Eastern, where communal ties are stronger and where communities are more traditional.

On the other modes, difference by background variables were slight, save for ethnic origin, which, in addition to the community mode, also registers differences on the search and external modes. That students from Western background were higher on the search mode than those from Eastern background can be explained by the difference between the "market situation" in Israel and the United States. As indicated earlier, in Israel religious alternatives other than Judaism (Christianity, Islam, Bahai, Hare Kirshna, Scientology, etc.), although available, are scarce items. They are at the periphery of public consciousness. Moreover, the search pursued by students from Western background requires a degree of mobility and economic support generally not available to Israelis. Furthermore, a milieu of seeking exists in the United States, which assumes the plurality of choices and the legitimacy of pursuing spiritual options. Despite the limitations built into the situation in Israel as a "religious market," a number of Israeli baalei teshuvah did "shop" occasionally outside Israel and more often within the country, and arrived at teshuvah after a search involving several stops.[12]

5
Return to the New

Seeking and Homecoming

The delineation of the search and community modes permits us to describe two dominant motifs characteristic of and peculiar to baalei teshuvah. These are *seeking* and *homecoming*, elements present in varying degrees in the accounts of all baalei teshuvah. Seeking dominates among the Americans; homecoming is more prominent among the Israelis.

The seeker is one whose teshuvah is the final stage in a process of quest, which may have included intermediate steps—stopovers at other religious groups. Or the search may have led directly to Judaism. The seeker decides consciously and autonomously at a certain moment that he is dissatisfied with what he is, what he believes, or how he carries on his life. He embarks upon a quest, which may be either short or prolonged. It is experienced as a passage from one form of existence in search of another.

The figure of the religious seeker is well known in the contemporary United States. Writers discussing the "cultic milieu" in which new religious movements sprout and grow also describe one of its inhabitants— the permanent seeker.[1] This is a person who is prepared to pass from one form of heterodox religion to another, experimenting, investing conditionally, and moving on. Once these religious groups are taken to have a partial or relative hold on truth, there is little difficulty practically and none theoretically in transferring one's belief, loyalty, and community from one to another.

The paths of search taken by students from the United States have been referred to previously. Here the search and stopovers of Israeli baalei teshuvah may be indicated in order to focus upon the movement and passage these people experience.[2]

An Israeli student, studying at Ohr Hahayim yeshivah, offered a rather lyrical version of the religious change through which he had passed:

The social and cultural emptiness cries out and the soul searches for its true place. The many vanities which are around satisfy only for a short hour and hardly that. The soul cannot be satisfied with anything less than Torah. Western culture cannot satisfy these things. The hardest thing in my life is to be a Jewish person. I think now that I was really born for labour—the labour of the Torah. Two years before I entered the yeshivah I had arrived at the conclusion that the true purpose of the life of the Jew is Torah. Every discussion about these matters caused a huge inner storm in me. There were many factors hindering my return. But finally, after the army, I decided that this is the true path. I found a yeshivah and entered. It was a long process of repair and of becoming whole.

Here the search led immediately to Judaism, but only after a two-year period of reflecting and hesitating. In a longer description by an Israeli woman of Tunisian background, the passage included a number of intermediate steps.

My interest in Judaism was on a low flame for two or three years. My home was traditional but during high school I ceased being interested in it altogether. I would say I was secular, even antireligious, and was influenced against religion by the philosophers I had started reading. Most of my friends were secular. During my second year at Bar Ilan University,* a friend told me about a guru at Tel Hashomer. I went with a boyfriend, but didn't like it at all. But this time my thoughts about religion started. However, I dedicated myself to studying literature and art. In thinking about religion I really didn't know where to start, and felt completely confused. Christianity was least interesting: it looked stupid to me. Islam seemed too masculine. I thought about studying Judaism, but gave the idea up. For a year I did nothing, just nothing.

In my third year at Bar Ilan I went to the guru and tried transcendental meditation in Bnei Brak. At the end of my third year, I started attending lectures in Tel Aviv given by a rabbi from Ohr Sameah. I had a religious boyfriend, who was moving away from Judaism. He wouldn't discuss anything with me. I didn't know how to deal with his confusions, and had a million questions to ask and no one to ask, so I went to see this rabbi. This was the beginning of the birth of Judaism for me.

In the university I had studied literature and loved the new young writers of Israel. Their message was nihilism, however. They seemed to lack a goal in their existence and wrote much about death. I identified with them—with their confusion and conflict, but *I wanted to end that state.* Today, I have content. Because I no longer need to identify with their views, I no longer identify with these writers.

*While Bar Ilan is a religious university, orthodox identification is not required of students there.

I still appreciate their forms, sympathize with them, and pity them. The other subjects which I used to like, and literature too, are important to me now only because they brought me to Judaism.

To the seeker, seeking is a valued way of being. To the baal teshuvah, it ceases being valued as such and is replaced by a desire for commitment, "to end that state" of confusion and searching. The object of commitment, an ancient religion and highly traditional interpretation of it, is not, moreover, a happenstance choice. It is not *any* religious group to which the baal teshuvah becomes attracted, although the precise cause of the turning, the particular event or time, may indeed be happenstance. The choice itself, however, is compelling because it resonates with part of the individual's biography. The baal teshuvah feels that he has "returned," has committed himself to something which was in fact really his all along.

The sense of "return" in contemporary teshuvah is in many ways an experience of self-discovery. The baal teshuvah discovers a self he feels was his by birthright and of which he was deprived. Underlying his feeling of "return" is an implicit sense that somehow the individual, no matter what his specific biographical experiences, participates in a historical, spiritual, and ethnic heritage. And this because of the peculiar nature of Judaism as a religion whose carrier is a natural people. Belonging to the Jewish people involves not merely biological or kinship ties but also ties to a historic religious culture. The baal teshuvah feels that he has awakened to the meaning of his being Jewish, that he has discovered the Jewish community, that he has come home.

A Moroccan student expressed this experience of homecoming in very clear imagery: "A man taps on the door of his neighbor's house and asks for an item missing in his home. Sometimes he stands at the threshold and is afraid—it isn't a nice feeling! When a Jew stands at the door of the yeshivah, he is not knocking at the door of a stranger's house, but his own. This is a return to the essence." Door, house, essence—when he enters the yeshivah the baal teshuvah enters his own home and feels that he recovers his "essence." "I feel I am returning to the values and practices followed by my grandparents." "I have returned to the religion that I was cut off from by my parents, who themselves had been exposed to Orthodox Judaism."

The nonreligious generations in the background of the baal teshuvah, no matter what his ethnic origin, are few. The hiatus is short and can be leaped with ease. The baal teshuvah does not have to travel back very far to find a family to which he can return. Moreover, baalei teshuvah can recognize their grandfathers or great-grandfathers in the figures encountered in the yeshivah or in the streets of Jerusalem. In fact, those who become his spiritual mentors, replacing his natural father in certain ways, may resemble his grandfather more than his natural father did.

As another student, a woman, put it: "There is a world which may be absolute truth, and I am obligated to know it, because, in the end, that is *the place from which I have come*—without it, I would not be." This insight impelled this woman to leave university in the middle of her third year in order to study in a school for women baalei teshuvah. The woman continued by telling how a year before she had attended a seminar in which "something had been kindled" in her: "In the beginning the meeting with religious people and the wrestling with their ideas repelled me. But at the end it was an inner call, and an unconditional call, which told me to go. Where? To the place from which I have come."

The same sentiment was expressed symbolically by a young student who asked that his parents in New Mexico search their attic for a picture of his grandfather, which had lain hidden there for years. The picture of a silver-bearded man dressed in rabbinic clothes now stands on the student's table in his room in Jerusalem. The student himself appears and dresses much as his grandfather did. And his values and activities may be closer to those of his grandfather than they are to those of his parents.

The American student returns to his family roots. At the same time, he feels that he returns to the geographical and cultural roots of his people. The center of his existence changes to Jerusalem and to the yeshivah. The Israeli's homecoming is experienced as strongly, although it does not involve the physical transfer of a center. It is a return home, nevertheless, because it is experienced as a return to the real self. A description of this sense of teshuvah was given by an Israeli who underwent the experience himself years ago: "In spite of the vast range of ways in which a Jew can alienate himself from his past and express himself in foreign cultural forms, he nevertheless retains metaphysically, almost genetically, an imprinted image of his Jewishness. To use a metaphor from the world of botany: a change of climate, of soil, or other physical conditions, can induce marked alterations in a plant's functioning, and even the adoption of characteristics of other species and genera, but the unique prototype persists."[3]

It is in this context that it is possible to understand the controversy over the very application of the category baal teshuvah. In discussions with rabbis or with observers of the contemporary teshuvah phenomenon, the question is often asked as to whether the contemporary baal teshuvah can be called a baal teshuvah. It has been suggested that another category, one used in the Talmud to describe a Jewish child taken captive by non-Jews and raised outside the structures of Judaism, would be more appropriate to those returning to Judaism today. This is the talmudic concept *tinok she-nishbah*.[4] Such children, captured by non-Jews, who grew up outside the Jewish community, had no knowledge of the halachah and, therefore, were not obligated to do teshuvah for the sins they had committed while captive.

The issue here is much wider than the legal question of whether the baal teshuvah is in the same position as a "child captured by the gentiles" and therefore not obligated to undergo teshuvah. The issue is the consciousness of the contemporary baal teshuvah and the phenomenology of his experience which leads him to accept the label and define himself as a baal teshuvah.[5] And this is precisely the point. The baal teshuvah does see himself as such.

Schuetz, in describing the stranger, stated that

> to be sure, from the stranger's point of view too, the culture of the approached group has its peculiar history, and this history is even accessible to him. But it has never become an integral part of his biography, as did the history of his home group. Only the ways in which his fathers and grandfathers lived become for everyone elements of his own way of life. Graves and reminiscences can neither be transferred nor conquered. The stranger, therefore, approaches the other group as a newcomer in the true meaning of the term. At best, he may be willing and able to share the present and the future with the approached group in vivid and immediate experiences; under all circumstances, however, he remains excluded from such experiences of its past. Seen from the point of view of the approached group, he is a man without history.[6]

Total "historylessness" is rarely a condition of the Jew, whatever his religious background and whether he be from Israel or New Zealand. He is a stranger and yet not a stranger. In a certain sense the graves and reminiscences are part of his biography but must be "conquered" and reappropriated. He is a seminewcomer. From "the point of view of the approached group" he is a newcomer and must learn everything from the beginning. And yet he is not a stranger to them because he is a Jew who can discover himself and restore himself to himself and to the community. From his own point of view, he is a newcomer in the sense that he has never been where he is going. And yet he is also coming home, rejoining his own past, returning.

The homecoming experience of the baal teshuvah resembles the gnostic process of throwing off the alien in response to a call from the good god, followed by the return to the world of light and life. In Gnostic religion, gnosis allows one to know oneself, return to oneself, and to save oneself from enslavement.[7] The baal teshuvah, too, acquires knowledge which enables him to free himself from what he feels is a false and corrupt world. He views himself as passing from one world to another, one of which he considers his home and truly his. It is as if the home had been hidden from view by secular culture, by foreign forms, languages, styles, values, and beliefs. Breaking through them, the baal teshuvah feels that he is returning to his true self and culture.

Old and New Self

This is accompanied by a sense of being changed radically, of beginning life anew. It is a feeling very similar to that associated in other religions with the experience of conversion. Teshuvah is in this sense a Jewish version of conversion. Conversion is an inner experience, a response to a perceived internal or external force, which leads to a major transformation in the existence of an individual or a group. It is experienced as renewal, even of rebirth. The past is felt to be annulled by the change, and a new future is embraced in which life is different, other, new. One who experiences this sense of rebirth has been called "twice-born" by William James. The experience has been described by Van der Leeuw as one in which "a second self stands over against the first."[8]

Teshuvah, insofar as it reverses transgressions and enables one to start again, as it were, is also an experience of rebirth. The baal teshuvah has been described in the tradition as one reborn: "A baal teshuvah is like an infant just born."[9] Teshuvah is described as wiping out the past and opening the possibilities for new life and new creation. In one source God says to Israel, "Repent in these ten days between the New Year and the Day of Atonement, and I will justify you on the Day of Atonement and will create you a new creation."[10] The great power of teshuvah is its regenerative force, its ability to overcome the past and enable the creation of a new future.

While teshuvah resembles conversion in this sense of rebirth, the element of *return* is quite specific to it. In traditional Jewish society the baal teshuvah literally returned to something he knew and had lived. And as we have noted, the baal teshuvah of today also experiences teshuvah as return. The self-consciousness of the contemporary baal teshuvah is not that of an altogether new person but of one who has discovered his true self, revealed his real past, rejoined his family. The modality is restoration—an experience of the actualization of the Jew who was there but hidden rather than the creation of a new person out of a new fabric.

The changes demanded by teshuvah in behavior and ultimately also in perceptions (or in perceptions and ultimately also in behavior) lead to disputes and realignments between the baal teshuvah and his family, his occupation, preoccupations, and aspects of his physical, social, and cultural existence. For example, and not as trivial an example as it may seem, whereas 50 percent of the baalei teshuvah stated that they engaged in physical activity (work, sport) to a great or very great extent before teshuvah, only 15 percent reported that they now do so. Yet overall, in areas asked about directly, the direction of change was to greater satisfaction. The percentage answering to a "great or very great extent" to select questionnaire items regarding their pre- and postteshuvah situation is as follows:

	Before Teshuvah (%)	"Now" (%)
To what extent do you participate in activities which expose your values and beliefs	40	78
To what extent do you feel your values and beliefs are in harmony with your environment	23	79
To what extent do you feel that the various beliefs you hold fit together	29	84
To what extent do you feel committed to a set of beliefs and values	36	89
To what extent do you have a sense of confidence in and belonging to your community	32	72

As can be seen, Judaism provides these baalei teshuvah with a sorely needed universe of significance and an everyday existence based on relationship to transcendence in the context of a community to which they have a sense of belonging and which for them is the embodiment of sacredness and purpose. Not surprisingly, baalei teshuvah feel that they are in passage between worlds, moving from the false, nonreligious, non-Jewish, Western, and forbidden reality of their past to a newly discovered world, good, true, holy, and commanded. The distinction is so sharp that in a real sense life is experienced by the baalei teshuvah in binaries.

Because Judaism makes a total claim on the life of an individual, teshuvah affects a transformation that filters into every aspect of existence. A change in the perception of ultimate values and meanings calls for a reevaluation of what is considered penultimate. The implications of the ultimate relationship which is at the heart of teshuvah must be worked out in everyday life, when everyday values are measured by values considered to be derived from an ultimate source.

The contrast between the worlds is felt in many ways. It may be experienced in the very encounter with the yeshivah, an institution totally different from any the baal teshuvah had ever known. It may be experienced in the contrast between the community of which the yeshivah is a part and the community of which the baal teshuvah is a part. The perception of differences between worlds emerges lucidly from the following account by an American baal teshuvah:

When I got to the yeshivah I couldn't relate to anything. Despite all my learning in Hebrew school, attending shul, davening, and kashrut, I didn't understand anything. Then they said come to the beit midrash. I saw a Talmud and didn't know what it was. I walked in and the room was full—impressive. Twenty-five couples of guys, bent over books, learning. If it was Plato it would have had the same effect upon me. Or if they were learning a Theodore Roethke poem. It was out of will that they were standing over the text and trying to learn.

I was put with someone for *hevrusah,** and was totally bored. But then I began to feel guilty. I was so enthusiastic about the place, but totally out of it, foreign to it, and didn't know what to do. So I kept trying, very impressed by the externals, Hebrew, books, and Aramaic and by the logic of the arguments. But I wasn't ready to make a decision, so I went back to the university. I started another ulpan. I finally realized that it was drudgery, that I was sick of college, grades, courses, and wasn't going to whittle my life away.

On Shavuot I went back to the yeshivah. That night we stayed up all night studying. It was the book of Ruth, to which I could at least relate. The next day I was invited to a family in Mea Shearim where they like to invite baalei teshuvah. It was a lovely family, seven kids. They draped a towel over our laps because they couldn't afford napkins. As I walked back through the streets of Mea Shearim I kept thinking that I did not want to be like these people. As I walked along the streets I felt I was going through different worlds. God—is this what I would be? I was frightened by the whole business and didn't want to be part of it. I got back to the yeshivah and spoke to normal guys. I really liked these people. Don't forget—it was the late sixties and early seventies. It was a hip place—eleven out of the fifty

*Study companion.

guys were vegetarians, music loving and grass smoking. They weren't
that far away from my past.

I saw there were two ways: synthesize or break. If there weren't
the first possibility, I would have quit. I wanted to develop my
writing. I knew that I wanted to do Jewish writing but all I had was
Christian symbols. So I wanted to change my symbology or myth-
ology. This was the excuse which allowed me to stay at the yeshivah.
I didn't think about it then as a life forever. Basically, I liked what
we did. I liked to daven three times a day and put on tefillin. But I
didn't wear tzizit. This was the symbol for me of embracing the
whole thing. Putting on a *yarmulke* was just a commitment to the
institution.

I had a wonderful *rebbe* —an incredible pedagogue and I made
fantastic progress. I was entirely involved in study. The commitment became a habit. *Benching* [prayers after meals] everyday,
washing before meals. Besides, en principe, I was not against this
stuff. I figured you had to do the whole number. From morning till
midnight, I studied with top guys. It was an exemplary community—it wasn't that I was devoting my life to learning petty details, I
felt I was devoting life to changing my symbol system.

I continued like this until I hit a certain inner crisis. I came to feel
that maybe I was performing a cultural surgery on myself. I seemed
to be too much to switch cultures like this. I went to speak to my
rebbe, who said immediately that if I felt I was committing some
kind of intellectual suicide while studying in the yeshivah, he would
be the first to pack my bags and send me off. Then he described his
own relationship to this learning. He said that he felt attached to the
divine when he did this stuff. This didn't impress me—the divine
part. I wasn't too much into the God thing. What did impress me
was that he was devoting his whole life to study because he had a
feeling. I had admired him so much because of his powers of reason,
his rationality. And now I saw that it all rested upon a feeling.

I realized that I simply didn't know enough to make a judgment.
I didn't know if I had that feeling, so I decided to stay and learn
more. My leap of faith came from the example of this rebbe. That
was the breaking point, and then I became frum, which means that
the business ceased being an exercise in changing symbol systems.

"I couldn't relate to anything" was his first response to the yeshivah.
The streets of Mea Shearim passed through other worlds. The students
in the yeshivah were still "normal," but only because they were still in
the yeshivah—not yet part of those other worlds in the orthodox communities. The contrast between worlds, and between the yeshivah and
the past of the student, would have broken him if he did not think it
possible to synthesize the two rather than supplant one by the other.
In the case of this student, the desire was not to abandon the past completely, not to negate totally, but to reach a synthesis of some kind.

Even with this goal, and the support of his teachers, the path was not clear or secure. What were clear, however, were the blatant contrasts between past and present, between one world and another. The significance of experiencing religious reality through a neighborhood, a synagogue, or through contact with a person cannot be overstressed when describing the factors important in contemporary teshuvah. Israelis and Americans who happen to encounter a reality they experience as new, overwhelming, yet somehow theirs, point to that encounter as the moment that they began to consider teshuvah as a possibility for them. A desire to draw close to that new reality, to become part of it, coupled with awareness of the drastic changes commitment to it would entail sets in motion a process of conscious deliberation, a weighing of worlds. An account by an Israeli woman enables us to focus for a moment on this point in the teshuvah process.

I was born in Haifa and received a secular education. My parents had been raised orthodox, but had rebelled. They had gone to Hashomer Hatzair kibbutzim. I served in the army in a unit on the Golan Heights, where I met a girl whose mother had become religious. The mother had moved to a religious neighborhood in Jerusalem, Bayit va-Gan, and was attending a baal teshuvah institution there, Nevei Yerushalayim. My return was really built around this woman.

After the army I attended the Hebrew University, studying psychology. I went to visit the mother of my friend. The first time, I walked up the main road to Bayit va-Gan, and entered the neighborhood on the main street there. The air and the atmosphere were different from anywhere else I had been—they gave me a feeling of faith. What is faith? It is something found in everyone, but which is felt more or less. It made a huge impression on me. Still, I got up and went home. I thought that what had happened was just an experience and perhaps an illusion.

Three years passed and nothing happened. My friend returned from London and together we went to visit her mother. This visit was really something. Something entered me. I felt that I was on a high for sometime afterward. It made me certain that I was somehow going into this thing. A spark in me answered—responded to my friend's mother. I decided to go back once or twice to discuss Judaism with her. I went to the synagogue with her on Rosh Hashanah, and it hit me again. Then I went to synagogue on Yom Kippur and nothing happened.

I really didn't change until Purim, after I finished my work at the university. A little before Purim I started attending classes at the baal teshuvah school. By Pesah [Passover] I had decided to attend full time. The more religious I became, the more questions I had to ask. I am not a natural nonconformist and am not particularly an individualist. I am a simple person with strong social needs. I do not like to oppose the views of others. In Bayit vaGan I found a community which supports me, and which welcomed me in.

I don't know really how I began to believe, but it just flowed. I can't put my finger on anything. And throughout the process there was a little fly which buzzed in my head with doubts: maybe they are all mistaken. This was a short period. Faith is not something which is or is not. It is like the parable of the tree with roots and branches. It grows and develops. Slowly, faith envelops all areas from the roots up. It keeps blooming in all directions. In the summer of 1978, the year before my teshuvah, I had been in London. I had tried to read the Bhagavadgita, but it was not for me. Finally, the light burst through with God's help.

In teshuvah doubts about the truth or nature of religious principles exist and remain. The leap taken is less one of faith than of action— does one want to live a certain way, accept certain patterns of doing and not doing? Does one want to make a neighborhood one's own? Something "hit her," making the woman certain that she was "going into this thing." An experience of a sacred presence overwhelmed her and determined her turning. In the previous description, the model of the rabbi and the young men studying in the yeshivah also "hit" the potential baal teshuvah, and he decided to "become frum". The decision is made to act, to join the community and to adopt its ways of living. It is a decision that allows doubts about specific theological problems to be suspended.

All or Nothing

Given the emphasis in Judaism upon action it is not surprising that most baalei teshuvah do not make belief a precondition for entering the yeshivah or beginning to participate in its life. Neither, of course, do the yeshivot. But since the religious identity chosen is an all-encompassing one, the baal teshuvah, having made the decision to act, comes under pressure to reject compromises. A half-way house situation will not do, not for him and certainly not for the community he wishes to become part of. He is thus pressed to enact greater changes, intensify separations, heighten the perceived divisions between past and present.

I feel myself still on the bridge. This is expressed externally in the wearing of a maxi, which I think is the special mark of the baal teshuvah. I like to wear a maxi, a hat in the summer, a certain type of belt, and to appear loose and sloppy. I admit that this is especially me—it is my connection to the loose and nonconformist past. I buy my dresses in the Old City, and do this so that I won't appear part of the ultraorthodox world. It is a double value or two worlds. How long can this last? Years.

For a long time I forced myself not to listen to Israeli folk music as part of divorcing myself from Zionism and that sort of thing. The music was associated with a period which I did not want to remember, I was not afraid of a regression but a fall. When I heard that music, I became immersed in it and then fell into a black mood. During this period, I threw out all my cassettes. Now, I can turn on the radio and if I happen to hear this kind of music, nothing happens. . . . There is a period of weakness, when one fears regressions and depressions, and then one builds up. This requires time. I am insecure—there is always the option to return.

Awareness of the fragility of the new structures informs this description. The hazards of "falling" while crossing the bridge between worlds are such that it is best to eliminate all distractions and temptations. The sense of moving in one direction is dominant, but with awareness of the ever-present risk that the process might be reversed. Both senses, of forward movement and the danger of slipping back, are characteristic of baalei teshuvah in passage.

In recalling his reaction to seeing the film *The Champ*, an American baal teshuvah stated, "I cannot do that again. It filled me with the past. Passions. You can't live in two worlds and have it both ways." This baal teshuvah was aware of the fact that orthodox Jews attend films. Those who do not do not refrain because it is forbidden by Jewish law but because it is deemed inappropriate according to customs of the community or because it is considered a waste of time. For the baal teshuvah, however, a different issue was involved—the threat of the past overwhelming the present. To protect his new self, or the self he was in the process of constructing, he resolved to avoid the conflict by avoiding films. "You can't live in two worlds. . ." In one form or another that is the conclusion baalei teshuvah repeat when discussing the transformation taking place in their daily existence. To strengthen a fragile present, the past must be pushed aside or behind.

An Israeli baal teshuvah, today a rabbi in a yeshivah for baalei teshuvah, cast further light on this matter: "Attachment to the outside world and to the things of that world depends on each individual. It must continue for a certain amount of time. It gradually stops because interests and language change, and one cannot understand each other anymore. This is a natural process through which we all go—the only difference is the pace." The rabbi continued by stating that in his view a "serious" baal teshuvah will seek to avoid situations "in which he may not be strong enough." The goal must therefore be to minimize contacts with the outside, with the secular, in order to protect the new existence against activities which are seen as threats to it. Activities that actually conflict with the halachah must cease, obviously. Activities that do not actually conflict but seem inappropriate or threatening because of their "secular" character are also abandoned, even if gradually. He described the process as he experienced it, drawing prescriptive conclusions for baalei teshuvah in general:

> Certain hungers not normally permitted may be satisfied, even though it is not what God wants. A man changes slowly in every way. When I entered the yeshivah I slept on a mattress on the floor, since that is what I preferred. My entire life was "low." After a while I wanted and accepted a bed. Once I was at a party arranged by women friends. All were kosher and OK, but Bob Dylan music was playing in the background. I felt it was wrong—it wasn't in place anymore. You must change these things and the little things sometimes are the hardest. Clothes are a part of a mentality, express a mentality, and so one must change from jeans. You have to have one thing in your head—to do what God wants.

Bob Dylan and kosher food seem to represent two different mentalities, one secular and one religious. The baal teshuvah feels that he cannot cope simultaneously with the claims of two worlds, which do not mix. Under these circumstances the claim of the new existence is felt to be exclusive. Polarizing the choice, the baalei teshuvah opt all out for the religious world as they see and understand it—the one presented in, through, and by the yeshivah. The atmosphere of the yeshivah is intrinsically one of totality, for in it is a community of those who dedicate themselves fully to the Torah. As bahurei yeshivah (yeshivah students; literally, yeshivah lads) they symbolize total dedication to the highest values of Judaism. That baalei teshuvah encounter Judaism in the yeshivah means that they meet a Judaism more demanding than less, extreme rather than moderate, total rather than partial. The framework formed by the yeshivah and its staff and encompassing the baal teshuvah leads him to define Judaism as a tight and totalistic system. If he binds himself to this system, it seems to him that he binds himself out of any other: "Their problem is that they try to live in two worlds, to have both sides, and it can't be done, if you want to learn and be really frum. All of the truth is in Judaism, so why read anything else. I have given away my books of Hebrew literature. I don't want my children to read Bialik and be filled with questions and doubts. Why should they have the problems I had." This statement expresses the conclusion to which most baalei teshuvah arrive. "It can't be done." If one wants to be frum, one must choose. And having chosen, one might as well eliminate doubts to the extent possible, both from oneself and for one's children.

Baalei teshuvah, drawn to the conclusion that one chooses between worlds of clashing fundamental values, tend to strike the contrast between their past and present harshly. They tend to view their past as a period of moral and spiritual confusion, an inferior existence basically off-the-mark. "I miss nothing of my past. Now I have a sense of the spiritual order of the world, a better knowledge of the difference between right and wrong, and the challenge of recognizing the supreme and absolute truths. Recognizing and knowing these things has given me a sense of purpose and I no longer have the empty feeling of those who thrive on materialism alone."

Other baalei teshuvah aspire not to cut themselves off from their past totally, and do not believe that this is even a realistic possibility were it desirable. The past indeed represents a different order and one inferior to the religious order of the present. This does not mean, however, that one does not feel drawn back to the past nor that one does not miss aspects of it.

Part of my being is the experience I had in the secular world. To deny that would be to deny part of me, which, whether it was legitimate or not, that was who I was. I never saw the process of teshuvah as destroying my being but as redirecting it. I also felt that I had a responsibility to maintain myself in the secular world as a bridge. My personal history was the bridge. It was not necessary to cut, but rather, to maintain connections without destroying either side or negating my personal being. It does not have to be a total personality change, which is very scary. The change is rational and step-by-step. It can be without a trauma. I still do what I used to but less, and I don't value it. There is still a certain amount of guilt now in going to movies and in listening to records. You can't really live in this frum community without adopting the view that learning Torah is the highest value. Therefore, I go to fewer movies, and have to rationalize when I do go. It is not a value, but it is also not an evil. I say I can do it if I am tired of studying.

Here the baal teshuvah clearly sees his present as a continuation of his past. He does not believe that he has rejected his old self totally. And yet, he admits that the activities of his past life, which conflict with the religious way he has accepted, he can no longer value. Gradually, he diminishes his participation in such activities. Further, he describes how he has changed in conformity with the definition of frum framed by the orthodox community. The community continues to press in upon the newcomer. "You can't live in this community without...." It forces a reevaluation of all behavior according to its standards. The contacts with the past which are maintained must be psychologically rationalized. Moreover, the scope and force of these contacts must be diminished if one is to be absorbed fully into the community. And they do diminish, even for a baal teshuvah who aspires to hold onto his past. He may still be part of it—but it is a past trimmed and clipped by the norms of the community to which he now feels he belongs.

Another testimony to this process from an American student adds to the picture of the struggle through which the baal teshuvah passes and the direction in which it inevitably goes.

I began to study more and more, and finally decided I had to come to the yeshivah. Nothing can reverse me now, but the problem is how I will relate to secular society. Am I going to be an academic as I planned? I had this strong desire to return to the past after the boorishness and philistinism of American life. I knew that we had to be Jews no matter what. This is what we were commanded at Mt. Sinai and that's it. I do not feel that this is something I can choose. I must accept everything of the Oral Law. I understand that. My problem with being *haredi** is not that. I have a feeling one must be immutable before time and that I cannot change because of socio- logical or technological factors. Change has never affected the Jews. Technological change is not even a threat. My only problem with the haredi position is that I have roots in the secular world. My friends will always be from both worlds. What I want to do is to fight to bring more Jews to their awareness of the necessity of accepting or rejecting orthodoxy. I want to make others recognize that they must choose and what the ramifications of their choices are: TV or *Pirkei Avot*,† the beach on Shabbat or studying Maimonides.

The push and the pull—back and forth from the past and the present, from the secular to the sacred. The baal teshuvah feels that the change toward what he regards as the haredi option is inevitable, but part of him fights it. This is the process most typical of teshuvah. The choice is seen as *Pirkei Avot* or TV, the beach or Maimonides. Because the dominant thrust is toward the past, and because the determination is to be immutable before time as Jews have always been, in the opinion of this student, the roots in the secular world will be loosened and eventually pulled out as completely as possible.[11]

This painful process is illustrated clearly through the question of the relationship to Zionism. As stated earlier, Zionism is a problem for every orthodox Jew because it raises the question of the meaning and significance of a secular Jewish state. Some orthodox Jews have accorded sacred, even redemptive, value to the Zionist enterprise and consider

*Ultraorthodox.
†*Ethics of the Fathers.*

the state a religious value. Others deny all religious value to the state because it is secular, and condemn the Zionist movement as a carrier of secularism.

Baal teshuvah yeshivot which are oriented to the ultraorthodox community embody the latter view toward Zionism and transmit it to their students. Some baal teshuvah yeshivot are oriented in a more moderate direction and direct their students toward a religious view of Zionism and Israel. In either case, however, baalei teshuvah undergo a fundamental change in their relationship to Zionism and the state: one sanctifying both and one negating both.

As indicated earlier, most of the yeshivot are oriented to the ultraorthodox position and community. This includes Ohr Hahayim, Aish Hatorah, Dvar Yerushalayim, and Nevei Yerushalayim, to mention only the largest. Machon Meir and Yeshivat Hamivtar present another option, which is attractive to a minority of contemporary baalei teshuvah. This minority stands firm on a positive evaluation of Zionism. Even within the ultraorthodox yeshivot, there are students who maintain a positive attitude toward Zionism or who do not adopt the negative attitude the institution propagates. The rejection of secular values, and the translation of this rejection into every aspect of an individual's existence, is more widespread than the total rejection of Zionism.

A few figures on the issue of Zionism can shed some light on the attitude and relationship of baalei teshuvah on this sensitive subject. It should be noted at the outset that all baalei teshuvah associate their present relationship to Zionism with the teshuvah they have recently undergone. Of the 135 Israelis reviewed, 43 percent stated that they felt positively toward Zionism at present. Of the 217 Americans, 67.5 percent were positive, 10.6 percent indifferent, and 15.3 percent negative. Overall it may be stated that students from the United States are less caught up in the issue of Zionism than the Israelis.

Moreover, in the yeshivot for Diaspora students the issue is almost always avoided; it is discussed only where the attitude of the yeshivah toward Zionism is positive.[12] Symptomatic of the delicate situation in which Diaspora yeshivot for baalei teshuvah find themselves concerning this issue is the attitude taken on Israel's Independence Day, when something must be said about the State and Zionism. In two yeshivot, Machon Meir and Yeshivat Hamivtar, prayers for the State are recited. At others, no special prayers are added, reflecting the view of the staff that no holiday is being celebrated. At one yeshivah, where for internal political reasons there is a desire to avoid the issue, prayers are not held at all on Independence Day.

As is apparent from the figures cited above, a large percentage of all students maintain a positive attitude toward Zionism redefined, however, in religious terms. Several basic justifications recurred among those who described their relationship to Zionism as positive or extremely positive. Among Israeli students the religious value of the land and the commandment to settle in Eretz Yisrael was repeated again and again. Some linked these values with the messianic process, with which teshuvah was also linked. Thus, an Israeli male from Machon Meir stated, "Zionism is the realization of national teshuvah, a return to roots, an increase in Jewish pride, and strength of position among non-Jews. And, most importantly, it is one of the signs of the beginning of the period of the coming of redemption."

Here redemption and teshuvah are linked to a return to roots and pride in one's self and one's people. Other simpler and direct interpretations stress the messianic dimension. The following are all taken from statements of students of Machon Meir: "Zionism is the beginning of the ingathering of the exiles, the beginning of the rebuilding of the land of Israel, and the beginning of the messianic period." "Zionism is the redemption and teshuvah on a national-universal scale."

Over and over again, in the descriptions of Israeli baalei teshuvah, the secular is transformed and made meaningful by the messianic vision.

Zionism is the beginning of redemption, the rebuilding of the kingdom of priests and holy nation. Zionism is part of the end of days, and we must help the Holy One, now at the end, to breathe life into the material body which has been created. This foundation is the economic system, the police force, and other functions of the state. Now I feel we are establishing the redemptive kingdom.

Secular Zionism was a necessary stage in the building of the Land. But, now its task is over. That stage has climaxed, and is in a state of disintegration. Now, after the rebuilding has been completed, we must breathe the real breath into the body which was asleep for so long in the *Galut*.

This last statement expresses most clearly the basic position of religious Zionists. The secular phase was important, but its time has passed. The secular must be transfigured if the state is to be justified as a Jewish state.

These and many other citations reflect, quite obviously, the influence of the redemptive theology of Zionism taught in Machon Meir, and which has also penetrated wider circles of orthodox Jews. Nothing is added by baalei teshuvah to the fundamentals of this position. The innovation is the transformation of their earlier views about Zionism into religious nationalist categories and concepts.

American baalei teshuvah, far less drawn to the messianic dimension or interpretation of Zionism, accord positive value to the State and to Zionism because of the sociological framework which they provide for a full Jewish life. Thus, "Zionism led to the creation of a grand potential for Judaism and Israel to fulfill the destiny of the Jewish people. The creation of a moral world order, observant of absolute laws, and designed to create a messianic order on earth in order to perfect the world under the rule of God." "It is important for Jews to have a homeland where they can develop their culture—political, social, and religious. In this way, they are not constantly compromising and apologizing for their ways of life. They are expressing Judaism as a people and as a way of life in the positive sense. In the long run, this is the only way Judaism can survive." In both these statements of American male students Zionism and Israel are portrayed as the arena where the Jewish people can fulfill its ethical and religious vocation without being pressured toward compromise by the influence of non-Jews. This is the view of the great majority of Americans who enter baal teshuvah institutions concerning the positive value of the Jewish state.

Those baalei teshuvah who do not accept the religious Zionist position claim that no secular Jewish state is legitimate, even as a transitory phenomenon. They also claim that there can be no hope of transforming the secular and that the only appropriate response to the secular Jewish state is maximum withdrawal from it. The statements of baalei teshuvah who reject Zionism on religious grounds, almost entirely Israelis, reflect a grave disappointment with the reality of the state as they perceive it. They articulate their disappointment in the categories and terminology of the traditional idiom provided by the yeshivot where they study. They chose these yeshivot not accidentally but because this particular idiom is one that expresses their own feelings and insights about the State.

From the critical statements issued by Israeli baalei teshuvah about Zionism, two main sets of claims emerge. First, Zionism is secular and therefore negative. Second, the product of the Zionist movement, the State of Israel, is actually destructive of religious life. The following citations convey something of their anger and disappointment vis-à-vis the State and Zionism:

> Zionism—it distanced the Jews from their Judaism. The Zionists
> established a movement which is collapsing today and which is leav-

ing behind it a state which is rotten to its core. This rottenness is particularly visible among the youth, who are confused and don't know why they were born, why they are Jews, and what a Jew is.

My understanding of Zionism is very negative because it led many Jews to secularism and did not fulfill what it promised to be.

Zionism led to the Jews' breaking with God. This is frightening. In my view, families who suffered during the Holocaust should be even more anti-Zionist than I am. Whoever reads this remark will feel that it is impossible and unnecessary to expand. However, I would like to indicate that this view is one which developed within *me* and *alone.*

Zionism distanced the Jews from their roots, made them forget Judaism, and distorted its image.

It denies Torah and claims that we should be like every other nation. But I must admit that it has accomplished great things.

It gives Jews a cop-out from being Jewish. The essence of life should be coming close to God and not Israel.

Zionism is against the spirit of the Torah and causes the Jewish people to degenerate and the state to be destroyed.

This anti-Zionist rhetoric articulates discontent, disappointment, and anger with secular society. Ambivalences toward the secular are channeled into the idiom of a community whose positions are well known and which run deep. That idiom appeals to the baal teshuvah because it expresses his experiences and responses. The dominant issue for the baal teshuvah is Western culture. Zionism, a highly sensitive issue which cannot be avoided, is actually secondary. Zionism comes to represent the efforts of the Jewish people to modernize itself, to enter history as a people responsible for itself and its own history, and to develop a new culture for itself. As such, Zionism seems to the baal teshuvah to be a betrayal of Judaism and of the vocation of the Jewish people.

Baalei teshuvah reenact in microcosm what the Jewish people has been doing for centuries. The Jews have set themselves apart from the nations. Baalei teshuvah set themselves apart from that part of themselves that was formed in imitation of the nations. Jews have very resolutely constructed boundaries with which they divide reality into that of the chosen and that of the others, the outsiders. The baal teshuvah did not inherit these boundaries but discovers and appropriates them for himself. Separating himself from his past, he crosses the fences, which for one born into an orthodox framework have always formed boundaries, and he consciously places himself within the bounded area.[13]

Separating

The secular preteshuvah past is made past by changes in daily life imposed by the assumption of the commandments of Jewish law.

The tendency among baalei teshuvah is to take upon themselves a high standard of observance, in order to put their secular preteshuvah past behind them as assuredly as possible and to demonstrate and underscore the break with that past. They not only accept the "yoke of the Torah" but desire to accept it in a most disciplined and maximalist form. If a choice is available between an easier or more difficult way of performing a commandment, the baal teshuvah will choose the more difficult. Given a choice between assuming certain duties slowly or quickly, he would opt for the quick path.

This tendency to extremism among baalei teshuvah was noted by a rabbi who teaches in a school for women:

> Another one of the toughest problems with which we cope all the time, especially with beginning students, is the tendency toward fanaticism. They tend in this direction for many reasons. One is because it offers greater security to see things black and white. The school's philosophy is that the individual is central and that a balance and control must be maintained. But it is a continuous problem. The issue is not the halachah, but the boundaries at the end of the line. There is lots of room between the permitted and the forbidden. The more learned the girl is, the more she recognizes this and the less fanatical she is. In the beginning, they accept the definition that more strict is more religious and if something is harder, it is better. This even creates competitions within the school among girls. This is difficult for newer people.
>
> Another source of fanaticism is the families which the baalei teshuvah visit and which set standards for them. We can't seal off the girls hermetically. The tendency is not just religious but also social. They tend to see that it isn't a closed system and that there is no one answer. The challenge is the interaction between the individual and the system. We don't want people to feel guilty about their reading a book at night. First, it is not considered *bitul Torah** for girls, since the requirements for men in this regard are not the same for women. Second, after a full day studying, they will either go up the walls or read something not connected with learning. So we should let them, and without guilt.

*Waste of time.

We know that people have different needs. We once had a
musician for whom we arranged classes at the musical academy in
Jerusalem, although it cut off class hours. The question is one of
framework and that must be analyzed for each person. Everything
depends on the extent and degree. All of their past life was not
corrupt and bad. They must channel it and build their selves—that
is the goal. Most of us suppress our selves, but that ought not be the
goal.

While stating his views of the ideal course teshuvah education should
take, the rabbi reveals that the course it actually takes is quite different.
To his students, stricter means more religious, and the less of the past,
the better. Students prefer to suppress themselves rather than try to
channel the past into the present. And, by his own admission, the community within which the students live and within which they hope to
be integrated reinforces their interpretations and aspirations. The communities themselves are not moderate. And they are not moderate vis-
à-vis the baal teshuvah. They expect a high standard of religious behavior from him as demonstration of the thoroughness of his new commitment.

For most, self-transformation—the goal set by the baal teshuvah for
himself but equally for the community within which he wishes to live—
is a slow and difficult process. Not all the changes demanded are enact-
ed with ease. One area where external and internal changes are most
evident, most intimate, and often most painful is the family. Another
is sexual life and norms. Teshuvah brings about strains in the relation of
the baal teshuvah with his parents and with the opposite sex.

Relations between parents and children are upset on several grounds.
A baal teshuvah finds it difficult to eat in the home of his parents who
do not observe the dietary laws of Judaism. He finds it difficult to
spend the Sabbath and holidays with his parents who violate the religious proscriptions and prescriptions regarding their observance. By
assuming the "yoke of the Torah," the baal teshuvah not only separates
himself from the non-Jew, he may also force a physical separation between himself and his parents, deeply disturbing to both parties. The
impact of teshuvah on family relations on this level is greatest for
Israelis, who have much closer contact with their parents than the
Americans living thousands of miles away from theirs. And it is felt
more intensely by Israelis of Western family background than Eastern,
perhaps because the latter's parents are themselves more traditional or
less disturbed by the changes.

When I started to observe the Sabbath my parents said my health
would suffer because I couldn't ride with them to the beach and

swim. Then I broke up with my boyfriend over matters related to the *mitzvot* (commandments) and my parents were very angry. The problem was that I didn't want to fight. I wanted to preserve *shalom bayit'*.* But, the house was not kosher. Second, I couldn't stand the transistors on Shabbat. I got my own dishes, and finally became a vegetarian to resolve the kashrut problem. My mother could at least respect that. When it came to Pesah, I took over the kitchen and changed all the dishes and made sure the meal was kosher.

The vegetarian solution served many a baal teshuvah well. Other issues, such as the observance of the Sabbath and holidays, were not so easily resolved. In most cases, baalei teshuvah moved out of the homes of their parents and set up their own apartments, as in this Israeli's account:

> My parents opposed my going to visit the people on a religious kibbutz, saying that they were all missionaries and that I would lose my critical sense. When I said that I wanted to observe the Sabbath, my father said that I would destroy family unity, but my brothers were sympathetic. In the army I gradually moved toward a religious life, starting with observing the Sabbath. Because of my parents I could not keep kosher. But then I took an apartment with my brother and we made it kosher. By now my parents are reconciled.

The issues go beyond pots and pans. Students described situations in which they feared they would no longer be able to communicate with their parents because their interests would no longer be the same. American students focused on two specific problems as a source of conflict with their parents. One was the possibility of immigration to Israel, or actual immigration, which disturbed parents. Another was interruption of career plans or university education, which also disturbed parents.

Baalei teshuvah fight out the entire range of issues with their parents, arriving at some sort of modus vivendi. The staff of the yeshivot are often consulted both by parents and children to aid in working out living arrangements and to help bring about mutual understanding. The ideal is not to break families apart.[14] On the contrary, because of the place of the family in Judaism, the ideal is to work toward a resolution of problems that would enable sound and solid relationships to be maintained between parents and children. Whatever the ideal and the degree of achieving it, the fact is that for at least half the baalei teshuvah this is an area of conflict, tension, and pain.

It should also be noted, however, that a minority of baalei teshuvah claim that their teshuvah led to an improvement in relations with their

*Peace at home.

parents. They believe this to be the result of recognition on the part of parents that teshuvah was beneficial to them.

The issues around sex, intimacy, and modesty, the norms governing premarital and postmarital relationships between the sexes, are where the clash between preteshuvah and postteshuvah behavior is most pronounced. The standards for these accepted by the orthodox community differ profoundly from those common today on the campus, in suburbia, or in most neighborhoods in either the United States or Israel. That is well-known. The questions, however, are, How do baalei teshuvah resolve the clash between contemporary Western mores and halachic norms? How do they adjust to the rules governing premarital intimacy and to the standards of sexual modesty? How do they cope with the traditional division of sexual roles?

In the orthodox communities within which baalei teshuvah live, not only is premarital celibacy the absolute rule, but any physical contact between man and woman prior to marriage is proscribed. Baalei teshuvah are expected to conform to this norm as to any other. Conformity here, however, in many cases means that a man will dissolve a relationship unless he is willing to marry the woman with whom he has been living. Or it may mean that the potential baal teshuvah does not move to the yeshivah dormitory because he is not prepared for such a dissolution. He is forced, therefore, to fragment the sexual area from the rest of his "progress" and to handle it at another pace and according to looser standards. Rabbis in baalei teshuvah yeshivot, recognizing the peculiar sensitivity of this area, treat it with great care. Thus, they may allow students to live away from the yeshivah temporarily, seeking to bring them into conformity with the halachah in the sexual area gradually according to the special situation of the individual.

Baalei teshuvah who find it necessary to move slowly in conforming their own behavior to the demands of the halachah are the exceptions. Those involved in premarital relationships almost always break them off as part of the changes undergone in the initial stages of teshuvah. The strain of maintaining a relationship that violates the codes of traditional Judaism and clearly conflicts with the standard of the yeshivah is considered not worthwhile by nearly all students. Moreover, such a relationship, because it violates the norms being voluntarily assumed, creates an inner contradiction with which students cannot live. The result is that sexual relationships formed prior to teshuvah are ended either through marriage or the separation of the couple.

Given the restrictions on premarital contact between men and women, "arranged" marriages are quite customary within the orthodox world. In the ultraorthodox setting, such arrangements are an unchallenged norm. Baalei teshuvah, drawn toward this community, fit themselves to the system. They accept the limitations on contact. They also accept the notion that friends, rabbis, or teachers may be best able to arrange matches, given the knowledge they have of both sides and given the limitations on other ways of making initial contact. Meetings arranged by persons tied into the social networks of the orthodox community are all the more useful, and necessary, given the fact that most of the baalei teshuvah do not themselves have wide contacts in that community.

The idea of a *shiduch,* an arranged marriage, is novel and strange to baalei teshuvah. They become passive actors, as those who know them consider with whom they might be best matched and when to arrange the first meeting. From the first meeting onward, however, they take an active role in the progress of the relationship. They determine whether a second or third meeting is worthwhile or desirable; they decide whether or not to pursue the relationship to marriage. Courting in this system follows strict rules. The kind of free experimentation common in the nonreligious world is obviously not permitted. Engagement and marriage are also governed by strict regulations and procedures, in contrast to the mores of the secular world. Nevertheless, and despite the strangeness and contrasts with familiar patterns, no baal teshuvah objected to the shiduch system. On the contrary, those who commented on it indicated its virtues over the open courting game in which they had previously engaged.

> The shiduch idea is a big adjustment. There are new ground rules. In some communities you can't even be alone with girls. We meet girls who are friends of the rabbi's wife. She introduces us to orthodox families, which befriend fellows, invite you for shabbos. If they don't want you to marry a girl, they tell you so.... The idea here is not self-denial. But there is the idea that you must use strong self-discipline while at the yeshivah. Long hours of study. There are temptations and celibacy is difficult—but look at Jacob and Isaac. There is the midrash that their wives were three or four years old when they were brought into their homes. They taught them the ways of the family and then married them. The forefathers were old men when they got married, and they waited the whole time. I take this midrash symbolically and not literally, but I use it as a model.

> The shiduch system is great. First, I have no way to search for a fellow since I have no entrée to the schools. A rabbi who knows me chooses a boy. They search throughout all the yeshivot. I can ask them to hurry. I meet him and see if he is favorable toward me. This

is totally different than the secular world. Flirting doesn't determine, but what I know about his character. The reasons for choosing
are cold rational ones.

Baalei teshuvah accept the tradition's way of handling these issues.
Many are pleased by the shiduch system as a counter to the tensions
and difficulties they had experienced or imagined as part of the "ro-
mantic-love" system. Given the constraints of the life they have adopted, and their desire to marry, the shiduch system seems practical,
reasonable, and fairly successful. This is not to say that all baalei teshuvah accept suggested shiduchim, but that they accept the shiduch
principle.

It should also be noted that shiduchim are not arranged in a manner
whereby "personal compatibility, not to speak of romantic attachment," are not taken into account.[15] On the contrary, in the case of
contemporary baalei teshuvah, the element of personal compatibility is
very seriously considered by those friends or teachers who attempt to
make the match. Furthermore, romantic attachment may well develop
before marriage, although its development remains constrained by the
limitations imposed by the halachah. The shiduch system in practice
within the baal teshuvah community should not be viewed as a medieval anachronism, wholly at odds with modern practices and tastes. The
actual meeting of the two people involved is not spontaneous, and this
is indeed contrary to modern conceptions of romantic relationships.
The reasons the two decide to marry, however, may indeed be the same
as that of any two people who decide to marry.

Furthermore, the restrictions governing sexual contact, the marriage
customs, and the definition of sex roles appeal to baalei teshuvah precisely because they seem to defy modern trends and practices. Part of
the appeal of Judaism is that it is not "up-to-date" in these areas, and
apparently has no need to be trendy or "relevant" to modern expectations. Its immunity to these influences is taken as a sign of its
strength. Ancient precepts and practices, it turns out, may seem quite
acceptable to those eager to oppose contemporary mores and assump-
tions.

It must be noted that most shiduchim arranged for baalei teshuvah
are with other baalei teshuvah, and for two obvious reasons. Yeshivot
for male baalei teshuvah are linked with institutions for women. The
pool of marriageable people is easily available. Rabbis in schools for
men consult rabbis in the associated school for women in order to
locate suitable partners, or the reverse. In an institution such as Dvar

Yerushalayim, where men and women study separately but within the same organization, the wife of the head of the yeshivah arranges marriages between the students, all of whom she gets to know by inviting them to her home during the course of the year.

It is not just the technical factor of availability of pools of interested partners that creates the phenomenon of the inmarriage of baalei teshuvah. It is also the shared background and experiences of baalei teshuvah that seem to make marriages between them both appropriate and likely. The matter goes even deeper, however. The baal teshuvah carries a stigma that makes orthodox families hesitate before welcoming him or her as a mate for a daughter or son. Suspicions about the marks a secular past have left on the baal teshuvah exist and cause orthodox families to close the door in this most intimate matter. This does not mean that marriages between orthodox people and baalei teshuvah do not occur. They do, but infrequently and exceptionally.

The shiduch is the pride of the baal teshuvah institution. It is of great importance in the social life of the yeshivah. Weddings between baalei teshuvah are celebrated by the schools of each partner. They are large and joyous affairs, marking not simply the marriage of a couple but another critical step in the teshuvah process. Marriage, especially through a shiduch, epitomizes the values of the baal teshuvah yeshivah. It is taken as a sign of the completion of a process. The couple will settle in an orthodox neighborhood, will fulfill the standards of family life demanded by Jewish law, will have children (many are expected), and will educate them in orthodox schools. Such a marriage signifies the final throwing off of the loose ethic of the secular world in sexual matters and family life, and the commitment of yet another couple to the ranks of orthodoxy.

The redefinition of the woman's role in life is another area in which separation from the standards and values of the secular world and acceptance of new standards and values is most clear. This is true for men as well as for women. While the role of the woman was highly respected within Jewish society, praised in certain sources, highest status was reserved for the male. Women were obligated to perform only a few ritual commandments. The obligation to study Torah was not incumbent upon them. Separate and distinct functions were established for men and women corresponding to what were accepted as separate and distinct natures.

Baalei teshuvah come to accept the traditional definitions and distinctions. They also come to accept the carefully defined expression-inhibition balance which guards standards of propriety and modesty in orthodox Jewish society. More American than Israeli baalei teshuvah described the process of coming to accept these perspectives and practices as difficult. Nevertheless, they too overcome the difficulties and in the end adopt the orthodox view: "It comes slowly. Things are built up. At certain points one wants to be like a man, study as many hours, etc. But then one recognizes that one receives a certain spirituality through the man, and that there is a division of roles. There is an infinite range of possibilities for a woman." A more detailed and poignant version of the education process through which women baalei teshuvah pass was offered by an Israeli woman of Yemenite background:

> It is very difficult for me to accept the position of the woman because I was built differently from what I am becoming. The difficulty is in what is expected of the orthodox woman: she is supposed to sit at home, to be the symbol of modesty, to serve her husband. This is the revolutionary thing vis-à-vis the secular world. All the functions are the opposite in the secular world. I also felt that from the viewpoint of intellectuality, I wasn't developing. I used to think this was unfortunate, but now I understand it deeply. Many rabbis spoke to me about this and I read about the place of the woman in Judaism. My view has changed. I used to think that the religious woman was obtuse, closed, and could never develop. Now I see the beauty in her position. What won me over was the family, the mutual respect, love, warmth—it's amazing. It's something one rarely sees in nonreligious couples. The restraint is what is beautiful and highlights real love. . . . One who observes the purity laws doesn't demonstrate more love but more appreciation and admiration. There is an essential difference and the psychologists agree about this. The separation and return to each other increases admiration. It also guarantees that love will be a love of friends as well as physical love."

In these accounts initial reservations about accepting the orthodox norms are openly admitted and then tempered by rational explanations for accepting them. The purity laws, for example, heighten the love relationship between man and woman. The main point, however, is that "all the functions are the opposite of the secular world." To accept the new standards is to oppose secular values with another superior system. That is the crucial element.

It is important to stress the resistance among many men and women baalei teshuvah regarding the woman's role in Judaism as presented in the yeshivot. While it is true that this resistance breaks down and the role is accepted eventually, it is necessary to marshal apologetics and seek justifications to legitimate what conflicts at first with the baal teshuvah's sensibility. A sample of the apologetics is presented below:

A man or a woman cannot live alone without being a half-person. They have two separate functions: the male gives and influences, the woman receives and is influenced. These should not be mixed up. Therefore, there is no sense of being suppressed. A chicken does not want to be an egg.

I think the role of a woman in Judaism is very positive. I don't see that as a "frum woman" I am prevented from doing anything which I wouldn't want to do in the first place or which I realize I shouldn't be doing at all. I see that the role of the woman in the Jewish home is very important—and any discontent and/or belittling of this role usually stems from a misunderstanding of the options open to her and of the role of the Jewish woman in general.

Basically, it seems in harmony with the female nature. Just like any structure, it doesn't prevent one from pitfalls like becoming a slave to the house and children, stagnation intellectually and emotionally, etc., but I believe the way of life of women to be generally sound.

The first statement, the strongest in defense of a division of natures and functions, was by a Yemenite woman, a university graduate, who reached the conclusion that a total division, biological and social, is natural and right. The other explanations are not nearly as positive or forceful. The last speaker even acknowledges that there are dangers in her new situation and is determined to avoid them. A few women baalei teshuvah express even stronger reservations and hesitations about the role assigned to women:

In most ways of being tied to apron strings I don't like the position of the woman very much. The husband has an attitude that he is better than the woman. If the attitude were that both are equal but have different roles—or that the woman is the backbone of the husband and that the family is superior—then it would be fine.

Right now I think it is very unfortunate that the division has become great between roles in Judaism. The woman has been designated the worst part. I would want men and women to both observe mitzvot and have equal opportunity in learning. I would like men to take a more active role in household life and women be freed of having to take care by themselves of the household and the children.

This last statement by an American male student expresses the aspirations of only a small group of baalei teshuvah. When asked how they felt about those differences, which exist between men and women in the obligation to observe mitzvot, 49 percent felt very positively about such differences and 33 percent felt positively. There were no significant differences between males and females in their response.

The only area where differences between males and females in the performance of commandments was not accepted as positively was the area of learning. Because of the traditional view of the inferior capability of women as well as the view that women's time is limited by their ascribed functions, limitations have been placed upon the study demands and opportunities for women. Thus, women are not obligated to study. Those who do study are not taught Talmud and do not study in a yeshivah—traditionally a male province. These restrictions are less easily accepted by baalei teshuvah than were other differences between the sexes imposed by Jewish law. Only 65 percent felt positively toward the differences between men and women in the area of study.

The baalei teshuvah were also asked about their overall degree of comfort with changes in their relationships to men or women. Sixty-three percent stated first that the change in these areas had indeed been great or very great, while 25 percent stated that they had changed somewhat in such relationships. Fifty-eight percent felt comfortable with the change to a great extent, 21 percent to a certain extent, and only 8 percent admitted being uncomfortable with the change.

To understand this "comfort" with and overall acceptance of traditional practices and mores in this area, the nature of the commitment baalei teshuvah make must be recalled. The commitment is total. It is a commitment to a tradition, not to selected parts of it. A structure is presented to the baal teshuvah as a whole. Times of prayer, how to pray, laws of purity, laws of ethical conduct, what to eat, times when foods can be eaten, how to dress, what to read—all form a unity.[16] The structure is not something that can be unpacked and reassembled by the individual. Rather, it is a full spiritual, ethical, and ritual system totally interwoven with a community. The people surrounding the baal teshuvah seem to function within the whole and be part of it. The community may not be united in its theological interpretation of particular points. It is, however, solid and united in the fulfillment of the law, its vision of the whole, and its opposition to those who do not fulfill the law. The baal teshuvah thus sees before him an all-or-nothing choice. Those who make the choice would not destroy their relationship to the total system because they find parts of the whole disturbing or unpleasant. They tend to accept the whole, act within it, suspend doubts while they are so acting, all within the context of the total package.

And in understanding the baal teshuvah's willingness to enact the changes demanded of him, the modes and motives of teshuvah must be recalled. The baal teshuvah, feeling repelled by his secular existence, encounters a religious-cultural-communal entity. He does not distinguish between these interlocked elements both because they resist attempts to cleave them, and because such an all-encompassing entity is precisely what he seeks. Everything about teshuvah is total and all-encompassing. Turning is not a partial movement but one which involves every aspect of existence. The law and the community demand total commitment and encompass the total person. Finally, the goal of teshuvah for the baal teshuvah is complete integration in a community, which, as indicated, is compact, demanding, and total.

Not only are baalei teshuvah prepared for a major transformation in their lives, the yeshivah they enter is geared to educate for such a change. The assumption in the yeshivah is that students have arrived because they want to change themselves and that the task of the institution is to present a clear formula, a clear pattern, and a clear definition in order to facilitate that change. There is no hesitation within the yeshivah about what is right, true, and authentically Jewish. The options are painted in black and white terms, directly and indirectly. Students are made to see that the halachah is all-encompassing. While they may not be urged to make rapid or hasty decisions, and are certainly not encouraged to feel guilty about their pasts, cumulatively they are urged to make a radical rupture with the past.

The end station is clear to the baal teshuvah from the moment he enters the yeshivah. The insight of those rabbis who founded the yeshivot for baalei teshuvah in the mid-sixties was precisely this—that a population of young Jews willing to make this transformation did in fact exist. Those who enter the yeshivah and do not head for the exit are those ready to appropriate a whole system of commandments, instructions, and signals. What explains the willingness to make this investment? We must recall the fundamental discontent expressed by baalei teshuvah of all backgrounds. Biting social and cultural critiques of both Israeli and American society were issued, and this deep discontent was one major force pushing potential baalei teshuvah toward a search which ended, sooner or later, in teshuvah. In fact, the discontent was a precondition of teshuvah.

The specific turning, however, depends upon an encounter of the individual with Judaism which exercises compelling power over him. We have described how baalei teshuvah are struck by the force of the sacred as revealed to them in the beit midrash, in ritual life within the contexts of the yeshivah and the family, in the exemplary character of teachers, and in the exemplary character of the relationships between teachers and students. The potential baal teshuvah is bound by the charismatic power of the community and by its way of life. The immediate emotional attraction forms the ground for the commitment that follows as the baal teshuvah becomes convinced of the intellectual sense and moral excellence of the system with which he is presented.[17] Those who remain in the yeshivah are those who are overpowered by its sacred qualities and who are willing to meet the demands and assume the obligations which go with participation.[18]

The great investment which teshuvah involves is made because to the dissatisfied and seeking person it is intrinsically worthwhile. It is worthwhile because it provides moral certainty, cognitive meaning, and spritual direction within a community whose way of life seems to be a direct counter to that which so dissatisfied the baal teshuvah previously. Moreover, the community which he adopts feels like home. He has traversed worlds to return to the ancient ideals, world view, and ways which were his people's and which were lost to him. He has thus returned to his existential center and recovered for his life and that of his family the sacred core which had always justified Jewish existence. Having done so, thereby saving himself, he turns toward the world to work for its change.

In the next chapter we shall discuss the baal teshuvah's relationship to the nonorthodox world around him. We shall also attempt to discuss the tensions in the baal teshuvah's position in between worlds and the significance of the entire phenomenon.

6
Relation to the Old

Crossing

In analyzing the relationships of baalei teshuvah to nonorthodox Israeli society, we return to our earlier depiction of Jerusalem as a city of neighborhoods and seek to relocate baalei teshuvah within them. Almost all yeshivot for baalei teshuvah are located in orthodox neighborhoods. That is significant partly because of the psychological value of the religious neighborhood for the baal teshuvah. A solitary community with uniform norms, in which life can be lived in relative isolation from nonreligious Jews, is a source of support for the baal teshuvah. This is especially so while he is in the transitional stage between his nonreligious past and his religious future, a situation similar to that referred to by Turner in liminality,[1] of being on the threshold. The existence of a clearly bounded, ultraorthodox neighborhood replicates on the ground the new boundaries of the baal teshuvah's existence.

The physical demarcation of neighborhoods, moreover, mirrors a social-cultural demarcation established and recognized in Israel as somehow representing reality. Israelis divide their society into "religious" and "nonreligious," the terminology and imagery referring not only to individuals but also to groups. In fact, Israelis view their society as divided into distinct camps whose positions on a variety of issues conflict and whose fundamental ethics are opposed. The religious world and the nonreligious world are perceived as living according to different and conflicting visions, ideals, and values. The neighborhoods are a physical manifestation of this Israeli "zoning" of their world.

The religious-nonreligious dichotomy as it is presently used in Israel conceals as much as it reveals about the groups identified, for it covers only two groups neatly: those who accept the halachah as normative and absolute and who live according to its precepts, and those who deny any relation to the Jewish tradition. Between these clearly defined camps, however, is the bulk of the Israeli population, which relates to the Jewish tradition in some positive way but does not accept its absolute authority. These Jews, who relate positively to Judaism and to the Jewish tradition, are not orthodox and observe the halachah selectively;

they are referred to in Israel as "traditionalists."[2] No systematic study of the religious ideas or practices of these Jews exists, although it is certain that neither unity nor uniformity in belief and practices among them is to be found.

Despite the existence of the large traditionalist bloc of Jews in Israel, popular language and imagery insists upon dividing society into "religious" and "nonreligious" camps. As indicated, the dichotomy, because it lumps all nonorthodox Jews into the residual category of secular, obscures the actual continuum that predominates in Israel among Jews in their relationship to the Jewish tradition.[3] Nevertheless, the representation of two camps holds, and baalei teshuvah as well as their teachers understand themselves in relationship to it.

In Israel switching has very great significance for the individual involved. Donning a kippah and being willing to define oneself as religious is no light matter. Nor is it a private matter. Given the long cultural battle between religious and nonreligious Jews and its special intensity in Israel where it involves the fate and meaning of central Jewish symbols, switching is a social and cultural declaration. It is understood as such by the baal teshuvah and by the orthodox community and by the nonorthodox public. Only because it is seen in this way has contemporary teshuvah aroused the interest it has in Israel.

The Mission: Offensive against Secular Culture

What does the baal teshuvah himself conceive to be the significance of his teshuvah and of the teshuvah phenomenon generally. On the whole, baalei teshuvah accept the basic designation assigned them by the orthodox community of being people who have abandoned one camp to join another. Moreover, they appreciate the symbolic significance of this designation of people in both camps. Second, baalei teshuvah generally do not see themselves as isolated individuals who have undergone a personal subjective and private transformation. Rather, they view themselves as a group, an ever-growing group which is the vanguard of the generation.

Baalei teshuvah are not political revolutionaries seeking to bring about the transformation of the Jewish people through political change. The majority of American baalei teshuvah who state that once they were interested in politics profess disinterest today. The same is true of Israelis in relationship to Israeli politics. This lack of interest is linked obviously to the baalei teshuvah's total preoccupation with new tasks, new interests, and new relationships. Their chief concerns are understanding and adapting themselves to a religious culture which the yeshivah filters to them and becoming part of the social life of the orthodox community with which the yeshivah involves them. These tasks demand the full attention and energy of the newcomers, necessarily drawing them away from other concerns and interests.

The lack of interest in politics, however, is more deeply rooted and cannot be accounted for simply by lack of time. It is linked, rather, to lack of desire, which is itself linked to the radical change of orientation baalei teshuvah have undergone. Religious concerns come to constitute the center of existence for baalei teshuvah—a center which leaves little space for anything else.

"Ninety percent of all baalei teshuvah are joined to the Torah. That is the point. Secular Jews come from another world where experiences are central. All they want is more experiences. We know that only through the Torah can one find truth. We become sons of the Torah."[4] This Israeli baal teshuvah, Uri Zohar, may have exaggerated his figures but not his basic perception. To be "joined to the Torah" is the experience of baalei teshuvah throughout their stay in the yeshivah. They are completely occupied with learning and living within an orthodox world that is detached in many ways from secular culture and society. Within the yeshivah, where baalei teshuvah spend most of their hours, they live in a reality that is to them both new and extraordinary. Their attention is focused upon the texts and community. As newcomers to both they must invest themselves fully and tend to reject activities or concerns that would distract them.

Moreover, because they have entered the yeshivah out of dissatisfaction with the secular world, they willingly cut themselves off from it. Politics, as a central activity in that secular reality with which they were dissatisfied, is viewed by baalei teshuvah as morally suspect, immoral, or as simply lacking in meaning.

This is not to say that baalei teshuvah may not be engaged in political activity at all. On the contrary, they may be enlisted by their rabbis to support a particular political position. This is true almost only among Israeli baalei teshuvah, who as citizens of the State may be more easily involved in political activity than noncitizens. Thus, Israeli baalei teshuvah have appeared at the head of demonstrations in two different contexts mustered by their teachers for the occasions.

Baalei teshuvah who study in yeshivot oriented to the ultraorthodox community are enlisted to promote a specific interest of the community. Thus, in recent demonstrations against permitting motor vehicle traffic on the Sabbath on a major highway in Jerusalem, or against permitting archeological digs in the City of David, baalei teshuvah were visible and prominent. Such political activity, however, is elicited and directed by teachers of the baalei teshuvah and is short-termed.

A second path of political involvement is taken by baalei teshuvah trained in the religious Zionist yeshivah, Machon Meir. This institution teaches a nationalist-religious ideology that is translated politically into a demand to settle Judea and Samaria and to establish Israeli sovereignty over these territories. It is not surprising, therefore, to find baalei teshuvah in the midst of demonstrations for settlements, or in the midst of actual settlement activity such as the populating of homes in Hebron by Jews.

Even that small group of baalei teshuvah that engages in political activity is not interested in politics per se. Nor does that small group expect to achieve its ultimate goals through political action. Baalei teshuvah are determined to change Jewish society. They are not, however, either political or religious revolutionaries. Their political activity is very limited. Their religious activity in the direction of bringing about change is also very limited. They seek to educate, slowly, toward a gradual transformation of the Jewish people in the stamp of their own transformation. The goal is to return all Jews to true authentic Judaism and to a strictly orthodox way of life. The vision of baalei teshuvah is radical. The means considered to bring about the actualization of the vision are nonradical; they are, in fact, traditional.[5]

Baalei teshuvah accord themselves a vital function in the transformation of the Jewish people they envision. In their view, they constitute a bridge between worlds on which traffic flows in all lanes in one direction—away from the secular world and toward the religious. Baalei teshuvah believe that, encouraged by them, others will travel in their path. They propose this role for themselves, that of forming a bridge, on the grounds of their peculiar past. They claim that, because they have lived a secular existence, they are best qualified to speak to the secular public and to lead others toward orthodoxy. Conscious of the difference between themselves and orthodox Jews who were born orthodox, baalei teshuvah turn the difference to an advantage. In the effort to bring about a social cultural transformation, who is better placed than they to serve as key agents?

> I can show religious people that unreligious people need a little push to make them religious. I can show the nonreligious that to be religious is what every Jew should be. How is it possible to belong to the Jewish people and not be religious? They shouldn't think that to be religious means not to belong to the present, or that to be religious means to belong to the past without moving forward.

> Baalei teshuvah can tie the two worlds together and show the nonreligious Jews that to be religious is a personal thing and not a degenerate state. I can show that the religious Jew is truly a free thinker. We can show the religious Jews that it is possible to bring

the messiah by being a living example of the potential that exists amongst our nonreligious brothers and sisters, and that it is possible for nonreligious Jews to be understood and be moved by religious Jews.

Baalei teshuvah know the language, the claims, the slogans. They know the brainwashing of the media, they passed along the whole way. They know the darkness and the high road to light. Because of the past, and although they wish to forget it, baalei teshuvah can show the way to others. They can return Jews to their own people.

To explain to the free thinkers [non-religious Jews] that they are mistaken and that they are on a false path.

We have passed through everything in life, we have tasted the nonreligious portion, and now the religious.

We can explain ourselves better because we know all in life and have found that the Torah is the true path in life for all Jews.

We can strengthen the religious. And we can show the nonreligious that they are in darkness and that it is not too difficult to emerge from it with God's help.

Some baalei teshuvah adopt a more aggressive vocabulary and more aggressive imagery to describe the breaking down of barriers separating religious from nonreligious Jews.

I can demonstrate a serious and positive approach to the problems of life; can be a model of good social life. Looking further ahead, we can destroy the relations between religious and nonreligious totally by destroying the concept of 'non-religious.'"

To destroy the walls which were built upon a foundation of lics by nonreligious education. Many times external appearance puts off the secular Jew. We can break down this block.

We can show that there are not camps totally distinguished but that there is a constant stream from the secular—which lacks all spiritual challenge—to the religious camp. And here the religious must prepare themselves internally to receive those from the outside.

Despite the more active tone, nothing other than education is suggested. Baalei teshuvah believe that once nonreligious Jews are exposed to Judaism they will return. The task is to open eyes, to arouse interest, to bring more Jews to the yeshivot, and thereby effect a slow but widening transformation. And they see the task as theirs.

Four-fifths of those interviewed stated that they intended to work personally for the return to Judaism of other Jews; 60 percent stated that they felt more Jews would return both in the United States and in Israel; 70 percent said they felt they were living in the beginning of a messianic process. Repeatedly, baalei teshuvah focused on the wider processes occurring within the Jewish people that would lead to teshuvah. Their statements reveal not only a thirst to know the future but also to know that they constitute its driving edge.

While the main interest of baalei teshuvah is to influence secular Jews to turn toward Judaism, they are also interested in affecting the orthodox community. They stressed the need to open the orthodox world to the outsider and to press orthodox Jews to encourage a teshuvah phenomenon. The underlying conception here is that the greater the effort to encourage teshuvah, the greater the success, because the time and the conditions are ripe. Baalei teshuvah are well aware of the tendency of orthodox Jews to turn inward and to ignore the secular world or "protect" themselves against secular influences. They support the minority who want and are driven to turn outward in an attempt to attract secular Jews to orthodoxy.

In their perception of their own role and in their view of the historical processes occurring around them, baalei teshuvah reflect the views of their rabbis and teachers. The latter too regard themselves as participating in a mighty teshuvah process, the significance of which lies in reversing a historical trend, namely, secularization, and in rebuilding the Jewish people. They feel themselves called to the special task of rescuing those who know little or nothing about Judaism and returning them to their sources. They perceive the institutions they have established as the critical agent in working this great process of return.

The wider historical context must be recalled if one is to appreciate their sense of mission. For more than two centuries there has been a steady abandonment of Judaism by large numbers of Jews. The result is that orthodox Jews are today a minority within the Jewish people, defending what they consider to be true Judaism. Within this perspective, orthodox Jews view their task to be continuing the battle to preserve their own forces and working for the return of other Jews to orthodoxy, or at least educating them in Judaism.

In Israel and in the United States the defenses of the minority have indeed been fortified. Until the past decade, however, little progress was noticeable beyond the borders of the established orthodox camp. For this camp, the current teshuvah phenomenon appears as one step in the direction of educating the Jewish people in the ways of Orthodox Judaism.

The Orthodox View: Counteroffensive

The teshuvah phenomenon in Israel during the past decade is viewed by some orthodox as a significant sign of progress in reaching out and

returning secular Jews to Judaism. Suddenly and unexpectedly, products of the secular world have turned around and moved toward the
religious world. From the perspective of the orthodox, this is a great
historic event, marking perhaps a turnabout in the processes which have
been occurring since the Enlightenment.

It must be recalled that during the initial stages of the teshuvah
phenomenon, in the sixties, there was little support within the orthodox establishment for institutions aimed at baalei teshuvah. Rabbis who
envisioned the emergence of a teshuvah phenomenon and who wished
to found special institutions for baalei teshuvah worked against the
stream. Conservative and suspicious, the orthodox establishment in
Jerusalem doubted that a major teshuvah phenomenon could develop
and, perhaps more critical, that secular Jews could be transformed into
reliable orthodox Jews on any large scale. Reservations broke down
only after the yeshivot were established, the number of students increased, and "graduates" produced who were demonstrably reliable and
legitimate.

By now the teshuvah phenomenon has gained general support within
the orthodox world of Israel. Such support is evident in published
articles that take pride in the phenomenon, in funds raised for the
yeshivot, and in conversations or lectures in which rabbis describe the
current phenomenon as the first sign of the triumph of orthodoxy over
secular values, education, and world view. A rather exemplary expression of this sentiment is a discussion of the significance of the current
phenomenon in a book entitled *Petah Ladofkim Beteshuvah* by Rabbi
Yoel Schwartz, who teaches in a yeshivah for baalei teshuvah.[6]

In the view of this rabbi, the Six Day War was the beginning of a
change in attitude toward Judaism on the part of the nonreligious Jews
in Israel and in the Diaspora. The miraculous character of the victory,
the reunification of Jerusalem, and the return of the sacred lands of
Judea and Samaria caused many to reconsider the connection between
the Jewish people and their Torah. The renewed interest and awareness
was expressed by secular figures in references to sacred texts, such as
the chief of staff's message that "this is the day which God has made,
let us rejoice in it": or the utterance of the chief education officer of
the army, "There can be no other meaning than the Jewish meaning,
the simple meaning, the nation of God."[7]

However, the intoxication of victory clouded these insights, and the
only marked religious return was among Jews from the Diaspora. The
Israeli awakening came after the Yom Kippur War; it "exploded the
many idols which ruled in the Jewish street, such as military strength
and the worship of leaders. Secular society was undermined, and many

doubts filled the hearts of Israelis."[8] The result of these doubts and confusions was a steadily increased search after Judaism among secular Jews, which has led to the current teshuvah phenomenon.

> We witness an increasing quest after knowledge of Judaism which has caused many public institutions like the kibbutzim (even Hashomer Hatzair) to be interested in Judaism: the army, the public schools, and educational institutions. The general evaluation of religion has changed for the better. It may be that the present situation is the beginning of the process described in the Talmud (Sanhedrin 76): "Rabbi Nahman said to Rabbi Yitzhak: Who told you when the 'fallen one' will come? Who is the fallen one?" Rabbi Nahman answered: the messiah. He asked: And is the messiah called the fallen one? He answered: yes, as it is written, "In that day I will raise up the *sukkah* of David which has fallen." It would seem that rising up comes from the essence of having fallen.[9]

The fact that people from kibbutzim of the antireligious socialist movement, Hashomer Hatzair, are awakening to Judaism and that some are even returning signals a messianic event. The claim is made that the great thirst for Judaism evident today is a direct consequence of the great distance from Judaism which has been the lot of large sectors of the Jewish people since the Haskalah. In the view of Yoel Schwartz, because that distance is so great the steps toward teshuvah must be gradual. He illustrates the plight of modern man attempting teshuvah by citing a story from an earlier period about the inner struggles of persons attempting to change their attitude toward Judaism:

> Not everyone absorbed things. Thousands of us, despite everything, did not reach what *Navordeck* * and Reb Yisrael wanted. The sins mounted. It was not in our power to renounce this world. We wasted our days in vanities, we became empty-headed, turned away from good deeds and *musar*.† Even more, we became more possessive and ravenous. But there was not one of us before whom the gates of teshuvah were closed. There was not one of us who, from the depths, from distant roads, after years and years, would not wake up in the middle of the night to musar. We had lost ourselves and had released all constraints. But one pillar was still within our grasp, although weakly and from a great distance. There was no mud in which we had not plunged, no idol to which we had not bowed down, no desire which we did not fulfill. Sins filled our days, weeks, and years. Yet, musar awakens in us and does not let us rest. Suddenly, involuntarily, we stand in a corner of our rooms crying. All the ties of Haskalah and education fall from us and void opens

---

*Musar yeshivah.
† Special ethical discipline.

before us, between imagination and reality, and from it emerges teshuvah. Where are we? Have we not met, friend? From everywhere we are pulled back to *Mesillat Yesharim.**[10]

The parallels between young men during the musar movement and young people during this period of teshuvah are taken by the author to be transparent. Modern young people are far removed from Torah and Judaism. And yet, they too cannot escape the call when they are within hearing distance of it. They too have immersed themselves in every form of evil offered by the foreign cultures of the West. And yet, teshuvah awakens in them, modern Jewish youth, as teshuvah and musar awakened in young people who heard the words of Rabbi Yisrael Salanter or read *Mesillat Yesharim.* The author of *Petah Ladofkim Beteshuvah* is confident that teshuvah can be effective and that the period is one of "communal teshuvah." He sees not only individuals with biographies, he views the entire society and the historical processes taking place within it. The greater the number of individual baalei teshuvah, the greater the hope that the entire generation will return and thereby prepare the way for redemption.

The link between teshuvah and redemption established in *Petah Ladofkim Beteshuvah* is stressed in classical sources on teshuvah. The author's innovation is not here but in perceiving the movement in Jerusalem today as the vanguard of a general mass movement, which is linked to the final redemptive process. "All the prophets commanded teshuvah, and Israel will not be redeemed without teshuvah. The Torah has promised that in the End, Israel will do teshuvah and will be redeemed."[11] The messianic motif is meaningful to contemporary baalei teshuvah, who seek a connection between their own radical act, that which they undertook as individuals, and the historic destiny of the Jewish people. They believe that a historic change is taking place before their own eyes and that they are agents in its progress.

The orthodox position concerning baalei teshuvah emerging from such discussions and articles is clear: Jews are sobering up from their intoxication with non-Jewish culture and are coming to recognize its intrinsic weaknesses and fundamental falseness for Jews; Orthodox Judaism, which has been on the defensive among Jews, can now launch a counteroffensive. Baalei teshuvah are a sign of the disappointment and disenchantment spreading among those very Jews who previously had been intoxicated by secular culture and society. They are also a sign of the positive strength and power of revival of orthodoxy. Those

---

*Book on religious ethics and piety written by the founder of the Musar movement, Rabbi Israel of Salant.

Jews working in the teshuvah movement see themselves as bringing true enlightenment to Jews who had been lost in Western culture and who are now seeking "true identity, which is bound up with the spiritual Guide of the nation of Israel."[12]

As is evident from the public relations material distributed by yeshivot, the goal is to halt Judaism—rejecting assimilation to Western culture. On the other hand, the goal is also to open religious Jews to the notion that it is possible to "return" the Jewish people and that efforts should be expended to do so.

> First and foremost, one must create an awareness of the needs of the Jewish people among the religious population. This group must know that the time has come to turn toward the whole Jewish people. One must not be content to battle for the needs of the religious (battles which are surely legitimate). We must set up lines for action within the entire population."[13]

The call issued in this statement and in many others is to gather the spiritual forces of orthodoxy and to work toward bringing about the return of the entire Jewish people. No doubt exists among those issuing the call as to the readiness and openness of the generation to receive and respond to it. It is assumed that others will follow the baalei teshuvah who have already taken the path. The tone within the yeshivot is one of total confidence about the possibility of success in what is formulated as a counteroffensive against secularism, Western culture, and assimilation.

Proofs of the success are offered by all yeshivot. First, secular Jews who have become baalei teshuvah are widely available for show. Second, notices of great "victories"—such as pilots from the Israeli Air Force becoming baalei teshuvah, children of generals from the army becoming baalei teshuvah, a politician attending lectures at the yeshivah—are spread privately in conversation and publicly in newspapers. The yeshivot have become a lobby within religious circles and parties. They have not only gained considerable support for their efforts but have become bywords among the religious public for what is taken to be a major change in the cultural climate in Israel—an openness toward Judaism among secular Jews—and in the balance of power between the religious and secular camps. In the view of some orthodox Jews, the boundaries between the camps have now been opened up and traffic has started moving from the nonreligious toward the religious camp.

And, as indicated, baalei teshuvah themselves envisage and bear witness to this process. They have self-consciously and deliberately crossed borders. They come to affirm the reaffirmation of tradition made constantly by those born into a community on the defense. They bring their own testimony about the nature of secular society and disappointments with secular culture, and thereby reinforce the community they join not only in number but also, as it were, in conviction.

Baalei Teshuvah and Israeli Society

Given the fact that the current teshuvah phenomenon comes to fortify a highly traditional community, which is also non-Zionist, and that it represents a rejection of secular Israeli culture and a crossing over to the other camp, one might expect a highly negative view of the phenomenon on the part of the secular Israeli population. This is not the case, however. In fact, Israeli society supports the teshuvah phenomenon indirectly. In order to understand the relationship of nonorthodox Israeli society to the teshuvah phenomenon, and the significance of the latter in this context, one must turn to the experience and effects of the Six Day War.[14]

The war was a catalyst for changes already in process, which marked a major shift in the economic, political, social, and cultural directions of the country. The war created a new geographic and political reality in Israel. It led to the influx of Arab labor, open borders, and rapid economic expansion. It gave rise to messianic national-religious sentiments within orthodox and nonorthodox circles, and bolstered the expansionist territorial claims of religious and nonreligious forces. A sharp ideological debate opened within Israel regarding the future of the country and the meaning and vision of Zionism—an ideological debate that began after the June 1967 war and was intensified after the Yom Kippur War of 1973.

The period since the Six Day War is to be seen against the background of the decline of socialist Zionism as an ideology that held the loyalty of the majority of the population and was capable of responding successfully to new challenges and tasks.[15] Socialist Zionism had accomplished, at least partially, those tasks it had set out and which were most necessary if a Jewish state were to be established. The basic economic, political, social institutions of the new state were molded by the socialist elite dominant since the early immigrations from Europe. An autonomous Jewish state had been founded, which had demonstrated ability to defend itself, govern itself, absorb immigrants, and to develop new cultural forms in the conditions of a modern sovereignty in the Middle East.

Secular socialist Zionism never captured the minds or hearts of the large numbers of Asian and African immigrants who came to form the numerical majority in Israel. The Jews from Muslim countries were highly traditional and religious people for whom ideological secularism had little resonance. The new immigrants felt they had little stake in established socialist institutions and stored up resentment against the governing elites of the country, their symbols and ideology. Thus, the Zionist movement—that had aspired to create a society of equality and social justice in which a new Hebrew culture would emerge—was rejected by those who experienced actual social and economic inequality and who felt alien to secular Western cultural forms that had emerged in the settlement and had even become its hallmark.

The withering of the hold of revolutionary socialist Zionism occurred within the ranks of its own Israeli-born children. The original tasks of settlement and institution building were largely accomplished. New challenges arose to which the older established institutions and leadership had difficulty responding. Thus, internal inequality, the "social gap" between ethnic groups in Israel, was not narrowed. Further, urbanization, economic mobility, and the communications revolution produced needs and aspirations among a new generation not satisfied with the collective orientation, symbols, and ideology of socialist Zionism.

A turning toward older traditions occurred when those which had come to replace them appeared thin, worn-out, and outmoded. Even before the June 1967 war, signs of a change of attitude toward Judaism emerged among people not identified with the religious camp. Thus, in 1959, Zalman Aran, labour minister of education, sponsored a bill in the Knesset, which passed, to further the "Jewish consciousness" of Israeli children in nonreligious public schools. The program's conception reflected a concern among a growing number that "the Government shall be concerned with the deepening of Jewish consciousness within Israeli youth, to enable this youth to take root in the past of the Jewish people and its historical heritage, to strengthen its moral attachment to Jewry through an appreciation of the common destiny which has united Jews the world over, in all generations and all countries."[16]

It must be pointed out immediately that among socialist Zionists there were always two distinct views toward Judaism.[17] One was negation of religion and tradition, reflecting a conviction that Judaism represented a primitive survival that braked the progress of the Jewish people and had to be abandoned if the work of national reconstruction was to reach fulfillment. The second approach toward Judaism was much more complex and ambivalent. It rested on a deep attachment to the Judaism of Eastern Europe and on a belief that Zionist realization was the actualization of core elements of the Jewish tradition. While viewing themselves as the builders of a new Hebrew society, socialist pioneers also considered themselves to be a vital link in the historical continuity of the Jewish people. However, at the same time as this approach aspired to maintain historical continuity and even to receive legitimation from Jewish history, it also involved conscious dismissal of the religious tradition. Socialist settlers certainly did not define themselves as religious Jews and would not have accepted a religious self-definition of the national enterprise in which they were engaged. On the contrary, the context of a national settlement undertaking facilitated and made real a transition from a religious to a national self-definition. If there was a sacred in their lives, its locus was the new society they were building in the historic "holy land." Values derived from the tradition were resanctified as nationalist values.

Thus, the Bible retained its sacred quality for the pioneers as a national cultural monument. The Bible was a link to Jewish history, a legitimator of Jewish claims to the land of Israel and a source of Jewish humanist and universal ideals. The specific religious significance of the Bible as revelation and as the source of God's authoritative word was abandoned. Other values, such as Hebrew, formerly linked to a total religious culture and valued because of their connection with the whole, were split off from any specific religious content and value.[18]

Secularization and guarding the tradition on the part of "secular" Jews are both parts of the background that must be recalled when one considers the basic tacit agreement between "religious" and "secular" Jews that the symbols, ideas, and values—which are the products of Jewish historical religious culture—would be central to and constitutive of the society being built. Differences in interpretations and often grave disagreements over the policy implications deriving from this foundation of Jewish national unity have emerged throughout the history of the state. Despite them, the entire history of Zionism has demonstrated that Jewish ethnicity cannot be split off from Judaism and that both are a source of meaning and identity for Israel. This double role of Judaism in Israel, based upon the complex configuration of Judaism-Jewishness, must be recalled in analyzing the renewal of interest in Judaism today. This renewal does not spring as a phoenix from a bed of ashes but from a foundation which has been present since the earliest days of the "secular" settlement.

The Six Day War was experienced as a dramatic and traumatic victory against forces of annihilation. The situation prior to the war had recalled only too live memories of the Holocaust. The paradigmatic

Jewish condition seemed to be relived—the threat of utter destruction, the sense of being alone in a hostile world, and the sense of being an abnormal people destined to bear a peculiar fate even as a sovereign and not exilic community. This time, however, the enemy was overcome, but the effects of having been thrust into the "Jewish situation" or of bearing the "Jewish fate" aroused deep sentiments of identification with a historic past, loyalty to the Jewish community, and antagonism toward the non-Jewish world.

Not only the military victory but the sudden encounter with sites sacred to Jewish religious-cultural history struck Israelis deeply and with great force. Return to the holy places went hand-in-hand with return to historic sources. Among religious Zionists, the conquest was interpreted as a further step in the messianic process begun with the modern Zionist resettlement of the land and the ingathering of the exiles. Judea and Samaria had to be held and settled by Jews if the redemption process were to be continued. Among nonreligious Zionists the conquest offered an opportunity to realize the long-held ideal of the establishment of the Jewish state within the historic biblical borders—or at least up to the West Bank of the Jordan river.

Thus, the war led to a rise of historical and religious consciousness, translated by some into imperatives for political action. It also initiated a period of self-questioning regarding the very legitimacy of the Jewish state, the attachment to the land, the relationship to the Arabs, to world Jewry, and to the nations of the world. In the years following the war, searching and questioning took place on all these questions among intellectuals, political leaders, and cultural figures. The shock of the Yom Kippur War served only to increase discussion and self-examination.

The journal of the kibbutzim, *Shdemot,* reflects in its many articles by young kibbutz members a new interest in Judaism and a driving pressure to work out a new relationship between Judaism and Zionism. Moral, political, and religious questions were raised in its pages which are far from theoretical in an effort to find a way to relate traditions and sources to the realities of nonorthodox Israeli existence. In other journals and in works of Israeli authors from the Left and the Right, the questions of the legitimacy, meaning, and vocation of the Jewish state, and the relationship of the sources and traditions of Judaism to the modern Jewish state have been dealt with incessantly since the Six Day War, in a period characterized as that of unease in Zion.[19]

Baalei teshuvah emerged in this period, reflecting in their own biographies the uneasiness, search, and questioning. The reaction of the secular Israeli public to the current teshuvah phenomenon must be understood in light of these same conditions. Since the Six Day War, in the context of both enthusiasm and self-questioning, an openness to the religious option and a greater appreciation of a traditional way of life exists among those who do not choose that option themselves and who do not live a traditional life themselves.

This openness is greater than it was in pre-1967 Israel. It is reflected in the fact that the *kulturkampf* atmosphere of the fifties and early sixties has virtually disappeared in the late sixties and seventies. The open hostility between warring camps, the "religious" versus the "secular," has diminished to a great extent, reflecting a reconsideration of the significance and value of the religious factor in Israeli society. None of this is to suggest that the war is totally over nor that the Israelis stand ready to "return," to undertake teshuvah in a traditional sense, or to commit themselves to the halachah. What it does indicate, however, is a greater sympathy for those who do determine to undertake teshuvah than might have been the case in a period of greater national self-certainty and confidence.

No full-scale study of how the nonreligious public views baalei teshuvah has yet been undertaken. However, to gain some measure of the public reaction to the phenomenon, we piggybacked on the public opinion survey conducted regularly by the Israeli Institute of Applied Social Research. As a result, in November 1978 a short series of questions related to baalei teshuvah was presented to a small sample (532 respondents) of Israeli urban residents.[20]

The respondents were asked their assessment as to whether Israeli society was in need of a strengthening of religious values. They were also asked whether the baal teshuvah way was, in their view, the way to effect such a strengthening of values. Sixty-eight percent responded that Israeli society did need a strengthening of religious values, and 51 percent stated that the baal teshuvah way is the way to accomplish it. Moreover, 46 percent reported that the teshuvah phenomenon has a positive influence on Israeli society, while only 4 percent attributed a negative influence to it. Given the extreme position represented by the baalei teshuvah, so high a level of positive response is truly surprising.

Four factors were listed as bringing people to teshuvah, and respondents were asked which of these they considered decisive. The factor attributed most weight as leading toward teshuvah was the desire to give meaning to life. Fifty-five percent credited it to a considerable extent or a very great extent with bringing people to change their relationship to Judaism. Personal problems and awakening of religious feelings were credited to a considerable or very great extent by 44 percent and by 39 percent, respectively, and disappointment with Israeli society by 34 percent.

The baalei teshuvah as individuals were described in positive terms by the overwhelming majority of those who expressed an opinion on the subject (about 80 percent of the respondents). Thus, 58 percent felt that baalei teshuvah were happy, and 7 percent thought them to be unhappy; 53 percent thought they were balanced, and 14 percent thought them unbalanced; 48 percent courageous, 14 percent weak.

Although these responses include a percentage of "religious" respondents, they indicate a basic tolerance for the teshuvah phenomenon, an appreciation of its social impact, and a positive evaluation of the baal teshuvah himself among all Israelis. It is clear that Israelis do not view baalei teshuvah as deviants nor as dangerous to the general welfare of the society, nor do they oppose the phenomenon as potentially subversive, despite its blatant non-Zionist or anti-Zionist character. It should be recalled that in the United States the tension between society and the new religious cults is such that because the cults are considered deviant the courts have legitimated the "kidnapping" and "deprogramming" of converts.[21]

Given the complex and deeply rooted relationship of Israelis to Judaism, it is not surprising that the teshuvah phenomenon arouses positive chords and elicits positive responses. Baalei teshuvah have a special hold on that large part of the Israeli public which recognizes, tacitly or manifestly, that Judaism is somehow constitutive of Israeli identity. To the Israelis who are neither self-proclaimed orthodox or secularists but whose relationship to Judaism has been described as "traditional," baalei teshuvah do not represent deviant norms or behavior. Rather, they represent values and behaviors central to Judaism and to Jewish self-definition.

Neither kidnapping, deprogramming, nor ostracism are feasible within the Israeli context. More than that, it is not feasible to relate to the teshuvah phenomenon as a deviant cult phenomenon. The large body of traditionalist Jews can hardly oppose teshuvah, in whatever form it assumes, and obviously the self-defined orthodox population is highly favorable to the phenomenon. Ideological secularists may oppose teshuvah but have not done so vocally or forcefully.

Moreover, a state which defines itself as Jewish, linked with and dependent upon the cultural tradition of Judaism, is unable to delegitimate the teshuvah phenomenon. Baalei teshuvah are people who identify with a constellation of values which are at the symbolic center of

Israeli society. Although in doing so they cut themselves off from other central values, their rejection of values of the westernizing secularizing majority is in the name of norms that same majority recognizes as legitimate. The steps they have taken and the framework they adopt, therefore, have great symbolic power over the majority.

This is the setting within which the teshuvah phenomenon occurs today, and which backs it up. Nonorthodox Israeli society is tolerant of baalei teshuvah. Orthodox society is extremely supportive, viewing baalei teshuvah as living proof of the collapse of secular values and as one visible sign of the triumph of Torah values. While certain ambivalences toward baalei teshuvah may exist, the public stance of orthodoxy, and that which baalei teshuvah perceive, is positive. And yet, even within this setting the position of the baal teshuvah is difficult and often tension-ridden.

Abiding Tension

The baal teshuvah chooses to join a community which is highly traditional and highly defensive in its traditionalism. It is a community engaged in a constant struggle to maintain what were once naturally accepted and self-evident boundaries and structures. Baalei teshuvah attempt to become members of this community. They begin as outsiders, marked by the secular world, and attempt to become insiders, fully integrated within the orthodox world. The problematic of having once been part of a secular reality and of carrying that past into the present, if not actually bearing its stigma, remains with the baal teshuvah. In this section we shall examine aspects of this problematic.

The attitude of the baal teshuvah toward his own past has been discussed earlier. We have seen that some baalei teshuvah claim they have totally cut themselves off from the past, or at least aspire to such a total break. Others are proud of certain continuities they are able to maintain with their pasts. They insist that they can continue careers, that they can preserve old friendships, and that they can somehow combine worlds. Their very insistence is characteristic of one caught in a tension between the old and the new.

In fact, all baalei teshuvah have broken ties, left friendship circles behind, and assumed new interests. They have oriented themselves to a community very different from any they have lived in previously. They make a tremendous investment in conforming to the demands of this community. The idea of reversing, of returning to their former selves, seems utterly impossible to them. Even those who guard continuities notice that these diminish in force and number.[22]

And yet, no matter how they proceed in adapting, changing, and conforming to the orthodox reality as they see it, and as it is transmitted to them by their teachers, baalei teshuvah remain "betwixt and between."[23] They remain baalei teshuvah—noticed, known, recognizable. They remain in the position of struggling to master a culture, struggling to become frum, and struggling to be accepted. They remain on a bridge, in a liminal position, despite all efforts to be integrated and absorbed totally.

There are many examples that could be cited to illustrate the betwixt and between position. We will begin with a dramatic portrait of the problem, conceived by the baalei teshuvah themselves.

The occasion was Purim, when it is customary for yeshivah students to present sketches satirizing the yeshivah, the rabbis, and themselves. Adopting this custom, the students in one baal teshuvah yeshivah presented a sketch about the conflict between their past as students in universities and their present as baalei teshuvah in a yeshivah. During the year they had studied a certain talmudic passage that deals with the status of stolen objects. The issue is whether a thief is required to return a stolen object. The Talmud in the tractate Baba Mezia rules that if it be judged that the stolen object has undergone a change of nature after being stolen, no obligation exists to return it. If it has undergone a change which is reversible, not an essential change, the thief is obligated to return it to its owner.[24]

The play acted out on Purim depicts three students studying. Suddenly they are kidnapped by a deprogrammer, whose goal is to change them back to their former selves. The deprogrammer is sure that the changes that have occured to the baalei teshuvah are only temporary and external—clothes, affections in speech, and so on. These, it would seem, could be reversed so that the baal teshuvah could return to his former and real self.

The deprogrammer tries several ploys. In one he appears dressed in "drag" and introduces himself in Mae West style: "Hi boys, I'm Alma, Alma Mater. Come back, come back to my side..." The students respond: "We are not like that anymore." Alma Mater tries to lure them with a sexy voice, bumps and grinds, suggesting attractions such as Latin, math, and other seductive intellectual subjects. For naught. The students repeat in almost robot fashion: "We are frum...." In the face of this reply, Alma Mater turns and runs away. The deprogrammer then admits that an essential change has indeed occurred in the nature of the students, and he departs.

Hence the struggle of the baal teshuvah is portrayed with utmost clarity. The temptation to return, the attraction of the university, rings in the ears of these students, but they resist. They insist that they are frum and will not be lured by seductive figures. They will not return to their old world. Their resistance and insistence is in fact what distinguishes the baalei teshuvah. They have left the past behind, but it apparently has not yet let go of them. And so, they must discuss whether an essential or reversible change has occurred and whether it is or is not a final change. They are aware of the fragility of their situation and identify the tensions they experience. And as the play indicates, they can treat that situation with humor.

Consciously or unconsciously, gradually or quickly, painfully or with ease, it is realized that teshuvah is a major investment demanding a radical break with the past. It is judged to be not only right and true but also the most worthwhile investment a person could make. It is an expanding investment and leaves less and less time for former interests and occupations and less will to pursue them. The greater the investment, the deeper and more extensive the change and the more difficult to reverse the process, were there will to do so. To the baal teshuvah the transformation seems inevitable and providential. He feels that his past was preparation for this process, which must be allowed to take its course even if that be, as it seems, toward a radical break with the past. The tension lies in the shadows of the past which remain, willy-nilly, or which the baal teshuvah aspires to preserve despite the transformation he has undergone.

Teshuvah alleviates certain problems, delivers from certain difficulties, and activates others. While the baal teshuvah discovers a universe of meaning, a system of values, and a community to which he can commit himself fully, he also unleashes insecurities, raises questions, and suffers doubts. As we have noted, one dominant response to these anxieties and tensions is the tendency toward extreme religious behavior and attitudes. By maintaining an extreme and closed approach to religious ideas and behavior, baalei teshuvah can protect and support their new and perhaps still shaky commitment. They can also submerge "temptations" and overcome lures back to their past.

Uri Zohar, the most well-known baal teshuvah in Israel today, was a highly successful and popular TV personality, entertainer, and actor. Over the course of several months he acted out the struggle toward commitment on Israeli TV before a very wide audience. Attending classes with Rabbi Noah Weinberg, he gradually moved toward teshuvah. As he did so, the signs of the change were projected on the TV screen. He referred to Judaism and to teshuvah more and more, appeared with tzizit first and later with a kippah, finally, and to the surprise and consternation of many viewers, he announced the complete break, that he was withdrawing from entertainment altogether and going to study in a yeshivah for baalei teshuvah.

Uri Zohar symbolizes the 180-degree-change baal teshuvah. He left TV, left movies, left the public eye, entered a yeshivah, and moved to an ultraorthodox neighborhood. He transformed himself and his family. His friend and predecessor, another popular entertainment figure, Mordecai Arnon, took the same path. He renounced secular activities, went to study, and is now an administrator of a large Israeli baal teshuvah yeshivah. For Mordecai, not only renunciation but denunciation has been part of the teshuvah process. He delights in condemning secular society and culture in Israel, of which he was once an outstanding part and exemplar. The predecessor of both Uri and Mordecai, Ika Yisraeli, also found renunciation necessary in order to complete his transformation.

The break-continuity tension is evident in another tendency among baalei teshuvah. It is important to American baalei teshuvah that Rabbi Dr. Mordecai Goldstein teach them, that Rabbi Chaim Lifshutz, who studied with Piaget, be identified as a psychologist who works with baalei teshuvah, and that others associated within the teshuvah institutions have university degrees. The degree indicates competence in the secular sphere. It also indicates that its bearer could have worked elsewhere but chose the yeshivah. Moreover, the degree represents status to those who come from the secular world and who have not completely detached themselves from its standards, roles, values, and rewards.

And then there is the language of the baal teshuvah institutions. Baalei teshuvah quickly pick up a peculiar yeshivah language, which mixes idiomatic Yiddish or Hebrew expressions with English. In the case of Hebrew speakers, Yiddish expressions and the special "study" language are mixed into normal talk. One could almost speak of a peculiar "frum" language that has emerged among baalei teshuvah, which reflects both the transformation and their origin. Teachers who deal with baalei teshuvah also speak in a way not common among rabbis and teachers in standard yeshivot. They mix "hip" language, expressions from the popular youth culture, expressions from the secular street, as it were, with their normal discourse, in order to demonstrate that they have a sure footing in both worlds.

The emergence of musical bands in major baal teshuvah yeshivot is another sign of the distinctiveness of these institutions and of the distinctive tension of the contemporary teshuvah experience. The band offers an opportunity for baalei teshuvah who played prior to teshuvah to continue. The long-haired, bearded guitarist or pianist, now a reformed person, with peot, kippah, and tzizit channels his rhythms into a peculiar new Jewish soul music. The bands are extremely popular, play throughout Israel and the Diaspora, win prizes, carry the yeshivah's name wherever they travel, and bring in income for the yeshivah. The baal teshuvah yeshivah band is a peculiar phenomenon in the yeshivah world—an expression of both continuity and break. The music is the music of the seventies—pop or folk. The words are psalms or prayers. The players move or sing as any pop or folk musicians would, but appear in respectable yeshivah garb. Although the sound and the appearance form a striking incongruity, the baalei teshuvah create a congruity for themselves by channeling an old need and source of realization into avenues approved by the new framework. And yet, the tension remains. Standard yeshivot do not have bands, and standard yeshivah students do not leave the study hall to travel and play.

The tension between the new self and the old, between the sacred and the secular period, is also exemplified by a picture on the wall of the main office of a large baal teshuvah yeshivah. The picture represents the conflicts and ambiguities not only of the yeshivah where it hangs but of all baal teshuvah institutions. A picture of an Israeli air force jet, it symbolizes the achievements of secular Israel. It has been given to one of the rabbis of the yeshivah and to the yeshivah for services rendered to a unit of the Israeli air force. The gift is a sign of an arrangement between this yeshivah and the armed forces, through which soldiers and officers spend hours in the yeshivah hearing lectures and observing yeshivah life. The Israel Defence Forces (IDF) arranges this study period as part of the training course of soldiers. The yeshivah gladly participates, gaining contact with an esteemed echelon of secular Israel and perhaps an opportunity to influence soldiers.

Thus, the picture symbolizes a double dependence. The IDF turns to a yeshivah where the staff seemingly understands secular reality. the yeshivah seizes the opportunity to welcome soldiers into the study hall, anxious to establish contact with key sectors of Israeli society. The same desire motivates the yeshivot to reach out to secular kibbutzim. They are anxious to demonstrate that they can reach out and bring to themselves members of these elites. This is indeed the raison d'être of a baal teshuvah institution. At the same time, while denying the value of secular activities and values, the yeshivot demonstrate an implicit appreciation of both. They may denigrate secular Israel but still feel a need to remain in contact and in communication with it. For, paradoxically, it remains the measure of success.

For rabbis and teachers who are themselves products of the higher yeshivah world, but who have chosen to teach in a baal teshuvah institution, contacts with the secular world legitimate their choice vis-à-vis their own past yeshivah world. These rabbis have chosen a task and work which is not traditional, and which demands a sacrifice yeshivah students in standard yeshivot, or rabbis in standard yeshivot, would not make. For their own self-image as baal teshuvah rabbis, therefore, it is important that they have continued successes to their record or the record of the yeshivah with which they are associated. The baal teshuvah enterprise is an offensive action, as it were, of the orthodox world. The need to bring in air force pilots and other "stars" indicates a defensive motif vis-à-vis the secular world, which is present alongside the offensive one.

The distinctive features of the baal teshuvah yeshivah itself also reflect the ambiguities of the baal teshuvah situation and the problematics of continuity with the secular world. When one enters a baal teshuvah institution, one is struck by constant movement, action, and noise. Rabbis and students are in the offices discussing theological problems as well as how to arrange lives. Rabbis discuss expansion plans for the yeshivah, plan operations in kibbutzim and in the army. They discuss opportunities to present the yeshivah on television or radio. They discuss the effect on their students of involvement with ultraorthodox Jews in throwing stones at nonreligious Jews who drive past their neighborhood on the Sabbath. A yeshivah is a place to sit or stand and study. A baal teshuvah yeshivah is much more than that. It is a place where lives are changed and where people think they are creating a social change. Both are excellent reasons for walking around and talking a great deal.

The atmosphere of walking and talking, however, reflects other realities of the teshuvah phenomenon. It reflects the fact that the front door of the baal teshuvah institution is open. Many potential students enter and many leave. People walk in to look, to inquire, and many walk out soon after. Those who stay are forced to struggle against the temptation to walk out themselves.

The milieu of movement and activity mirrors the fundamental nature of the teshuvah process, which itself is one of movement, passage, and of becoming. The setting for acting out this process is not a quiet, withdrawn retreat but a busy and noisy community, involved in numerous programs and plans. The religious and nonreligious worlds are both present in the baal teshuvah yeshivah, mirroring the subjective condition of the individual baal teshuvah. This dual resource also enables those who wish to maintain contacts, to keep one foot partially in their former world. In a sense, walking and talking is a continuation of a former life-style within an institution which is a bridge between worlds. The baal teshuvah institution is noisy and full of movement because of the enormous amount of activity going on within it—teaching, advising, hosting groups of outsiders, meeting with parents, introducing newcomers to the facilities. Rabbis, who are educators, advisors, and administrators move around constantly. Individual students too walk and talk throughout the day. When studying they get up to seek advice. They walk out of the beit midrash for special classes and in to work alone or with a tutor. They may even leave to attend a class at the university and then return to the beit midrash.

The movement and activity mark the specificity of the baal teshuvah yeshivah. It is an institution whose fundamental task is to move people. It is an institution whose fundamental characteristic is process and ongoing change. It is an institution whose very existence marks and heightens the distinctiveness of the baal teshuvah.

Contributing further to the ambiguous position of baalei teshuvah is the continued suspicion of the orthodox community toward them. That community has a problem in fully accepting the baal teshuvah, the symbol of change, into its midst. The baal teshuvah carries a history which poses a threat to the wholeness of the orthodox world and which cannot be brashly overlooked in a great welcoming motion. Therefore, despite all the public pride and pleasure which orthodoxy displays regarding baalei teshuvah, ambivalence remains.

Baalei teshuvah are well aware of the suspicion which exists toward them and which remains even after they have undergone the changes which teshuvah demands. The following description of a woman baal teshuvah bears witness to the abiding tension inherent in the position of the contemporary baal teshuvah, deriving from the desire to integrate fully, and the actual strained integration: "Bayit va-Gan is not like Kiryat Zanz. The latter is much more closed. Both receive guests but in Kiryat Zanz they give without receiving in the sense that they are not willing to really let the baal teshuvah into their society. They go out and do everything for them, but when it comes to marriage, no. They are tolerant, but with fears."

Bayit va-Gan is a large almost totally segregated orthodox neighborhood inhabited by both neoorthodox and ultraorthodox Jews, Zionists
and anti-Zionists. It is a community where the baal teshuvah feels at
home and where he is welcomed to the point of intermarrying, according to this student. Kiryat Zanz is a small totally segregated neighborhood in Jerusalem, one of a series of small districts which are symbols
of the ultraorthodox rejection of modernity and Zionism. In the experience of our student, Kiryat Zanz is a neighborhood that welcomes the
baal teshuvah to a certain extent, but closes its doors before intermarriage because of an underlying suspicion of those who have lived within
a secular framework.

Another reason why they are more closed in Kiryat Zanz toward
baalei teshuvah is because they remember what it was like in the
state twenty years ago. There is an almost pathological fear of secular Jews which comes from the antagonistic attitude of the secular
toward the orthodox. The secular Jews actually attacked orthodox
kids who wandered into a secular neighborhood. It is hard to free
yourself from the fears of twenty years.

Once there was a group of girls who wanted to live in Kiryat
Zanz, baalei teshuvah. The Kiryat Zanz people said no because they
were afraid of the appearance of the girls and the men they might
bring in. Their appearance was not modest enough. The orthodox
Jews were afraid for their own young men. At first I was angry with
their attitude but I understood them. The real reason for their fear
is the fact that the *hozer be-teshuvah* carries with him his secularity,
residues, from which he always struggles to free himself. It is recognizable on some level—externally with some people in the way they
dress, although this can be changed; internally in the style of speech,
although this too can change; in forms of thinking such as a wider
perspective, a tendency to ask questions and to criticize, and this
doesn't change. For the haredim certain questions are taboo and
never arise. The hozer be-teshuvah continues to ask questions, even
if he knows they are taboo. An example of this difference is a friend
of mine who went to the home of a rabbi for the holidays. My friend
asked the daughter of the rabbi, who was eighteen years old, why
bother to live if life can be meaningless. The daughter said she had
never thought of such a question and would ask her father. The
latter made a joke, since he was busy, and asked if my friend would
wait five minutes since the question had waited five thousand years
for an answer. Then he went on to explain . . .

In this perceptive and sensitive statement not only are the suspicions
of the orthodox identified but the dilemma of the baal teshuvah is described: because he carries his past with him, in a certain fundamental
sense he remains an outsider. Maximal acculturation cannot eliminate

this existential baggage. And it is precisely this fact that concerns some orthodox Jews and causes them to separate themselves from baalei teshuvah when it comes to marriage.

As Jewish converts who adopt not only new beliefs and practices but also mannerisms, a new style of dress, and often also a new Hebrew name, baalei teshuvah bear the strains and wrestle with the dilemmas of converts to any new faith. They appear extremely enthusiastic and yet are hesitant. They display great certainty and yet harbor inner doubts and questions. They aspire to righteousness and are often self-righteous. They aspire to piety and are pressed to extreme religious behavior.

While receiving legitimation as an orthodox Jew, the baal teshuvah feels that he has not quite made it. He often feels that he is not accepted as a fully orthodox Jew by orthodox Jews. Who has not heard the joke based upon the talmudic saying that "where a baal teshuvah stands even a fully righteous man cannot stand"? The question is then asked, "Why can't a righteous man stand there?" The reply is, "Because the place stinks." This nasty joke reveals in a most pointed way an ambivalence toward the baal teshuvah which exists among some orthodox Jews to a greater or lesser degree. It reminds one again of the ambivalence expressed in Jewish sources toward the non-Jewish convert to Judaism. Thus, a first-century rabbi wrote that a convert is naturally bad and will inevitably return to his old ways.[25]

The dilemmas are those of people who are not fully in but who are not out either. To the orthodox Jew, to the nonorthodox Jew, and even to the baal teshuvah, the liminality of the baal teshuvah is not a passing but a permanent condition. Because of the mark of the secular past, baalei teshuvah remain on the bridge—not quite in but not out. They may strain to intensify their observance and demonstrate their commitment—but somehow the efforts do not remove the fact that Shmuel was once Scott with all that that implies.

In summarizing this section on the tensions inherent in the situation of the baal teshuvah today, certain structural factors must be mentioned that increase the askewed position of baalei teshuvah. First is the existence of a large and visible subgroup of baalei teshuvah in Israel. One of the reasons for the existence of this subcommunity of baalei teshuvah is that they have not been fully absorbed within the orthodox communities of Jerusalem or elsewhere. Another is the feeling of ease and comfort baalei teshuvah have with each other but not with other orthodox Jews. They have in common experiences and background which those born into an orthodox world not only do not share but do not even suspect. For these reasons baalei teshuvah seem to prefer to seek marriage partners within the baal teshuvah subcommunity.

The scope of the current phenomenon is, paradoxically, another factor contributing to the marginal situation of the baal teshuvah. When individuals returned, even in modern times, they could be absorbed as isolated individuals. Special problems arise when large numbers return. It is difficult to find enough families within which they might be integrated. It is difficult to get them to blend, to assume the coloration of the community fully so as not to be noticeable externally. Finally, the relatively large number of baalei teshuvah enables a reservoir to be formed within which baalei teshuvah can swim among each other, even protecting themselves from having to swim outside.

The yeshivot themselves, as noted previously, contribute to this marginality by making the teshuvah phenomenon highly visible. In fact, it has been the explicit policy of the yeshivot to heighten their visibility whenever possible. The use of TV and radio to promote teshuvah, the encouragement of yeshivah bands that play throughout Israel, make records, and travel abroad are examples of this trend. By being so visible, they attract interest and attention and help themselves in getting recruits. They have, however, also helped to create a permanent subsociety of baalei teshuvah. It is as if they have ferried people from one side of the river but have not reached the other. The baal teshuvah yeshivah not only occupies a peculiar position within the world of orthodoxy, it also stamps its students with a mark of peculiarity.

Significance of the Teshuvah Phenomenon

The perspective within which the teshuvah phenomenon should be understood and its significance measured extends beyond Israel, Judaism, and Jewish history. The context within which contemporary teshuvah should be understood is the renewal of interest in religion generally and the resurgence of traditional religious forms specifically in both Eastern and Western countries. Teshuvah is an example of a wider phenomenon of traditionalist religious revival, which is grounded in a staunch rejection of crucial aspects of Western secular culture and society.

Dissatisfaction with a questioning of secular values is certainly not unique to the past few decades. "It was the best of times. It was the worst of times." With this opening sentence of the *Tale of Two Cities* Charles Dickens indicates the apprehensions and misgivings which existed even in the age when faith in reason, science, and progress was at its height. Goethe sounded a note of grave pessimism upon considering the

changes the West was undergoing. "Mankind will become cleverer and more perspicacious, but not better nor happier, nor more energetic. I foresee the day when God will no longer take delight in his creatures and will again annihilate the world and make a fresh start."[26]
Recognition of the ambiguities inherent in the modernization and secularization processes, however, has both deepened and become more widespread in the past two-and-a-half decades. The 1960s witnessed a resurgence, in both the United States and Western Europe, of the feelings of discontent with modern secular culture and society. A poignant expression of this discontent was the counterculture movement, which had both political and religious manifestations. New religious groups were founded and established traditionalist religious movements were reinforced, whose orientation and posture opposed the rational, technological, relativistic, pluralistic, and bureaucratic aspects of modernity. Two citations document this trend, one from a sociological and one from a psychological perspective.

> The alienating aspect of modernity has, from the beginning, brought forth nostalgias for a restored world of order, meaning, and solidarity. One way of stating this is that modernization and counter-modernization are always cognate processes.[27]

> When social trends have psychological effects at all, the result is either the precise reflection of social trends in personality structure or the exact opposite—a psychological "rejection" of ongoing social trends and the development of personality characteristics (and cultural products) expressive of such a rejection.[28]

The rejection of secularization is not a process isolated to Christian or Western countries but is found within the Islamic world as well. One factor underlying the rise of revivalist movements in various Islamic countries is disenchantment with disenchantment, and a consequent desire to restore pure Islam against the intrusions of Western culture. A variety of resistance movements have used political and often violent means to defend the faith and way of life of Islam. One need only point to the present situation in Iran as the most obvious example of a militant revival and resistance, or to the less well-known and less militant but equally determined movement in Egypt to restore traditional ways and order in rejection of Western values.[29]
The story of this reaction in the Islamic world, however, is a complex one, which we mention only to indicate one more point of background. In analyzing the teshuvah phenomenon our primary interest is the Western setting from which baalei teshuvah emerge. In this

setting secular ideologies, which replaced sacred world views, have lost their hold on large sectors of the population. In this situation some have attempted to resanctify their world by returning to a religious framework or building a new one.

The Jewish score with modernity can be viewed as a heavy one and is certainly one that has caused many to weigh the costs and some to reject them as too heavy. Modernity is a relatively recent experience for the Jews. For some, it is an experience of two hundred years and for others a generation. During the past two hundred years the Jews have gained the opportunity to participate in the cultural developments of the countries where they lived. Taking advantage of these opportunities meant abandonment, at least partially, of the traditional Torah culture. It meant sharing in the results of the technological, communications, and transportation revolutions which broke down the regularities of traditional life. It often involved heavy personal costs. "The Jews did not enter modern European society in a long process of 'endogenous' gestation and growth, but they plunged into it as the ghetto walls were breached, with a bang, though not without prolonged whimpers."[30]

More or less the same can be said about Jews from Eastern Europe, Asia, and Africa. With the traditional foundations of spiritual and ethnic unity threatened in the modern world, the very nature of Jewish being became a problem.[31] Many resolutions to this situation have evolved, but as the "to be or not to be" and the "how to be" of modern Jewry was being worked out and fought over, the catastrophe struck that wiped out one-third of the Jewish people. The Holocaust, in a most tragic way, forced the issue of the relationship of the Jews to modernity forward with deafening sounds.

Modernity is a historical situation which has impinged upon the Jewish people in every sense—physical, cultural, and social—shaking groups and individuals to the core. Responses to this situation today are different from what they were one hundred and fifty years ago or even thirty years ago. Profound and prolonged "whimpers" can be heard. Conscious of the costs, some Jews have begun to question the worth-whileness of the rupture with traditional structures and the radical re-organization of selves that modernity demands.

This ambivalence toward the situation of Jews and Judaism in the modern world is tapped by the teshuvah phenomenon today. The baal teshuvah is a manifestation of the wrestling of the Jewish people with modernity and represents one dramatic resolution of the encounter. Baalei teshuvah issue a "no" to secular values and culture, which is intended not only for themselves but for the Jewish people as a whole.

Baalei teshuvah claim and seek to demonstrate that secularity was an episode that exacted too high a cost and must be overcome.

It is at this point that the ultraorthodox direction teshuvah has assumed can be appreciated and understood. Let us cite at length two documents that have emerged from the current teshuvah movement because they depict the climate and indicate the claims which led baalei teshuvah toward ultraorthodoxy rather than toward other forms of religious renewal which are possible and available.

Being Jewish is a book by an American baal teshuvah which has become popular in yeshivot with an English-speaking population. The author presents his basic position at the outset.[32] "The author is a Jew, a product of mid-twentieth century American culture. He did not know what it meant to be truly Jewish. ... Although very much still a beginner, he is taken by the stark contrast between Western culture which he knew and the true Jewish culture he is now learning."[33] The book is built around a discussion of the ills of modernity, which are contrasted, each in turn, with true Jewish values. Throughout the discussion, one point is stated repeatedly: "Authentic Jewish culture and Western culture and society are 180 degrees apart."[34]

Specific areas in which Western values have collapsed, such as the family, education, sexual mores, are described. Beyond these, however, the author points to general Western processes which are destructive of the Jew and Jewish culture. Thus, overriding individualism merits repeated condemnation. "The core of Western society can be expressed in one word—the individual. He is the king. Whatever he likes, whatever is good for him, whatever he finds pleasurable, is the center of the Western value system.... thus, the culture is geared to discover and satisfy the individual's desires."[35] In the view of the author, Shimon Hurwitz, individualism leads to materialism, an unceasing pursuit of individual pleasures, and to an unceasing craving for material satisfactions. "Everyone is in life to see how much he can get out of it, how much he can enjoy it, how many of his tastes, desires, whims, fancies, dreams, he can satisfy."[36]

The culture which supports this is all "vanity" and life in it a "dead end." "An individual who has not been exposed to any alternative to the 'dead end' style to which he has become accustomed is not likely to devise one of his own. The author of *Being Jewish* certainly did not, and would have remained stuck in his ignorance if a chain of events had not placed him in a yeshivah, a place of learning where Jews study Torah. Torah is the written and oral heritage of our Jewish forefathers, which has existed since before the world began and was given in its present form to the Jews at Har (Mount) Sinai, 3,300 years ago. An alternative does exist to the emptiness and self-indulgence of Western culture, and it is totally different from the way the assimilated Jew lives. The core of Torah Jewish living is not the individual. The center for the Jew is Hashem (God), the Creator and Father of all."[37]

Another fundamental "sickness" of the West discussed in *Being Jewish* is the multiplicity of options available to an individual. "Since no one in Western society really knows what life is for, any answer, even no answer at all, is completely satisfactory."[38] Hurwitz describes Western people as living according to a "chartless path," switching from course to course, because none is right or really true. This situation of lack of clarity and definition is not only difficult to tolerate but, in the eyes of the author, essentially wrong. He would, however, have been satisfied with this pluralistic condition of "any answer or no answer" if he had not discovered the path of Torah.

Another more sophisticated version of the attack upon preponderant secular values is found in *The Road Back,* a book by an American baal teshuvah.

> The Western world, once the bastion of religious civilization has, under the influence of the Enlightenment and the subsequent plethora of secular ideologies to which it gave birth, slowly been losing its own justification for existence. The crusading, temporal dogmas which once inspired the soul of Western man appear, so to speak, to be running out of gas. No longer do peoples of America and Western Europe look forward toward a "brave new world" to be ushered in by spreading the doctrines of secular democracy, progress, technology, etc., to the far reaches of the globe. An alienated moral relativism has descended upon the world.... Torah Jews on all sides witness the results of the moral bankruptcy of secularization as it destroys the faith of the Jew and gentile alike ... where does the Jew who is comfortably situated in suburbia turn, when his children ask him the "whys" of life, which in his rapid pursuit of material gain the "bourgeois Jew" has never had time to examine? Where can the modern Jew turn when "Reform" and "Conservative" Judaism reveal themselves as illogical and unsatisfying, illusory sources of faith? In this twilight period of Western history, can the Jew find the road back?"[39]

The collapse of the Western world is self-evident to the author. Where can the Jew turn? Certainly not to Conservative or Reform Judaism, which are regarded as illogical and unsatisfying sources of faith. The author does not explain why they are so. Other baalei teshuvah have offered explanations all pointing to the accommodation of Conservative and Reform to the West as the source of their weaknesses.

They are compromises of Judaism, in the eyes of those who wish not to harmonize with but rather to reject the West.

Ultraorthodoxy appears not to be a compromise, and that is precisely its strength for those searching for a total change of the direction and a rejection of the secular. The ultraorthodox world represents to the baal teshuvah a strong and visible counter to the dominant values of Western society. The attraction of ultraorthodox neighborhoods such as Mea Shearim or Geulah is the denial they so manifestly symbolize. Externally and internally—the small size of the homes and apartments, the modesty of dress, the general poverty of the surroundings, the dedication to learning and piety—the entire ethos seems to deny the very same values against which the baalei teshuvah protest.[40] It is difficult to imagine a community better suited to satisfy the needs of those who wish to register a strong countercultural protest and seek to do so in a religious direction. Here is a miniworld which has been denying the modernization and secularization of the Jewish people ever since those processes began. That this bastion of traditional values and ideas is extremely attractive to those interested in issuing such a denial in these latter days is hardly surprising.

Yet another dimension of this attraction must be mentioned. For the baal teshuvah, there could be no more outstanding and obvious embodiment of the past, the authentic Jewish past, than this particular community. Here the baal teshuvah encounters his own grandfather, as it were, the world of his fathers of which he had been deprived by forces beyond his control. Now, his future in his hands, he can reserve those forces and return to this conservative traditional world. By affirming its battle lines, he attempts to erase the historical gap—often only one or two generations—that separated him from it.

The ultraorthodox community is oriented to the past, striving to preserve and defend a traditional structure against the onslaught of a nontraditional surrounding environment. This community becomes the "utopia" of the baalei teshuvah.[41] Their vision of an ideal and pristine Jewish reality is embodied in a historic community they actually see before them. Its attraction for the baal teshuvah is precisely the perception that this community's face is turned backward to an idealized traditional community of centuries past.

When speaking of the appeal of ultraorthodoxy we must add to its cultural appeal its psychological attraction. This is the appeal of consistency, certainty, and absolute sincerity, all of great importance for those in the midst of a process involving serious changes which must arouse doubts and even fears. The ultraorthodox community, because of its rigidity and extremism, meets the baal teshuvah's need for certainty and consistency. For similar reasons, the baal teshuvah may be drawn toward more dogmatic intellectual positions rather than to positions which reveal less than total decisiveness.

For those going through a process of fundamental change, firmness and resoluteness in what is considered to be truth is more desirable than tolerance, openness, and balance. For these reasons, identification with a dogmatic and rigid community, which has been unwilling to entertain compromise, is highly attractive.[42] The very monochromaticity, symbolized in uniform and dark dress, is its appeal. The attraction was described by Eric Hoffer long ago in his description of the true believer: "To be in possession of an absolute truth is to have a net of familiarity spread over the whole of eternity. There are no surprises and no unknowns. All questions have already been answered, all decisions made, all eventualities foreseen. The true believer is without wonder and hesitation."[43]

The movement of teshuvah is prototypically radical; it is a turnabout and turnaround, a total denial of one identity and a full assumption of another. It is also a denial of the mode of permanent seeking within a realm of choices, for it affirms absolute truth and the absolute hold of primordial roots. It is not accidental that the current teshuvah phenomenon has as its share entertainers and not intellectuals. In its current form, its call will not resound loudly for those unwilling to chop off their past, to turn their back totally on secular Western culture in search of absolute and sacred meaning and values.

Insofar as the function of an intellectual is to criticize the accumulated tradition of a society, that which is passed down from one generation to another and considered to be essential to society's cohesion, the intellectual is a potential subverter of social order. Baalei teshuvah are interested in conserving, not criticizing; in learning, not in critical analysis. Having determined to accept, practice, fulfill, and believe, they are not anxious to introduce rational criticism. While possibly agreeing that life ought to be examined, the sort of examination intended by baalei teshuvah would not be that which Socrates had in mind when he said that the unexamined life is not worth living. Self-examination within the moral and spiritual framework of the tradition, but not a fundamental inquiry into the ontological basis of the system itself. This ontological basis is presupposed and not open to debate.

Could the contemporary teshuvah movement have gone in another direction? Could it reasonably have been expected that the majority would not have been drawn to conservative communities defending themselves militantly against Western culture? Would it have been reasonable to expect a course other than frantic neotraditionalism? In other words, could the sensibilities, values, and insights of the secular world, the seedbed of the preteshuvah self, have been brought forward to be synthesized somehow with the newly assumed religious ideas and structures?

Judging from the historical record, the answer to these questions would seem to be negative. That record shows that efforts to evolve a synthesis between a hallowed tradition and changing historical currents occur when the specific historical and sociological context is favorable to the new. Thus, in the recent past, movements for religious liberalization have occurred in "optimistic" and "progressive" ages, when it seemed plausible that the religious tradition had much to gain from the new ideas and cultural trends. At such points in historical development, appropriation or updating was considered to be an opportunity for the creative growth of the tradition rather than a threatening concession by it. However, the last several decades have witnessed a renewal of religion in Western Europe and in the United States accompanied by disenchantment with aspects of secularization and modernization. Given this climate, it would be unlikely to find many baalei teshuvah working out ways to remain open to secular trends, integrating aspects of their secular past into a new religious present.

Moreover, baalei teshuvah take their signals from existing models and fit into existing patterns, and the communities toward which they are drawn demonstrate no interest in a synthesis to which they could contribute. The salient spirit of these communities is in the opposite direction—toward greater closure, toward more extreme religious behavior and the erection of further barriers, and toward reaching out only in order to bring in. Baalei teshuvah conform to the trends and expectations of these orthodox communities. The only peculiarity about them is their starting point: outside the system and outside the presupposed "plausibility structure." Having moved in, they behave as if they were always insiders.

It is not surprising, therefore, that the teshuvah phenomenon in Israel has not produced a figure such as Franz Rosenzweig, nor does it seem likely to do so. Rosenzweig was a Jew who underwent a dramatic and profound teshuvah experience in Germany on Yom Kippur in 1913.[44] He had been immersed in German culture and after this teshuvah experience never considered abandoning it. On the contrary, Rosenzweig maintained that it was necessary to preserve critical intelligence and Western cultural sensibility for the resuscitation of Judaism in modern times. Moreover, he did not think that critical intelligence, having advanced to where it had, could be dislodged. The problem for Rosenzweig was the establishment of belief, using the tools of modern European culture. He felt that the critical philosophical perspective would illuminate and revivify the ontological basis of faith, that tradition would be rekindled on this basis as a witness to ontological truth. Out of the contemporary teshuvah phenomenon have come apologetics, condemnations, and confessions. Translations of classical sources have been produced to help the newly interested in Judaism who do not read Hebrew. Manuals of instruction about the frum life have also been written. These are all books of piety and traditional learning, reflecting the character of this contemporary religious awakening and the needs of the students. They are interested not in Rosenzweig and Buber, for that matter, but in Luzzato, Rabbi Jonah of Geronda's *Gates of Repentance*,[45] in *The Reasons for Jewish Customs and Traditions*,[46] or in *Being Jewish*.[47]

In its militant negation of secular existence and determination to reverse processes that have embraced large parts of the Jewish people, the current teshuvah phenomenon recalls earlier moments in Jewish history. Coursing through that history is a perpetual tension between the demands of an ideal order determined by a transcendent ideal and those of mundane existence. This tension has produced a historic conflict within the Jewish people between those defending what they define as the uncompromised ideal and those willing to accommodate that ideal to the mundane or to abandon it altogether. The conflict between these forces is presented clearly in the Bible. Thus, the prophets struggled against the "secularizing" ambitions and life-style of the monarchy and upper classes as well as against the violations of the covenant law on the part of the Israelite masses. They projected a dire punishment for the entire nation if repentance and return were not undertaken.

In the book of Jeremiah, the Rehabites are described—a small clan who opposed imitation of Canaanite or any other culture and attempted to remain faithful to the Israelite ways of the nomadic period. Their very presence served to remind a more sophisticated and "secularized" society of the ideal of the covenant and of the vocation of Israel. At a time when social, economic, and political forms had changed and the ideals of the sacred ethnic-religious order seemed to be threatened, if not collapsing, the Rehabites stood as a model of ancient ideals and issued their call for a return to them.[48]

Later, during the period of the Second Temple, the Qumran community formed in protest against the "secularizing" ways of Jews in the cities of Judea. This community withdrew to the desert to defend and practice an uncompromising Judaism, opposing thereby the accommodations of both Pharisees and Saduccees.

Contemporary teshuvah is a reactive and radically antimodern statement. As such, it is not a path followed by large waves of Jews. At the same time that the path marked out is being taken by some, it has sent out signals to larger numbers open to reconsidering and reflecting upon their own way and the way of the people. Alongside the contemporary teshuvah phenomenon exist other phenomena of "return," which do not fit the teshuvah model as it has been developed by the yeshivot and cast in public consciousness. Thus, informal study circles and formal programs, which attract hundreds of people interested in a return to literary sources and sometimes in religious observance, have arisen in various centers of Jewish life, where a new relationship to a historic tradition is sought.

The contemporary teshuvah phenomenon, however, as it has actually emerged and been formed, is not a moderate movement of gradual intellectual search and constant wrestling. It is an extreme movement, founded upon an absolute decision, worked out in a total way in the daily life of the individual who has undertaken it. The baalei teshuvah are in a sense contemporary Rehabites. They hark back to an ideal of the past and attempt to reverse history in the name of a pristine idealized reality. That in a period of great social change and confusion their call and model attracts a few and interests many demonstrates both the hold an ancient paradigm has upon Jewish consciousness and the unsettled condition of that consciousness.

That is the background against which one may better understand the traditional direction taken by the teshuvah phenomenon. On the subjective level, teshuvah is a revolutionary experience of personal renewal. Yet, the revolution is quickly transfigured into a highly conservative form by a highly conservative community. This is because the moment of renewal is a moment of recovery, experienced by the baal teshuvah as restoration of the past of his ancestors. Since that past is thought to be represented by the forms and structures of a highly conservative, even fundamentalistic community, that community becomes the shaper of the contemporary teshuvah process and product.

These new and noticeable members of the orthodox community, Israelis or Americans, sought answers to questions Max Weber, a precursor of our era, posed years ago: "What shall we do and how shall we arrange our lives? Or in the words used here tonight: 'Which of the warring gods shall we serve; Or, should we serve perhaps an entirely different god, and who is he?' "[49] For contemporary baalei teshuvah the answer to these questions is a highly traditional form of Judaism that represents a paradigmatic Jewish stance toward secular culture and callings. "Turn away every one of you from your evil doings, and do not go after other gods to serve them, and then you shall dwell in the land which I gave to you and your fathers."[50]

This stance is and has the power of an archetypal ritual, ethical, and spiritual response. Baalei teshuvah reject the "iron cage"[51] of secular disenchantment of the world and the specific Jewish or Israeli versions of it through an act of religious return defined in normative categories. They join a community whose ethos was formed in the days of Ezra and whose specific adornments were forged in Lithuania, Hungary, Poland, and Jerusalem in the last century. They are not fully accepted in this community and yet feel themselves to be riding the tide of Jewish history. That they are at the edge of that tide and not merely buffeted by it is as hard and disturbing for many of us to believe as it is easy and necessary for them to believe. But at this juncture who is to say.

Appendix

Background factors of a sample population are presented here to provide information useful for understanding the baalei teshuvah. This sample is 66 percent male and 34 percent female. The proportion of women within the yeshivah population is approximately 25 percent, so that this sample is somewhat overbalanced in favor of women.

The following background factors offer some indication of the social profile of the students interviewed:

I. Age (%)
1. Under 18   6
2. 18–19   15
3. 20–21   19
4. 22–23   19
5. 24–25   18
6. 26–27   9
7. 28–30   7
8. 31–35   5
9. 36 and over   2

II. Education (%)
1. Elementary school   2
2. Junior high   4
3. Part of high school 14
4. High school   32
5. Part of college   34
6. College   11
7. Master's degree   4
8. Ph.D.   0

III. Education correlated with Eastern and Western cultural background (%)

	Eastern	Western
1. Elementary school	5.4	0
2. Junior high school	7.1	1.8
3. Part of high school	20.5	11.4
4. High school	21.4	36.0

	5. Part of college	24.1	38.6
	6. College	16.1	8.8
	7. Master's degree	5.4	3.1

IV. Family status (%)
1. Single 83
2. Married 15
3. Divorced 3

V. Ethnic background (%)
Country of father's birth
1. United States 38
2. Israel 6
3. Europe, Common-
wealth 37
4. Asia, Africa 18

Student's country of birth
1. United States 50
2. Israel 30
3. Europe, Common-
wealth 16
4. Asia, Africa 5

VI. Traditionality

Several questions were asked regarding the observance of ritual commandments in order to measure the degree of traditionality of the student's parents and the student himself before teshuvah. One such question is most revealing in a clear-cut manner regarding observance and hence traditionality: Did your father go to synagogue on Shabbat? If a person is religiously traditional in Judaism, he attends synagogue service on Shabbat.

The following picture emerged regarding father's attendance:

	Total (%)	Eastern (%)	Western (%)
1. Always	29	35.1	24.7
2. Usually	6	7.2	5.5
3. Sometimes	15	8.1	19.6
4. Rarely	19	15.3	21.5
5. Never	31	34.2	28.8

Another measure of traditionality is the degree of observance of the laws of kashrut, the dietary proscriptions of Judaism in the home of the students:

	Total (%)	Eastern (%)	Western (%)
1. Observed all laws of kashrut	24	31.5	19.5

2. Observed some laws
   of kashrut   37   28.8   43.0
3. Did not observe   39   39.6   37.6

Fasting on Yom Kippur is one ritual act which seems to persist despite secularization. In a sense, it is the lowest common denominator of traditionality. The following percentages emerged in answer to the question: Did your father fast on Yom Kippur?

	Total (%)	Eastern (%)	Western (%)
1. Always	72	75.9	70.4
2. Usually	5	2.8	7.0
3. Sometimes	5	4.6	4.2
4. Rarely	6	5.6	6.6
5. Never	13	11.1	11.7

VII. Affiliation

American students were asked with which synagogue movement their parents were affiliated in order to gauge again the degree of traditionality (in %):

    1. Orthodox   36
    2. Conservative 36
    3. Reform   18
    4. Reconstruc-
       tionist   1
    5. None   10

This measure must be taken with great reservation, since affiliation is not a necessary measure of endorsement of actual religious principles or practices, and since affiliation is expected in American religious society without implying commitment to specific positions.

   Students were asked about their own observances prior to teshuvah in two areas, attending services on Shabbat and fasting on Yom Kippur. The following were the results (in %):

Shabbat services

	Total	Eastern	Western
1. Always	15	13.6	16.3
2. Usually	13	8.2	16.3
3. Sometimes	22	17.3	25.1
4. Rarely	20	21.8	18.5
5. Never	29	39.1	23.8

Yom Kippur fast:

1. Always	53	48.6	56.9
2. Usually	12	9.9	13.3
3. Sometimes	10	11.7	9.3
4. Rarely	8	8.1	8.0
5. Never	16	21.5	12.4

Notes

Preface

1. Within orthodoxy a variety of movements emerged which expressed opposition to modernization and secularization. The pietistic Musar movement, founded by Rabbi Yisrael Lipkin Salanter (1810–83), is an example. A reaction to secularization among Lithuanian Jews, the goal of Rabbi Salanter, was to emphasize the spiritual aspects of Judaism through a program of moral and intellectual exercises focused upon the individual. The ideas of Salanter and his program spread within the yeshivot of Lithuania where a Musar movement developed which was definitely a force of resistance to secular ideas and life-style. Hasidism has been interpreted as a movement of resistance to the same trends. See Jacob Katz, *Tradition and Crisis* (Glencoe, Ill: Free Press, 1961), pp. 231–44.

2. The research project was supported by The Van Leer Jerusalem Foundation. Field work was conducted from 1977 to 1978 and analysis from 1978 to 1980.

3. The nature of the resistance is best illustrated by several short accounts of encounters with rabbis from whom I sought permission for access to their yeshivot. A date had been set with a certain rabbi, head of a major yeshivah, which was to take place in a crowded, disorganized room that served as the office of the yeshivah. The rabbi arrived a half-hour late, invited me and the research assistant with me to a classroom where we sat down to talk. Speaking in Hebrew, we introduced ourselves by our English names. As if rebuking small children mildly, the rabbi asked our real names. After a few moments in which signals of misunderstanding were passed, it became clear that *real* referred to our Hebrew names. It also became clear that trust in our ability to understand him and his institution had been undermined by this short introduction.

Another rabbi, with whom we spoke in the beginning of the project, told a story in response to the request we made. A tale, he said, was told about the famous rabbi, the Hafetz Hayim. A man was selling newspapers. The Hafetz Hayim approached him and said that he should stop his work and ring church bells instead. The Jew was amazed and asked how he could possibly do such a thing since he was Jewish. The Hafetz Hayim replied, "And how can you do what you are doing?" The message was clear: questionnaires, university studies, and an academic approach are goyish (non-Jewish) and as forbidden as reading news-papers or ringing church bells.

In another yeshivah where the rabbi had consented to be inter-viewed, he quickly became the interviewer, asking what the use of the proposed study was for his yeshivah and indicating that he was not interested in money. He added that he did not care whether non-Jews knew about the teshuvah phenomenon because he didn't care about non-Jews. And as far as Jews were concerned, those who wanted to know about it already did. It was suggested to him that the research could reach noncommitted Jews, interest them in the yeshivot, and thereby attract baalei teshuvah. This was accepted as a positive purpose. But, the rabbi wanted to know, who was advising the researcher, and from whom had the researcher learned about teshuvah and about Judaism generally? Trying to impress the rabbi with Jewish knowledge and specific background study on the subject of teshuvah, various books and sources were mentioned, among them *Hazal* [The sages] by Prof. E. E. Urbach (Jerusalem: Magnes Press, 1969). "He is not accepted by us; you should not have mentioned him," was the comment. Finally, the conversation ended when the rabbi stated that he could not give a final answer but would have to consult a known rabbinic authority, such as Rabbi Schach.

Chapter 1

1. Theodore Roszak, *The Making of a Counter Culture* (New York: Doubleday, 1969), p. 141.

2. Peter Berger, *The Heretical Imperative* (New York: Doubleday, 1979), p. 18.

Chapter 2

1. Teshuvah is a noun form derived from the verb "shuv," meaning to turn or return.

2. Lev. 17:11. For a discussion of expiational sacrifices, see Gerhardt Von Rad, *Old Testament Theology*, trans. D. M. G. Stalker (New York: Harper & Row, 1962), 1:262–72; Roland DeVaux, *Ancient Israel*, trans. John McHugh (New York: McGraw-Hill, 1961), pp. 418–21.

3. Maimonides, *Hilchot Teshuvah*, 77.5.

4. On the meaning of the term "teshuvah" in rabbinic thought, see E. E. Urbach, *Hazal* [The sages] (Jerusalem: Magnes Press, 1969), pp. 408–15.

5. Maimonides, *Hilchot Teshuvah*, 2.2.

6. Berachot 34b.

7. Maimonides, *Hilchot Teshuvah*, 1.1; 2.1; 2.5.

8. Ibid., 1.1.

9. The history of the establishment of the baal teshuvah yeshivah is an oral one gathered, sorted out, and put together from interviews with the rabbis of the major yeshivot. In places where versions clashed, the attempt was to gather other evidence and determine which version was more trustworthy.

10. The history of the Diaspora yeshivah is clouded with stories about the seizure of land on Mt. Zion by the yeshivah and the seizure of buildings beyond those given to the yeshivah by the Ministry of Religions. Rabbi Goldstein did nothing to diminish from the image that the yeshivah acquired its place by illegal action and that it attracted to it "deviant" types. The land issue has been solved most recently with deeds recognized legally.

11. A yeshivah named after Rabbi Avraham Yitzhak Kook, and a bastion of religious Zionism.

12. The work of the Lubavitch hasidic movement in various countries of the Diaspora, but especially in France and in the United States, must be mentioned when speaking of contemporary movements of religious renewal in Judaism. The Lubavitch movement has launched a campaign to "return" Jews to Judaism, employing many innovative techniques, including the establishment of "houses" on college campuses and the use of the media in their work. The Bretzlav hasidim have also worked to "return" Jews in various centers. Individual rabbis, such as David Ashkenazi in France or the Bostoner rebbe in Boston, have also worked with Jewish youth and have established centers of study and teshuvah. No study of the current teshuvah phenomenon in Diaspora countries exists. The current teshuvah phenomenon must be distinguished from any of its predecessors not only because of its size and visibility but because of the single and exclusive purpose of the enterprise, namely, teshuvah. It is the latter that distinguishes the current teshuvah phenomenon from a wide and large network of educational institutions established in Jerusalem in the past decade, whose purpose is to awaken interest in Jewish sacred sources and to train and educate Jews but not necessarily to create baalei teshuvah.

13. We refer the reader to the work of Mircea Eliade on the force and significance of the center in human existence in order to understand the significance of Jerusalem as the locus of Jewish religious return today (e.g., see Eliade, *The Sacred and the Profane* [New York: Harper Torchbooks, 1959b]).

14. This map and the figures in it were compiled in 1978–79. It is based upon information gathered at the yeshivot and information submitted to the Israeli Ministry of Education by them. The numbers are approximate because of the ceaseless traffic in and out, and because of the fact that precise statistics are not kept by the yeshivot. The administrations of these institutions fail to keep records that can be regarded as reliable, perhaps because it is in their interest to speak in terms of round numbers and inflated enrollment.

The following is a list of the Hebrew names of the Jerusalem yeshivot and their translation:

Yeshivat Hatefuzot (The Diaspora Yeshivah)
Tifferet Hateshuvah (The Beauty of Teshuvah)
Aish Hatorah (The Fire of the Torah)
Dvar Yerushalayim (The Word of Jerusalem)
Nevei Yerushalayim (The Dwelling Place of Jerusalem)
Ohr Sameah (The Happy Light)

Ohr Hahayim (The Light of Life)
Naase Venishma (We Will Do and Obey)
Machon Meir (The Institute of Meir, named after Meir Lifschutz, a
yeshivah student killed in the Yom Kippur War)
Machon Bruria (The Institute of Bruria)
Yeshivat Hamivtar (Yeshivah of the Mivtar, named for the neighbor-
hood, Givat Hamivtar, where the yeshivah was first located)
Darcei Noam (Ways of Peace)
Shappell Yeshivah (named after the man who contributed funds to
build the yeshivah)

The estimated number of students is taken from a survey conducted in
1978. Most of the yeshivot have expanded since that time. Yeshivot in
Tel Aviv, Bnei Brak, and other places are not included in the list because they were not part of the study.

15. For a comparison with the recruiting methods of contemporary
cults, see R. W. Balch and D. Taylor, "Seekers and Saucers," *American
Behavioral Scientist* 20, no. 6 (1977): 844–47; John Lofland, "Becoming a World Saver," *American Behavioral Scientist* 20, no. 6 (1977):
806–13; Carroll Stoner and Jo Anne Parke, *All God's Children* (New
York: Penguin, 1979), pp. 26–66.

16. Robert Lifton, *Thought Reform and the Psychology of Totalism*
(New York: Norton, 1963); William Sargent, *Battle for the Mind* (New
York: Doubleday, 1957); John Wilson, "Education and Indoctrination," in *Aims in Education*, ed. T. H. B. Hollins (Manchester: Manchester University Press, 1968); Barry Chazan, "Indoctrination and Religious Education," *Religious Education* (July-August 1972), pp. 243–52.

17. On the value of Talmud Torah in Judaism, see Urbach, pp.
254–78.

18. Edward Shils, *Center and Periphery: Essays in Macrosociology*
(Chicago: University of Chicago Press, 1975), pp. 127–32.

19. Compare the practice of withholding information in the cults.
See Stoner and Parke, pp. 29–66.

20. Quote taken from a pamphlet distributed by Yeshivat Hamivtar
in 1978.

21. For the notion of the talmid hacham, see Gerson D. Cohen, "The
Talmudic Age," in *Great Ages and Ideas of the Jewish People*, ed. Leo
W. Schwartz (New York: Random House, 1956), pp. 188–91; Gershom
Scholem, "Three Types of Jewish Piety," *Ariel Quarterly Review*, no.
32 (1973), pp. 78–83; Urbach, pp. 538–57.

22. Baba Mezia 2.11.

23. For a comparison with the position and style of cult leaders,
see Stoner and Parke, pp. 95–117; Balch and Taylor, pp. 839–44; Dick
Anthony et al., "Patients and Pilgrims," *American Behavioral Scientist*
20, no. 6 (1977): 872–79.

24. Max Weber, *The Theory of Social and Economic Organization*,
ed. Talcott Parsons (Glencoe, Ill.: Free Press, 1947), pp. 63 ff.; Max
Weber, *From Max Weber: Essays in Sociology*, ed. and trans. Hans H.

Gerth and C. Wright Mills (New York: Oxford University Press, 1976), p. 285.

25. Erving Goffman, *Asylums* (New York: Doubleday, 1961).

26. Philip Rieff, *The Triumph of the Therapeutic* (New York: Harper & Row, 1968), pp. 66-78.

27. The Forty-Eight Ways have been compiled in writing by a student of Reb Noah on the basis of class notes. The student remained anonymous. The comments in this section are based upon this manuscript and upon personal conversations with Rabbi Noah Weinberg.

28. Louis Schneider and Stanford Dornbusch, *Popular Religion* (Chicago: University of Chicago Press, 1958).

29. Ellen Willis, "Next Year in Jerusalem," *Rolling Stone,* April 21, 1977, pp. 65-66.

30. Gerald Cromer, "Repentent Delinquents: A Religious Approach to Rehabilitation," *Jewish Journal of Sociology* (December 1981).

31. The very name of the yeshivah, Ohr Hahayim, reflects this ethnic assertiveness. The name is taken from the title of a work by Rabbi Hayim ben Atar, a major rabbinic figure from Moroccan Jewry in the nineteenth century who led an immigration of Moroccan Jews to Palestine.

32. Lifton, p. 487.

33. Ibid., pp. 93, 101.

Chapter 3

1. Peter Berger, *The Sacred Canopy* (New York: Doubleday, Anchor Books, 1967), pp. 107-8.

2. Three books in which aspects of the process of secularization among the Jews is described are Azriel Shochat, *Im Hilufei Tekufat* [Beginnings of the Haskalah among German Jewry] (Jerusalem: Mosad Bialik, 1960); Max Wiener, *Hadat Hayehudit Bitekufat Haemancipatzia* [Judaism during the emancipation] (Jerusalem: Mosad Bialik, 1974); Jacob Katz, *Tradition and Crisis* (Glencoe, Ill: Free Press, 1961).

3. Jacob Katz, *Out of the Ghetto: The Social Background of Jewish Emancipation, 1770-1870* (Cambridge: Harvard University Press, 1973).

4. W. Gunther Plaut, *The Rise of Reform Judaism,* vol 1 (New York: World Union for Progressive Judaism, 1963).

5. Ezra Mendelsohn, *Class Struggle in the Pale* (Cambridge: Cambridge University Press, 1970).

6. Yehezkel Kaufmann, *Golah Venekhar* [Exile and alienation] (Tel Aviv: Dvir, 1961), 2:189-99.

7. Eliezer Schweid, *Bein Ortodoxia Lehumanism Dati* [Between orthodoxy and religious humanism] (Jerusalem: Van Leer Foundation, 1977), pp. 50-63.

8. Eliezer Schweid, *Toledot Hehagut Hayehudit* [History of Jewish thought] (Jerusalem: Keter Press, 1977b), pp. 291-309; Noah H. Rosenbloom, *Tradition in an Age of Reform:·The Religious Philosophy of Samson Raphael Hirsch* (Philadelphia: Jewish Publication Society, 1967).

9. Zvi Yaron, *Mishneto Shel Harav Kook* [The thought of Rabbi Kook] (Jerusalem: World Zionist Organization, 1974), pp. 189–230.

10. Schweid, *Bein Ortodoxia Lehumanism Dati* [Between orthodoxy and religious humanism], pp. 24–29.

11. Moses Sofer [Hatam Sofer], "Eleh Divrei Habrit" [These are the words of the Covenant] (originally published 1819), in *The Jew in the Modern World*, ed. Mendes-Flohr and Yehuda Reinharz (New York: Oxford University Press, 1980), pp. 32 ff.; see also Jacob Katz, "Contributions towards a Biography of R. Moses Sofer," in *Studies in Mysticism and Religion Presented to Gershom G. Scholem on His Seventieth Birthday*, ed. E. E. Urbach et al. (Jerusalem: Magnes Press, 1967), pp. 115–48.

12. On fundamentalism, see Ernest R. Sandeen, *The Roots of Fundamentalism* (Chicago: University of Chicago Press, 1970).

13. David Vital, *The Origins of Zionism* (Oxford: Clarendon Press, 1975).

14. Ben Halpern, *The Idea of the Jewish State* (Cambridge, Mass: Harvard University Press, 1961), pp. 81–94.

15. Zalman Abramov, *The Perpetual Dilemma* (Rutherford, N.J.: Fairleigh Dickinson University Press, 1976), p. 74.

16. Schweid, *Bein Ortodoxia Lehumanism Dati* [Between orthodoxy and religious humanism], pp. 29–41.

17. Jacob Katz, "Mevasserei Hazionut" [Forerunners of Zionism], in *Leumiut Yehudit* [Jewish nationalism] (Jerusalem: World Zionist Organization Press, 1979), pp. 263–84.

18. Yaron, pp. 231–84.

19. Abramov, pp. 64–74.

20. Ibid., p. 68.

21. Ibid., p. 71.

22. See Menahem Friedman, *Dat Vehevra* [Religion and society] (Jerusalem: Yad Ben Zvi, 1977).

23. Rabbi Noah Weinberg and Rabbi Nota Shiller studied at Ner Yisrael yeshivah in Baltimore, Maryland. Rabbi Mordecai Goldstein studied in New York City in the Hafetz Hayim yeshivah and then in Jerusalem. Others, with the exception of Rabbi Hayim Brovender who studied in the yeshivah program of Yeshivah University, studied in traditional yeshivot associated with ultraorthodox communities. The same is true of Israeli rabbis who work with baalei teshuvah, with the exception of Rabbi Dov Bigon who studied in Merkaz Harav yeshivah.

24. Taken from a public relations pamphlet of Nevei Yerushalayim.

25. Taken from an advertisement of Ohr Sameah.

26. Notice in the magazine of Dvar Yerushalayim yeshivah.

27. Yoel Schwartz, *Petah Ladofkim Beteshuvah* [Doorway for those seeking redemption] (Jerusalem: Dvar Yerushalayim, 1977), pp. 1–27.

28. Ibid., p. 12.

29. Natan Birenbaum, *Am HaShem* [The people of God] (Bnei Brak: Nezah Press, 1977), pp. 58–59.

30. Rabbi Avraham Yitzhak Kook, *Orot Hateshuvah* [Lights of redemption] (Ohr Ezion: Yeshivat Ohr Etzion, 1966), p. 36.
31. Pamphlet from Machon Meir.

Chapter 4

1. See Chap. 1.
2. As examples, see Kenneth Keniston, *The Uncommitted* (New York: Harcourt, Brace & Jovanovich, 1965); Kenneth Keniston, *Youth and Dissent* (New York: Harcourt, Brace & Jovanovich, 1971); John Searle, *The Campus War* (Middlesex: Penguin, 1972). Erik H. Erikson, ed., *The Challenge of Youth* (New York: Doubleday, 1963).
3. Eric Cohen, "A Phenomenology of Tourist Experience," *Sociology*, no. 13 (1979), pp. 179–201.
4. Charles Glock, "Consciousness among Contemporary Youth," in *The New Religious Consciousness*, ed. Charles Glock and Robert N. Bellah (Berkeley: University of California Press, 1976), p. 365.
5. A sample of books on these subjects written after the Six Day War includes: Yeshayahu Leibowitz, *Yahadut, Am Yehudi, Vemedinat Yisrael* [Judaism, the Jewish people, and the state of Israel] (Tel Aviv: Schocken, 1975); Muki Tzur, *Ledo Ketonet Passim* [Without a coat of many colors] (Tel Aviv: Am Oved, 1976); Moshe Unna, *Yisrael Vehe-Amim* [Israel and the nations] (Tel Aviv: Hakibbutz Hadati, 1971); Eliezer Schweid, *Hayehudi Haboded* [The lonely Jew] (Tel Aviv: Am Oved, 1974).
6. Kenneth Back, *Beyond Words: The Story of the Human Potential Movement* (Baltimore: Penguin, 1973); T. Robbins, "Eastern Mysticism and the Resocialization of Drug Users, the Meher Baba Cult," *Journal for the Scientific Study of Religion*, no. 8 (Fall 1969), pp. 308–17; D. Stone, "The Human Potential Movement," in *The New Religious Consciousness*, ed. Charles Glock and Robert N. Bellah (Berkeley: University of California Press, 1976), pp. 93–115; D. Suzuki, E. Fromm, and R. DeMartino, *Zen Buddhism and Psycho-Analysis* (New York: Evergreen Press, 1963).
7. Benjamin Zablocki, *The Joyful Community* (Baltimore: Penguin, 1971); Lewis Yablonski, *Synanon: The Tunnel Back* (New York: MacMillan, 1965); Rosabeth Moss Kanter, *Commitment and Community* (Cambridge, Mass: Harvard University Press, 1972).
8. Kenneth Keniston, *Young Radicals* (New York: Harcourt, Brace & Jovanovich, 1968); Paul Jacobs and Saul Landau, eds., *The New Radicals* (New York: Vintage, 1966); S. M. Lipset and S. S. Wolin, eds., *The Berkeley Student Revolt* (New York: Doubleday, 1965); Jack Newfield, *A Prophetic Minority* (New York: Signet, 1966); W. C. Smith, *The Meaning and End of Religion* (New York: Mentor, 1963), p. 124.
9. Rudolf Otto, *The Idea of the Holy*, trans. J. W. Harvey (London: Oxford University Press, 1950); Emile Durkheim, *The Elementary Forms of Religious Life*, trans. Joseph W. Swain (Glencoe, Ill.: Free

Press, 1954); Joachim Wach, *Types of Religious Experience* (Chicago: University of Chicago Press, 1951), pp. 32–33.

10. William James, *Varieties of Religious Experience* (New York: Random House, 1972), p. 193.

11. The four modes were derived from an SSA analysis of forty-four variables taken from the questionnaire. The variables were actually observed through direct questioning of the subjects and all contained ordered response categories, which could be interpreted unambiguously as ranging from "high" to "low" in respect to the manifestation of teshuvah-associated behavior. The procedure employed, the technique of the SSA, permits an empirically testable structuring of observed items and the concepts they represent. See Louis Guttman, "A General Nonmetric Technique for Finding the Smallest Space Coordinate Space for a Configuration of Points," *Psychometric* 33 (1968) pp. 469–506. For the geometric ordering of the variables, see Samuel Shye, *Theory Construction and Data Analysis in the Behavioral Sciences* (San Francisco: Jossey-Bass, 1978).

12. Peter Berger, *The Sacred Canopy* (New York: Doubleday, Anchor Books, 1967), p. 138.

Chapter 5

1. See R. W. Balch and D. Taylor, "Seekers and Saucers: The Role of the Cultic Milieu in Joining a UFO Cult," *American Behavioral Scientist* 20, no. 6 (1977): 839–61.

2. Recent articles describing the process of search and commitment to new religions or to renewals within traditional religious structures include: Charles Glock and Robert N. Bellah, *The New Religious Consciousness* (Berkeley: University of California Press, 1976); Robert S. Ellwood, *Religious and Spiritual Groups in Modern America* (Englewood Cliffs, N.J.: Prentice-Hall, 1973); James T. Richardson, ed., *Conversion and Commitment in Contemporary Religion, American Behavioral Scientist*, vol. 20 (1977); Richard Travisano, "Alternation and Conversion as Qualitatively Different Transformations," in *Social Psychology through Symbolic Interaction*, ed. G. P. Stone and M. Garverman, eds. (Waltham, Mass: Ginn-Blaisdell, 1970), pp. 594–606; I. Zaretsky and M. P. Leone, *Religious Movements in Contemporary America* (Princeton, N.J.: Princeton University Press, 1974); Max Heirich, "Change of Heart: A Test of Some Widely Held Theories about Religious Conversion," *American Journal of Sociology* 83, no. 3 (1977): 653–80.

3. Adin Steinsalz, "Repentance," *Shefa Magazine* 1, no. 1 (1970): 4.

4. The discussion of the problem of tinok she-nishbah, a "child taken into captivity," is found in B. Shabbat 68b and B. Makot 7b.

5. Interested in obtaining an halachic opinion on the question of the definition of a baal teshuvah today, we consulted with Rabbi Yosef Cohen, a recognized rabbinic authority in Jerusalem. He discussed the responsibility of contemporary baalei teshuvah to undertake teshuvah, compared them to a "child taken into captivity," and ruled that they

are indeed obligated to undertake teshuvah. The argument went as follows:

a) Is a "child taken into captivity" responsible for his deeds? This is said to be the most extreme case to which baalei teshuvah could be compared. If the "child" is responsible, then surely the baal teshuvah is responsible. The discussion in B. Shabbat 68b and B. Makot 7b applies to the subject. The question is whether "he who believes the forbidden is permitted is not responsible" can be applied in every case or only in the one case where this expression appears, which is the case of "cities of refuge."

b) The most commonly followed authorities, the Tosephot and Maimonides, restrict the application of the rule of responsibility to one case only. In every other area in which a "child taken into captivity among the gentiles" sins, he is required to do teshuvah.

c) Therefore, if the degree of responsibility is relative and there is no universal rule about the child, there is certainly no freeing of the baal teshuvah from undertaking teshuvah, even when he did not know what he was doing in the preteshuvah state. This is the opinion derived from Maimonides and the Tosephot.

6. Alfred Schuetz, "The Stranger," in *Identity and Anxiety*, ed. Maurice Stein and Arthur Vidich (Glencoe, Ill.: Free Press, 1960) p. 103.

7. Hans Jonas, *The Gnostic Religion* (Boston: Beacon, 1968), pp. 48–96.

8. William James, *Varieties of Religious Experience* (New York: Random House, 1972); G. Van der Leeuw, *Religion in Essence and Manifestation*, trans. J. Turner (New York: Harper Torchbooks, 1963), 3:533.

9. Mircea Eliade, *Cosmos and History* (New York: Harper Torchbooks, 1959a), pp. 74–86; Van der Leeuw, 1:529–35.

10. Yevamoth 22.

11. Peter McHugh, "Social Disintegration as a Requisite of Resocialization," *Social Forces* 44, no. 3 (March 1966): 355–63.

12. In only three institutions for baalei teshuvah was a positive evaluation of Zionism clear-cut and overwhelming. When asked their overall evaluation of Zionism, students in Machon Meir responded 98 percent positive or very positive and 2 percent indifferent, 85 percent of the students in Yeshivat Hamivtar responded positive or very positive, and 100 percent of the students at Machon Bruria responded positive or very positive. Proportions in yeshivot that have a non-Zionist perspective tended toward the negative side or toward neutrality. Thus, in Aish Hatorah the students responded 59 percent positive, 29 percent negative, and 4 percent indifferent; students at Har Zion responded 48 percent positive, 28 percent negative, and 16 percent indifferent.

13. Students from the American branch of Ohr Sameah, for instance, were instructed to fill in the open question on Zionism with the letters N.A. (No Answer).

14. See Mary Douglas, *Purity and Danger* (Middlesex: Penguin, 1969), pp. 54–72.

15. In contrast to possible ideal in cases of conversion, see Luke 8:19–21.

16. It is important to note that the process is total and also gradual. The sense of the wholeness of the process to the baalei teshuvah may be gauged by responses to the question, "To what extent does the change in your relationship to Judaism seem to you to be a unified and whole phenomenon, or one formed of different and separate phenomena?" Eighty-two percent answered "whole and united" to a great or to a certain extent. The following responses were given, according to ethnic origin, when asked to estimate the length of time it took to make the change in relationship to Judaism:

	East (%)	West (%)
One day to one month	35.6	17.0
Several months	27.9	31.1
One year to more than two years	36.6	51.8

17. Jacob Katz, *Tradition and Crisis* (Glencoe, Ill.: Free Press, 1961), p. 142.

18. Rosabeth Moss Kanter, *Commitment and Community* (Cambridge, Mass: Harvard University Press, 1972), pp. 68–74, 80–86.

Chapter 6

1. The concept of liminality was developed by Victor Turner in several books. See Turner's *The Ritual Process* (Ithaca: Cornell University Press, 1977), pp. 95–96, 106–7; Victor Turner and Edith Turner, *Image and Pilgrimage in Christian Culture* (Oxford: Basil Blackwell, 1978), pp. 1–40, 243–55.

2. Moshe Samet, *Hakonflict Odot Misud Erkei Hayahadut Be-Medinat Yisrael* [Religion and state in Israel], Papers in Sociology (Jerusalem: Hebrew University, 1979).

3. Zalman Abramov, *The Perpetual Dilemma* (Rutherford, N.J.: Fairleigh Dickinson University Press, 1976), pp. 326–27.

4. Lecture by Uri Zohar in Jerusalem synagogue (Zvi Yisrael), September 1981.

5. Bryan Wilson, *Magic and the Millennium* (London: Heinemann, 1973), pp. 26–30.

6. Yoel Schwartz, *Petah Ladofkim Beteshuvah* [Doorway for those seeking repentance] (Jerusalem: Dvar Yerushalayim, 1977).

7. Ibid., pp. 12–13.

8. Ibid., p. 16.

9. Ibid., p. 3.

10. Ibid., p. 21.

11. Maimonides, *Hilhot Teshuvah*, 7.5.

12. Pamphlet issued by Machon Meir.

13. Ibid.

14. Amnon Rubenstein, *Mi Herzl Le-Gush Emunim Uhazara* [From Herzl to Gush Emunim and back] (Tel Aviv: Schocken, 1980).

15. S. N. Eisenstadt, "Change and Continuity in Israeli Society," pt. 2, *Jerusalem Quarterly* (Winter 1977), pp. 3-11.

16. Eliezer Goldmann, *Religious Issues in Israeli Political Life* (Jerusalem: Jewish Agency, 1974), pp. 74-92.

17. David Canaani, *Haaliya Hashniva Haovedet Veyahasa Ledat Vela Masoret* [The relationship of the Second Aliyah to religion and tradition] (Tel Aviv: Sifriyat Hapoalim, 1977).

18. Ibid., pp. 47-55.

19. Ehud Ben Ezer, *Unease in Zion* (New York: Quadrangle, 1974).

20. Unpublished report edited by Ira Kahaneman (Israel Institute for Applied Social Research, December 1978). The material regarding Israeli attitudes toward baalei teshuvah was taken from this report.

21. Deprogrammers are those individuals who claim to be able to reverse the learning, indoctrination, or brainwashing that takes place in the cult. The most well-known deprogrammer is Ted Patrick, who wrote on the subject (see Ted Patrick and Tom Dulak, *Let Our Children Go* [New York: Dutton, 1976]).

22. Rosabeth Moss Kanter, *Commitment and Community* (Cambridge, Mass.: Harvard University Press, 1972), p. 80.

23. The term is used by Victor Turner in *Forest of Symbols* (Ithaca: Cornell University Press, 1967), pp. 93-111.

24. Baba Mezia 21.1.

25. Mishpatim, *Mekilta*, p. 20.

26. Cited in Karl Jaspers, *Man in the Modern Age*, trans. Eden and Cedar Paul (London: Routledge & Kegan Paul, 1951), p. 17.

27. Peter Berger, *The Heretical Imperative*, (New York: Doubleday, 1979), p. 20.

28. Vytaulas Kavolis, "Post-Modern Man: Psycho-Cultural Responses to Social Trends," *Social Problems* (1970), p. 436.

29. W. C. Smith, *Islam in Modern History* (New York: Mentor, 1957); Bernard Lewis, *The Middle East and the West* (London: Weidenfeld & Nicholson, 1964), pp. 95-114.

30. R. J. Zvi Werblofsky, *Beyond Tradition and Modernity* (London: Athlone Press, 1976), p. 42.

31. Shai Horowitz, "Leshealat Kiyum Hayahadut" [The question of the survival of Judaism], in *Perakim Beyahadut* [Essays on Judaism], ed. Jacob J. Petuchowsky and Ezra Spicehandler (Jerusalem: Neumann Publishing House, n.d.), pp. 185-204.

32. Shimon Hurwitz, *Being Jewish* (Jerusalem: Feldheim, 1978).

33. Ibid., p. 11.

34. Ibid., p. 12.

35. Ibid., p. 15.

36. Ibid., p. 16.

37. Ibid., pp. 20-21.

38. Ibid., p. 28.

39. Mayer Schiller, *The Road Back* (Jerusalem: Feldheim, 1978), pp. 211-12.

40. Ruth Blau, *Shomrei Hair* [Guardians of the city] (Jerusalem: Idanim Press, 1979), pp. 82–83.

41. Gershom Scholem, *The Messianic Idea in Judaism* New York: Schocken, 1971), p. 3.

42. Serge Moscovici, *Social Influence and Social Change,* trans. C. Sherrard and G. Heinz (London: Academic Press, 1976), pp. 120–39.

43. Eric Hoffer, *The True Believer.* New York: Harper & Row, 1968), p. 77.

44. Nahum Glatzer, *Franz Rosenzweig: His Life and Thought* (New York: Schocken, 1953), pp. 24–29.

45. Jonah of Geronda, *Shaarei Teshuvah* [The gates of repentance]. Jerusalem: Eshkol Press, n.d.

46. Abram I. Sperling, *The Reasons for Jewish Customs and Traditions,* trans. Abraham Matts (New York: Bloch, 1968).

47. Hurwitz.

48. Jer. 35.

49. Max Weber, *From Max Weber: Essays in Sociology,* ed. and trans. Hans H. Gerth and C. Wright Mills (New York: Oxford University Press, 1976), pp. 152–53.

50. Jer. 35.15.

51. Max Weber, *The Protestant Ethic and the Spirit of Capitalism,* trans. Talcott parsons (New York: Scribner's, 1958), p. 181.

Glossary

amei ha-aretz (Hebrew)   Uneducated Jews; literally, "people of the land."

baal(ei) teshuvah (Hebrew)   One who repents and atones for his sins and returns to full observance of Jewish law.

bahurei yeshivah (Hebrew)   Yeshivah students.

Bar Ilan (Hebrew)   The name of a religious university in Israel.

Bayit va-Gan (Hebrew)   Name of neighborhood in Jerusalem with heavy orthodox population.

beit midrash (Hebrew)   Study hall.

benching (Yiddish)   Reciting prayers after meals.

bitul Torah (Hebrew)   The act of spending time that could have been spent in studying Torah in nonvalued activies, hence, a waste of time.

Bratzlav hasidim   Followers of Rabbi Nahman of Bratzlav (1780-1845), who are centered today mainly in Bnei Brak, Jerusalem, and in the United States.

Breuer, Isaac (1883-1946)   Leader of German orthodoxy and theologian.

davening (Yiddish)   Praying.

frum (Yiddish)   Being pious, demonstrating strict devotion to the principles and practices of Orthodox Judaism.

galut (Hebrew)   Exile.

gemarrah (Aramaic/Yiddish)   The commentary upon the Mishnah found in the Talmud. Used commonly to refer to the entire Babylonian talmud.

goy(im)   Literally, nation or the nations; used primarily to refer to non-Jews.

halachah (Hebrew)   The corpus of Jewish law; literally, "the way."

haredi(m) (Hebrew)   Used to refer to an ultraorthodox Jew or to the ultraorthodox Jewish community; literally, one who is fearful.

Hashem (Hebrew)   Used by orthodox Jews as a substitute for the Hebrew word for God in order to reserve the latter for ritual uses; literally, "the name."

hasidism   Popular enthusiastic religious movement which arose in the eighteenth century among Polish and Lithuanian Jews, and which spread throughout the world.

Haskalah (Hebrew)   The process of westernization and secularization among the Jews; literally, "enlightenment."

hevrusah (Hebrew)   A group of two or three men who study Talmud together; literally, "comrades."

Hirsch, Samson Raphael (1808-88)   Leading thinker and organizer of neoorthodox movement in Germany.

hozer be-teshuvah (Hebrew)   One who repents and atones for his sins.

Humash (Hebrew)   First five books of the Bible, the Pentateuch.

kashrut (Hebrew)   Jewish dietary laws.

Katamon   Old neighborhood in Jerusalem inhabited largely by Jews of Asian and African background.

kibbutz   Collective settlement in Israel.

kippah (Hebrew)   Skullcap worn by orthodox males.

Kiryat Zanz   Ultraorthodox neighborhood in Jerusalem.

kotel (Hebrew)   Outside Western Wall of the Temple in Jerusalem sacred to Jews; literally, "wall."

Kuzari   Major philosophical work of the Middle Ages written by Rabbi Yehuda Ha-Levi (1075-1141).

Lubavitcher hasidim   An enthusiastic hasidic group that engages in missionary work among Jews, encouraging them to fulfill ritual commandments and to undertake teshuvah. Headquarters in Brooklyn.

Maimonides (1135-1204)   Moses Maimon, great Jewish philosopher, rabbinic authority, and codifier.

Mattersdorf   Ultraorthodox neighborhood in Jerusalem.

Mea Shearim   Ultraorthodox neighborhood in Jerusalem.

Mesillat Yesharim   Book on religous ethics and piety written by Rabbi Israel of Salant, founder of the Musar movement.

Mishna   Interpretation of the Torah, codified by R. Judah, the prince, as the official code of Jewish law ca. 200 A.D.

mitzvah (ot) (Hebrew)   Religious laws, commandments incumbent upon Jews to perform.

Musar (Hebrew)   Special ethical discipline cultivated by the Musar movement.

Navordeck   Major yeshivah of the Musar movement. It stressed ascetic discipline and devotion.

peot (Hebrew)   Sidelocks grown by men in accordance with the biblical prohibition, Lev. 19:27. The growth of long peot is a demonstration of particular piety in certain orthodox circles.

Pesah (Hebrew)   Passover festival celebrating the exodus from Egypt.

pesukim (Hebrew)   Biblical verses.

Pirkei Avot (Hebrew)   Mishnaic tractate known in English as Ethics of the Fathers.

Purim   Holiday celebrating the deliverance of Persian Jewry, according to the Book of Esther.

Ramot   Modern new neighborhood on outskirts of Jerusalem.

Ramot Eshkol   Modern neighborhood in Jerusalem.

rebbe (Hebrew/Yiddish)   Rabbi.

Rehavia   Jerusalem neighborhood identified by its older, middle-class, highly educated German Jewish population.

Rosh Hashanah   Jewish New Year.

Saadia Gaon (882–942)   Scholar and legal authority of Babylonian Jewry in Geonic period.

Salanter, Yisrael (1810–33)   Founder of the Musar movement.

Sebastia   Israeli settlement established by Gush Emunim in Samaria on the West Bank.

Shabbat, Shabbos   The Sabbath.

shalom bayit (Hebrew)   Maintenance of peaceful relations at home.

Shavuot   Festival celebrating the Revelation at Sinai.

shiduch (im) (Hebrew)   Arranged marriage(s).

shuk (Hebrew)   marketplace.

Shulhan Aruch   Codification of Jewish law completed by Joseph Caro; first printed in 1565.

sofer (Hebrew)   Scribe of sacred texts.

sukkah (Hebrew)   Hut used in the festival of Sukkot. The holiday symbolizes the forty years the Jews wandered in the wilderness.

tallis (Hebrew)   Fringed prayer shawl worn by males during religious services.

talmid hacham (Hebrew)   Wise man; referring to one who has mastered rabbinic literature.

Talmud   Interpretation of the Mishnah as set down by rabbinic schools in Palestine and Babylonia. The Babylonian version was accepted as authoritative throughout the Jewish world.

talmud torah (Hebrew)   The commandment and act of sacred study.

tefillin (Hebrew)   Phylacteries worn by males during morning prayers.

teshuvah (Hebrew)   The return to the total observance of the Jewish law.

tinok she-nishbah   Talmudic term referring to status of a child who has been taken into captivity by non-Jews.

tzizit (Hebrew)   Ritual fringes on the four corners of a small talis worn by Jewish males according to the commandment in Num. 15:37–41.

ulpan (Hebrew)   Hebrew language course given to newcomers to Israel.

yarmulke   Head covering worn by Jewish males during ritual occasions.

Yehuda Ha-Levi (1075–1141)   Medieval poet and philosopher.

yeshivah (Hebrew)   Academy for the study of Talmud.

Yom Kippur   Day of Atonement

Bibliography

Abramov, Zalman. *The Perpetual Dilemma*. Rutherford, N.J.: Fairleigh Dickinson University Press, 1976.

Anthony, Dick, et al. "Patients and Pilgrims: Changing Attitudes toward Psychotherapy of Converts to Eastern Mysticism." *American Behavioral Scientist* 20, no. 6 (1977): 861–86.

Back, Kenneth. *Beyond Words: The Story of the Human Potential Movement*. Baltimore: Penguin, 1973.

Balch, R. W., and Taylor, D. "Seekers and Saucers: The Role of the Cultic Milieu in Joining a UFO Cult." *American Behavioral Scientist* 20, no. 6 (1977): 839–60.

Bellah, Robert, N. *Beyond Belief*. New York: Harper & Row, 1970.

Ben Arzi Shlomo. *Shivti* [My Dwelling]. Jerusalem: Kiryat Sefer, 1967.

Ben Ezer, Ehud. *Unease in Zion*. New York: Quadrangle, 1974.

Peter Berger. *The Social Construction of Reality*. New York: Doubleday, 1966.

———. *The Homeless Mind*. New York: Doubleday, 1967.

———. *The Sacred Canopy*. New York: Doubleday, Anchor Books, 1967.

———. *The Heretical Imperative*. New York: Doubleday, 1979.

Bergson, Henri. *Two Sources of Religion and Morality*. New York: Anchor, 1956.

Birenbaum, Natan. *Am HaShem* [The people of God]. Bnei Brak; Nezah Press, 1977.

Blau, Ruth. *Shomrei Hair* [Guardians of the city]. Jerusalem: Idanim Press, 1979.

Canaani, David. *Haaliya Hashniya Haovedet Veyahasa Ledat Vela Masoret* [The relationship of the Second Aliyah to religion and tradition]. Tel Aviv: Sifriyat Hapoalim, 1977.

Carrier, Henri, S. J. *The Sociology of Religious Belonging*. London: Darton, Longmann, & Todd, 1965.

Chazan, Barry. "Indoctrination and Religious Education." *Religious Education* (July–August 1972), pp. 243–52.

Cohen, Eric "A Phenomenology of Tourist Experience," *Sociology*, no. 13 (1979), pp. 179–201.

Cohen, Gerson D. "The Talmudic Age," In *Great Ages and Ideas of the Jewish People.* Edited by Leo W. Schwartz, New York: Random House, 1956.

Cohn, Norman. *The Pursuit of the Millenium.* New York: Harper Torchbooks, 1961.

Coser, Lewis. *Greedy Institutions.* New York. Free Press, 1974.

Cromer, Gerald. "Repentant Delinquents: A Religious Approach to Rehabilitation." *Jewish Journal of Sociology* (December 1981).

Dessler, Eliyahu. *Michtav MiEliyahu* [Letter from Eliyahu]. Vol. 1. Jerusalem: Reem Press, 1978.

DeVaux, Roland. *Ancient Israel.* Translated by John McHugh. New York: McGraw-Hill, 1961.

Diner, Ben-Zion. *Baolam Sheshaka* [In the world which sunk]. Jerusalem: Bialik Institute, 1958.

Douglas, Mary. *Purity and Danger.* Middlesex: Penguin, 1969.

Durkheim, Emile. *The Elementary Forms of Religious Life,* translated by Joseph W. Swain, Glencoe, Ill: Free Press, 1954.

Eisenstadt, S. N. "Post-traditional Societies and the Continuity and Reconstruction of Tradition." *Daedalus* 102, no. 1 (Winter 1973): 1–28.

––––––. *Tradition, Change, and Modernity.* New York: Wiley, 1973.

––––––. "Change and Continuity in Israeli Society," pt. 2. *Jerusalem Quarterly* (Winter 1977), pp. 3–11.

Eliade, Mircea. *Rites and Symbols of Initiation.* New York: Harper Torchbooks, 1958.

––––––. *Cosmos and History.* New York: Harper Torchbooks, 1959. (a)

––––––. *The Sacred and the Profane.* New York: Harper Torchbooks, 1959. (b)

––––––. *The Quest.* Chicago: University of Chicago Press, 1969.

Ellwood, Robert S. *Religious and Spiritual Groups in Modern America.* Englewood Cliffs, N.J.: Prentice-Hall, 1973.

Erikson, Erik H. *Young Man Luther.* New York; Norton, 1962.

––––––, ed. *The Challenge of Youth.* New York: Doubleday, 1963.

Etkes, Immanuel, *Rabbi Yisrael Salanter Vereshitah shel Tenvat Hamusar* [Rabbi Israel Salanter and the beginning of the Musar movement]. Jerusalem: Magnes Press, 1982.

Festinger, Leon, *When Prophecy Fails.* Minneapolis: University of Minnesota Press, 1956.

Friedman, Menahem. *Dat Vehevra* [Religion and society]. Jerusalem: Yad Ben Zvi, 1977.

Geertz, Clifford. *Islam Observed.* Chicago: University of Chicago Press, 1968.

––––––. *The Interpretation of Cultures.* New York: Basic, 1973.

Gerlach, Luther, and Hine, Virginia. *People, Power, Change: Moments of Social Transformation.* Indianapolis: Bobbs-Merrill, 1970.

Glanz, David, and Harrison, Michael I. "Varieties of Identity Transformation: The Case of Newly Orthodox Jews." *Jewish Journal of*

Sociology, 20, no. 2 (December 1978): 129–41.

Glatzer, Nahum. *Franz Rosenzweig: His Life and Thought*. New York: Schocken, 1953.

Glock, Charles, and Bellah, Robert N. *The New Religious Consciousness*. Berkeley: University of California Press, 1976.

Goffman, Erving. *Asylums*. New York: Doubleday, 1961.

———. *Interaction Ritual*. New York: Doubleday, 1967.

Goldmann, Eliezer. *Religious Issues in Israeli Political Life*. Jerusalem: Jewish Agency, 1974.

———. "Darkei Teshuvah Beyamenu [Ways of teshuvah today]." In *Teshuvah Vashavim* [Teshuvah and returners]. Jerusalem: Jewish Agency, 1979.

Grade, Chaim. *The Yeshivah*. Translated by Kurt Levant. New York: Bobbs-Merrill, 1976.

Greeley, Andrew. "Religious Musical Chairs." *Transaction* (May/June 1978), pp. 53–59.

Guttman, Louis, "A General Nonmetric Technique for Finding the Smallest Space Coordinate Space for a Configuration of Points." *Psychometric* 33 (1968): 469–506.

Halpern, Ben. *The Idea of the Jewish State*. Cambridge, Mass: Harvard University Press, 1961.

Harrison, Michael I. "Sources of Recruitment to Catholic Pentecostalism." *Journal of the Scientific Study of Religion* 13, no. 1 (1974): 49–64.

Heirich, Max. "Change of Heart: A Test of Some Widely Held Theories about Religious Conversion." *American Journal of Sociology* 83, no. 3 (1977): 653–80.

Heller, Erich. *The Disinheritied Mind*. New York: Meridian, 1959.

Hoffer, Eric. *The True Believer*. New York: Harper & Row, 1968.

Horowitz, Shai. "Leshealat Kiyum Hayahadut" [The question of the survival of Judaism]. In *Perakim Beyahadut* [Essays on Judaism]. Edited by Jacob J. Petuchowsky and Ezra Spicehandler. Jerusalem: Neumann Publishing House, n.d.

Hurwitz, Shimon. *Being Jewish*. Jerusalem: Feldheim, 1978.

Jacobs, Paul, and Landau, Saul, eds. *The New Radicals,* New York: Vintage, 1966.

James, William. *Varieties of Religious Experience*. New York: Random House, 1972.

Jaspers, Karl. *Man in the Modern Age*. Translated by Eden and Cedar Paul. London: Routledge & Kegan Paul, 1951.

Jonah of Geronda. *Shaarei Teshuvah* [The gates of repentance]. Jerusalem: Eshkol Press, n.d.

Jonas, Hans. *The Gnostic Religion*. Boston: Beacon, 1968.

Kanter, Rosabeth Moss. *Commitment and Community*. Cambridge: Harvard University Press. 1972.

Katz, Jacob. *Tradition and Crisis.* Glencoe, Ill: Free Press, 1961.

———. "Contributions towards a biography of R. Moses Sofer." In *Studies in Mysticism and Religion, Presented to Gershom Scholem on His Seventieth Birthday.* Edited by E.E. Urbach et al. Jerusalem: Magnes Press, 1967.

———. *Out of the Ghetto: The Social Background of Jewish Emancipation, 1770–1870.* Cambridge, Mass: Harvard University Press, 1973.

———. "Mevasserei Hazionut" [Forerunners of Zionism]. In *Leumiut Yehudit* [Jewish Nationalism]. Jerusalem: World Zionist Organization Press, 1979.

Kaufmann, Yehezkel. *Golah Venekhar* [Exile and alienation]. Tel Aviv: Dvir, 1961.

Kavolis, Vytaulas. "Post-Modern Man: Psycho-Cultural Responses to Social Trends." *Social Problems* (1970).

Keniston, Kenneth. *The Uncommitted.* New York: Harcourt, Brace & Jovanovich, 1965.

———. *Young Radicals.* New York: Harcourt, Brace & Jovanovich, 1968.

———. *Youth and Dissent.* New York: Harcourt, Brace & Jovanovich, 1971.

Kook, Rabbi A. Y. *Orot Hateshuvah* [Lights of redemption]. Ohr Etzion: Yeshivat Ohr Etzion, 1966.

Leibowitz, Yeshayahu. *Yahadut, Am Yehudi, Vemedinat Yisrael* [Judaism, the Jewish people, and the state of Israel]. Tel Aviv: Schocken, 1975.

Lewis, Bernard. *The Middle East and the West.* London: Weidenfeld & Nicholson, 1964.

———. "The Return of Islam." *Commentary* 61, no. 1 (January 1976): 39–49.

Lifton, Robert. *Thought Reform and the Psychology of Totalism.* New York: Norton, 1963.

Lipset, S. M., and Wolin, S. S., eds. *The Berkeley Student Revolt.* New York: Doubleday, 1965.

Lofland, John. *Doomsday Cult.* Englewood Cliffs, N.J.: Prentice-Hall, 1966.

———. "Becoming a World Saver." *American Behavioral Scientist* 20, no. 6 (1977): 806–13.

Luckman, Thomas. *The Invisible Religion.* New York: MacMillan, 1967.

McHugh, Peter. "Social Disintegration as a Requisite of Resocialization." *Social Forces* 44, no. 3 (March 1966): 355–63.

Maimonides, Moses. *"Hilchot Teshuvah* [Laws of repentance]." In *Sefer Hamada.* Jerusalem: Mosad Harav Kuk, 1957.)

Matza, David. *Becoming Deviant*. New York: Prentice-Hall, 1969.

Mendelsohn, Ezra. *Class Struggle in the Pale*. Cambridge: Cambridge University Press, 1970.

Mirsky, Samuel, ed. *Mosdot Torah Beeiropa* [Torah institutions in Europe]. New York: Hahistadrut Haivrit, 1956.

Moscovici, Serge. *Social Influence and Social Change*. Translated by C. Sherrard and G. Heinz. London: Academic Press, 1976.

Mumford, Lewis, *The Transformations of Man*. New York: Harper & Bros., 1956.

Needleman, J., and Baker, G., eds. *Understanding the New Religions*. New York: Seabury, 1978.

Needleman, J.; Bierman, A. K.; and Gould, J.; eds. *Religion for a New Generation*. New York: MacMillan, 1973.

Newfield, Jack. *A Prophetic Minority*. New York: Signet, 1966.

Nock, Arthur Darby. *Conversion*. London: Oxford University Press, 1961.

O'Dea, Thomas F. *Sociology of Religion*. Englewood Cliffs, N.J.: Prentice-Hall, 1966.

Otto, Rudolf. *The Idea of the Holy*. Translated by J.W. Harvey. London: Oxford University Press, 1950.

Patrick, Ted, and Dulak, Tom. *Let Our Children Go*. New York; Dutton, 1976.

Plaut, W. Gunther. *The Rise of Reform Judaism*. New York: World Union for Progressive Judaism, 1963.

Rieff, Philip. *The Triumph of the Therapeutic*. New York: Harper & Row, 1968.

Richardson, James T., ed. *Conversion and Commitment in Contemporary Religion*, American Behavioral Scientist, vol. 20 (1977).

Robbins, T. "Eastern Mysticism and the Resocialization of Drug Users: The Meher Baba Cult," *Journal for the Scientific Study of Religion*, no. 8 (Fall 1969), pp. 308–17.

Robbins, T., and Anthony, D. "New Religions, Families, and Brainwashing." *Transaction* (May/June 1978), pp. 77–83.

———. "The Sociology of Contemporary Religious Movement." *Annual Sociological Review* 5 (1979): 75–89.

Rosenbloom, Noah H. *Tradition in an Age of Reform: The Religious Philosophy of Samson Raphael Hirsch*. Philadelphia: Jewish Publication Society, 1967.

Rosenzweig, Franz. *On Jewish Learning*. New York: Schocken, 1955.

Roszak, Theodore. *The Making of a Counter Culture*. New York: Doubleday, 1969.

Rubenstein, Amnon. *MiHerzl LeGush Emunim Uhazara* [From Herzl to Gush Emunim and back]. Tel Aviv: Schocken, 1980.

Samet, Moshe. *Hakonflict Odot Misud Erkei Hayahadut Bemedinat Yisrael* [Religion and state in Israel]. Papers in Sociology. Hebrew University, 1979.

Sandeen, Ernest R. *The Roots of Fundamentalism.* Chicago: University of Chicago Press, 1970.

Sargent, William. *Battle for the Mind.* New York: Doubleday, 1957.

Schiller, Mayer. *The Road Back.* Jerusalem: Feldheim, 1978.

Schneider, Louis, and Dornbusch, Stanford. *Popular Religion.* Chicago: University of Chicago Press, 1958.

Scholem, Gershom. *The Messianic Idea in Judaism.* New York: Schocken, 1971.

――――. "Three Types of Jewish Piety." *Ariel Quarterly Review*, no. 32 (1973).

Schuetz, Alfred. "The Stranger." In *Identity and Anxiety.* Edited by M. Stein and A. Vidich. Glencoe, Ill.: Free Press, 1960.

Schwartz, Yoel. *Petah Ladofkim Beteshuvah* [Doorway for those seeking repentance]. Jerusalem: Dvar Yerushalayim, 1977.

Schweid, Eliezer. *Hayehudi Haboded* [The lonely Jew]. Tel Aviv: Am Oved, 1974.

――――. *Bein Ortodoxia Lehumanism Dati* [Between orthodoxy and religious humanism]. Jerusalem: Van Leer Foundation, 1977.

――――. *Toledot Hehagut Hayehudit* [History of Jewish thought]. Jerusalem, Keter Press, 1977.

Searle, John. *The Campus War.* Middlesex: Penguin, 1972.

Shils, Edward. *Center and Periphery: Essays in Macrosociology.* Chicago: University of Chicago Press, 1975.

Shochat, Azriel. *Im Hilufei Tekufot* [Beginnings of the Haskalah among German Jewry]. Jerusalem: Mosad Bialik, 1960.

Shye, Samuel. *Theory Construction and Data Analysis in the Behavioral Sciences.* San Francisco: Jossey Bass, 1978.

Simmel, Georg. "The Secret Society." In *The Sociology of Georg Simmel.* Translated and edited by K. H. Wolff. New York: Free Press, 1950.

Smith, W. C. *Islam in Modern History.* New York: Mentor, 1957.

――――. *The Meaning and End of Religion.* New York: Mentor, 1963.

Sofer, Moses [Hatam Sofer]. "Eleh Divrei Habrit" [These are the words of the Covenant] (originally published 1819). In *The Jew in the Modern World.* Edited by Paul Mendes-Flohr and Yehuda Reinhartz. New York: Oxford University Press, 1980.

Soloveitchik, Joseph B. *Al Hateshuvah* [On repentance]. Edited by P. Peli. Jerusalem: World Zionist Organization, 1977.

Sperling, Abram I. *The Reasons for Jewish Customs and Traditions.* Translated by Abraham Matts. New York: Bloch, 1968.

Steinsalz, Adin. "Repentance." *Shefa Magazine* 1, no. 1 (1970): 3–8.

――――. *Teshuvah* [Repentance]. Jerusalem: Domino, 1982.

Stone, D. "The Human Potential Movement." In *The New Religious Consciousness.* Edited by C. Glock and R. N. Bellah. Berkeley: University of California Press, 1976.

Suzuki, D.; Fromm, E.; and DeMartino, R. *Zen Buddhism and Psycho-Analysis.* New York: Evergreen Press, 1963.

Stoner, Carroll, and Parke, Jo Anne. *All God's Children.* New York: Penguin, 1979.

Tiryakian, Edward A., ed. *On the Margin of the Visible.* New York: Wiley, 1974.

Travisano, Richard. "Alternation and Conversion as Qualitatively Different Transformation." In *Social Psychology through Symbolic Interaction* Edited by G. P. Stone and M. Garvermann. Waltham, Mass: Ginn-Blaisdell, 1970.

Tzur, Muki. *Lelo Ketonet Passim* [Without a coat of many colors]. Tel Aviv: Am Oved, 1976.

Turner, Victor. *Forest of Symbols.* Ithaca: Cornell University Press, 1967.

————. *The Ritual Process.* Ithaca, Cornell University Press, 1977.

Turner, Victor, and Turner, Edith. *Image and Pilgrimage in Christian Culture.* Oxford: Basil Blackwell, 1978.

Unna, Moshe. *Yisrael Veheamim* [Israel and the nations]. Tel Aviv: Ha-Kibbutz Ha-Dati, 1971.

Urbach, E. E. *Hazal* [The sages]. Jerusalem: Magnes Press, 1969.

Van der Leeuw, G. *Religion in Essence and Manifestation.* Translated by J. Turner. New York: Harper Torchbooks, 1963.

Van Gennep, Arnold. *Rites of Passage.* Chicago: University of Chicago Press, 1960.

Von Rad, Gerhardt. *Old Testament Theology.* Translated by D. M. G. Stalker. New York: Harper & Row, 1962.

Veysey, Lawrence. *The Communal Experience.* Chicago: University of Chicago Press, 1978.

Vital, David. *The Origins of Zionism.* Oxford: Clarendon Press, 1975.

Wach, Joachim. *Types of Relgious Experience.* Chicago: University of Chicago Press, 1951.

Weber, Max. *The Theory of Social and Economic Organization.* Edited by Talcott Parsons. New York: Free Press, 1947.

————. *Ancient Israel.* Translated by Hans H. Gerth and Don Martindale. Glencoe, Ill: Free Press, 1952.

————. *The Protestant Ethic and the Spirit of Capitalism.* Translated by Talcott Parson. New York: Scribner's, 1958.

————. *From Max Weber: Essays in Sociology,* ed. and trans. Hans H. Gerth and C. Wright Mills. New York: Oxford University Press, 1976.

Weil, Simone. *The Need for Roots.* Translated by Arthur Will. Boston: Beacon, 1952.

Werblowsky, R. J. Zvi. *Beyond Tradition and Modernity*. London: Athlone Press, 1976.

Wiener, Max. *Hayahadut Betekufat Haemancipatzia* [Judaism during the emancipation]. Jerusalem: Bialik Institute, 1974.

Willis, Ellen. "Next Year in Jerusalem." *Rolling Stone*, April 21, 1977.

Wilson, Bryan. *Religion in Secular Society*. Middlesex: Penguin, 1969.

———. *Magic and the Millennium*. London: Heinemann, 1973.

———. *Contemporary Transformations of Religion*. Oxford: Clarendon Press, 1979.

Wilson, John. "Education and Indoctrination." In *Aims in Education*. Edited by T. H. B. Hollins. Manchester: Manchester University Press, 1968.

Woods, Richard. *The Occult Revolution*. New York: Herder & Herder, 1971.

Yablonsky, Lewis. *Synanon: The Tunnel Back*. New York: MacMillan, 1965.

Yaron, Zvi. *Mishnato Shel Harav Kook* [The thought of Rabbi Kook]. Jerusalem: World Zionist Organization, 1974.

Zablocki, Benjamin. *The Joyful Community*. Baltimore: Penguin, 1971.

Zaretzky, I., and Leone, M. P. *Religious Movements in Contemporary America*. Princeton: Princeton University Press, 1974.

Index